PRESER
LOCOMOTIVES
OF BRITISH RAILWAYS

C000100823

ELEVENTH EDITION

Peter Fox & Peter Hall

Published by Platform 5 Publishing Ltd., Wyvern House, Sark Road, Sheffield. S2 4HG, England.
Printed in England by B. R. Hubbard Printers Ltd., Callywhite Lane, Dronfield, Sheffield. S18 6XP.

ISBN 1 902336 30 5

Taff Vale Railway Class 02 0-6-2T No. 85 leads "IVATT" Class 2MT 2-6-2T away from Keighley with a train for Oxenhope on 29 June 2002.
Les Nixon

CONTENTS

Front Cover Photograph: One of the highlights of 2002 was the use of LMS Coronation Class No. 6233 "DUCHESS OF SUTHERLAND" on the Royal Train on 11 June 2002. Here the train is seen leaving Llandudno Junction for Crewe. **Hugh Ballantyne**

FOREWORD TO THE ELEVENTH EDITION

Thanks to the support of those enthusiasts who put their hand in their pocket and purchased the tenth edition in the last year, it is now possible to bring you this fully updated eleventh edition of the essential guide to preserved locomotives and multiple units.

The past year has seen continual change in the railway preservation movement with many locomotives and multiple units on the move and further additions to the ranks of preserved diesel and electric locomotives and multiple unit stock. It has however been possible to shoe horn all this extra information into a book of the same thickness as the last edition whilst also including the larger trolleys, omitted from the last edition, and widening the coverage of overseas steam locomotives.

The numbers of diesel locomotives in preservation continues to increase. Private industrial users continue to purchase elderly diesel locomotives for further use with Class 08 shunting locomotives being particularly popular. All those that do not have 'vehicle acceptance' for operation on the Railtrack network are included in this book. Several main line diesel locomotives once considered to be preserved have returned to commercial operation, whilst others of similar types that would once have passed to preservationists find themselves with smaller commercial operators. Such locomotives are not included.

Readers will appreciate that updating a book of this nature is no easy task, no official lists of transfers, additions etc. being available. Thus the authors have been dependent on scouring enthusiast publications, the accuracy of which on occasions, leaves a lot to be desired, making contact with owners and site operators and most importantly personally visiting and confirming locomotives and multiple units to be present at the locations shown. Special thanks are therefore given to all those who have knowingly and unknowingly assisted in the updating of this book. Unfortunately the authors are not infallible and would welcome notification of any corrections or updates to the book of which readers have first hand knowledge. We certainly did very well last time judging by the fact that very few comments were received. Surely more of you know something we do not?

Regrettably, again it is necessary to mention the most common comment received from readers of the last and earlier editions of this book, this being the difficulties experienced in viewing and identifying locomotives, multiple units and other items of rolling stock at heritage railways and railway museums. This is something the authors continue to experience increasingly at first hand and find very annoying and disheartening. Many locations appear to hide behind the cloud of heath and safety legislation and use this an excuse to prohibit access to sheds and sidings. At the same time they appear to make little or no effort to display items in a way which gives visitors at least viewing access. Even at events aimed at the enthusiast the problem persists with many areas containing rolling stock of interest to the many visitors "off limits". Often polite requests to visit certain areas are met with hostility rather than an appreciation of fellow enthusiast interests. The situation has been made worse, at several railways, by the building of new storage sheds. These are often funded with lottery or similar finance, yet despite promising viewing galleries and similar in prospectuses, visitor access turns out to be very limited at best and often non-existent. Railways on the Greater Manchester/Lancashire border, Worcestershire/Shropshire border and in the Highland Region of Scotland appear to be mentioned most often by our readers but these are not the only ones by a long way where difficulties have arisen. Attention to the requirements of visiting enthusiasts, who often appear to be regarded as pests, would surely prove beneficial to the long-term survival of many sites. Indeed, it is these same enthusiasts who are presented with the begging bowl, frequently, to help fund various projects or give a lifeline when the "wolves are at the door". Pursuing an interest in railways encounters enough problems from society at large without things being made worse by those with similar interests. It has also been found from experience that the general public is just as interested to know something about the rusting hulk in the bay platform as the number-crunching gricer. Thus greater attention to labelling items would, the authors feel, greatly enhance the image of preservationists. That is, of course, assuming the preservationists actually know what they have preserved in the first place! The lack of readily available, comprehensive and accurate stock lists, which is often the case at heritage railways and railway museums, does not help matters.

Peter Fox, Peter Hall, November 2002.

INTRODUCTION

Perhaps before the reader continues it is worthwhile explaining the ground rules used to decide which vehicles are and are not included within this title. Firstly only locomotives and multiple unit stock, the latter including single powered vehicles, are included. Secondly the locomotive or multiple unit vehicle must have been in the ownership of, or operated under the jurisdiction of the British Railways Board, its constituents or its descendants. Thirdly only vehicles no longer in the ownership of the descendants of the British Railways Board or commercial railway companies are included, thus vehicles such as the Class 306 multiple unit, although preserved, still constitutes part of a leasing company fleet and is therefore excluded. Details of this and similar items are detailed in other Platform 5 titles. Fourthly, although the title suggests only 'preserved' vehicles are included, for completeness all vehicles still in existence are included, whatever their status, provided they obey the above rules.

In addition, included are locomotives and multiple units of London Underground and its predecessors, overseas steam locomotives preserved in Great Britain of minimum 750 mm gauge, locomotives once operated by the British military and locomotives which replicate those which would otherwise be included.

It has however been found necessary to include several vehicles which do not strictly obey the above set of rules. Thus industrial locomotives masquerading as British Rail or its constituent types are included at the appropriate place. Having allowed the War Department steam locomotives in it is only fair that steam locomotives of the United States Army Transportation Corps be included, but for these only those currently resident in Great Britain are shown.

GENERAL NOTES

This book has been divided into several main categories namely steam locomotives, diesel locomotives, petrol locomotives, electric locomotives, battery electric locomotives, gas turbine vehicles, multiple unit stock and overseas steam locomotives in Great Britain. Further details applicable to each category being given in the introductory paragraph of each section.

Details regarding technical details of the various locomotives and multiple units can be found in the introductory paragraphs for each section. A few details are, however, consistent for each section, these being:

Numbers

All numbers carried at various times by the locomotives are shown, except in the case of temporary identity changes for filming and similar events. For each railway, numbers are given in chronological order. Details are also given of the current identity if it had not previously been carried.

Names and Class Names

Names bestowed after preservation are shown in inverted commas. Official names and class names are shown without inverted commas.

Locations

The location where the locomotive or multiple unit is normally to be found is given if known. Fuller details of locations in Great Britain including OS grid references are given under 'List of Locations'. It is not uncommon for locomotives & multiple units to visit other locations for operation or display. Where such visits are of a long-term nature, the locomotive or multiple unit is shown as being at its host site with details of its home site being given as a footnote. Details of locomotives undergoing restoration away from their home site are also given as a footnote. (N) denotes a locomotive or multiple unit from the National Collection not currently located at the National Railway Museum York.

Build Details

For each locomotive the builder, works number (if any) and year of build are given. Private builder codes will be found in section 11.

Updates

Updates to this book are published in Platform 5's monthly magazine, **entrain**, available from newsagents or on direct subscription (see inside back cover).

1. STEAM LOCOMOTIVES

Almost from the birth of the railways to the 1960s, steam was the principal form of propulsion, its rapid decline in the 1960s being the impulse for much of the preservation movement. Steam locomotives are arranged generally in numerical order of the British Railways number, except that very old locomotives which did not receive numbers in the series pertaining at nationalisation in 1948 are listed at the end of each pre-nationalisation company section.

A select number of steam locomotives are permitted to work steam specials on Railtrack routes Such locomotives invariably spend long periods away from their home bases undertaking such duties. Other locomotives may also spend peiods away from their home bases as guests of other locations.

Wheel Arrangement

The Whyte notation is used for steam locomotives and diesel shunters with coupled driving wheels. The number of leading wheels are given, followed by the number of driving wheels and then the trailing wheels. Suffixes are used to denote tank locomotives as follows: T – side tank, PT – pannier tank, ST – saddle tank, WT – well tank.

Dimensions

These are given in imperial units for steam locomotives as follows:

B.P.   Boiler pressure.

Cyls   Cylinder dimensions. The diameter is given first followed by the stroke. (I) indicates 2 inside cylinders, (O) 2 outside cylinders, (V) 2 vertical cylinders and (3) 3 cylinders (2 outside and one inside) and (4) 4 cylinders (2 outside and 2 inside).

Wheel dias. These are given from front to back, i.e. leading, driving, trailing.

Weights   These are given in full working order.

Tractive Effort

This is denoted by "T.E." and for steam locomotives is given at 85% boiler pressure to the nearest 10 lbf. Phillipsons formula has been used to calculate these as follows:

$$T.E. = \frac{.85dsnp}{2w}$$

where   d = cylinder diameter (inches);
             s = piston stroke (inches);
             n = number of cylinders;
             p = boiler pressure (lb/sq. in.);
             w = driving wheel diameter (inches).

Brakes

Steam locomotives are assumed to have train vacuum brakes unless otherwise stated.

Valve Gear

Unless stated otherwise valve gear on steam locomotives is assumed to be inside, except Walschaert and Capprotti gears which are assumed to be outside.

1.1. GREAT WESTERN RAILWAY AND ABSORBED COMPANIES' STEAM LOCOMOTIVES

GENERAL

The GWR was the only one of the big four companies which was essentially an existing company. A number of smaller companies were absorbed at the grouping. These were virtually all in Wales and included the Cambrian Railways, Cardiff Railway, Rhymney Railway and Taff Vale Railway. Prior to 1923 the GWR had also absorbed smaller concerns at various dates.

Numbering & Classification System

The locomotives of the absorbed companies were given the lower numbers and GWR classes the higher numbers. Instead of arranging classes in blocks, the GWR adopted a strange system whereby the second digit remained constant within a class, e.g. the 0-6-2Ts numbered 5600–99 continued with 6600–99. Sometimes earlier numbers were filled in, e.g. 5101–99 continued with 4100–99. Classes were always denoted by the number of the first member of the class to be built, which was not always the lowest number in the series. GWR locos were not renumbered by BR on nationalisation.

Power Class & Route Restriction System

The GWR adopted a power classification letter code system which ranged from A to E in ascending order of power. Certain small locomotives which were below group A were said to be unclassified and the 'Kings' were classed as 'special' being higher than 'E'.

Route restriction was denoted by a system of coloured spots painted on the cabside. In ascending order of restriction these were as follows: Yellow, Blue, Red, Double Red. Where no restriction is specified, locomotives were unrestricted.

◄ A general shed view at Minehead on 10 July 2002 shows 7820 "DINMORE MANOR", No. 80136 and small Prarie 4160 preparing for their next duties.
J.C. Hillmer

CORRIS RAILWAY

0-4-2ST

Built: 1878 by Hughes Locomotive & Tramway Engine Works Ltd. as 0-4-0ST.
B.P.: 160 lbf/sq. in.
Wheel dias.: 2' 6", 10".
T.E.: 2670 lbf.
Cyls.: 7" x 12" (O).
Weight: 9 tons.
Gauge: 2' 3".
Valve Gear: Stephenson.

3	"SIR HAYDN"	Talyllyn Railway	HLT 323/1878 reb. 1901

CORRIS RAILWAY

0-4-2ST

Built: 1921.
B.P.: 160 lbf/sq. in.
Wheel dias.: 2' 0", 1' 4½".
T.E.: 3330 lbf.
Cyls.: 7" x 12" (O).
Weight: 8 tons.
Gauge: 2' 3".
Valve Gear: Hackworth.

4	"EDWARD THOMAS"	Talyllyn Railway	KS 4047/1921

VALE OF RHEIDOL

2-6-2T

Built: 1902 by Davies & Metcalfe (9) GWR development 1923 (7, 8).
B.P.: 165 lbf/sq. in.
Wheel dias.: 2' 0", 2' 6", 2' 0".
T.E.: 10 510 lbf.
Cyls.: 11½" x 17" (O).
Weight: 25 tons.
Gauge: 1' 11½".
Valve Gear: Walschaert.

BR	GWR	VOR			
7	7		OWAIN GLYNDWR	Vale of Rheidol Rly.	Swindon 1923
8	8		LLYWELYN	Vale of Rheidol Rly.	Swindon 1923
9	1213	2	PRINCE OF WALES	Vale of Rheidol Rly.	DM 2/1902 reb. Swindon 1923

No. 12

4wT

Built: 1926. Sentinel vertical-boilered geared locomotive. Returned to manufacturer after 3 months service.
B.P.: 275 lbf/sq. in.
Wheel dia.: 2' 6".
T.E.: 7200 lbf.
Cyls.: 6" x 9" (I).
Weight: 20 tons.
Valve Gear: Rotary cam.

GWR	Present		
12	49 "No. 2 ISEBROOK"	The Rosemary Vineyard, Isle of Wight	S 6515/1926

OXFORD, WORCESTER & WOLVERHAMPTON RAILWAY

0-6-0

Built: 1855. Following withdrawal in 1904 the cut-down frames, motion and four-coupled wheels were set up as an instructional model. It has been preserved in this form although presently dismantled.
B.P.: 140 lbf/sq. in.
Wheel dia.: 5' 3"
T.E.: 13 100 lbf.
Cyls.: 17½" x 24" (I)
Weight: 32.60 tons

GWR	OW&W		
252	34	Leeds Industrial Museum	EW 1855

TAFF VALE RAILWAY CLASS O2

0-6-2T

Built: 1899 by Neilson, Reid. Sold by GWR 1926. 9 built.
B.P.: 160 lbf/sq. in.
Wheel dias.: 4' 6½", 3' 1".
T.E.: 19 870 lbf.
Cyls.: 17½" x 26" (I).
Weight: 61.5 tons.
Valve Gear: Stephenson.
Power class: B.
Restriction: Blue.

GWR	TVR		
426	85	Keighley & Worth Valley Railway	NR 5408/1899

TAFF VALE RAILWAY CLASS O1

0-6-2T

Built: 1894–97. Survivor sold by GWR 1927. 14 built.
B.P.: 150 lbf/sq. in.
Wheel dias.: 4' 6½", 3' 8¾".
T.E.: 18 630 lbf.
Cyls.: 17½" x 26" (I).
Weight: 56.4 tons.
Valve Gear: Stephenson.
Power class: A.
Restriction: Yellow.

GWR	TVR		
450	28	Dean Forest Railway (N) Cardiff West Yard	306/1897

PORT TALBOT RAILWAY   0-6-0ST

Built: 1900/01. Survivor sold by GWR 1934. 6 built.
B.P.: 160 lbf/sq. in.   **Wheel dia.:** 4' 0½".   **T.E.:** 17230 lbf.
Cyls.: 16" x 24" (I).   **Weight:** 44 tons.
Valve Gear: Stephenson.   **Power class:** A.   **Restriction:** Yellow.

GWR	PTR		
813	26	Severn Valley Railway	HC 555/1901

WELSHPOOL & LLANFAIR RAILWAY   0-6-0T

Built: 1903. 2 built.
B.P.: 150 lbf/sq. in.   **Wheel dia.:** 2' 9".   **T.E.:** 8180 lbf.
Cyls.: 11½" x 16" (O).   **Weight:** 19.9 tons.   **Gauge:** 2' 6".
Valve Gear: Walschaert.

BR	GWR	W&L			
822	822	1	THE EARL	Welshpool & Llanfair Railway	BP 3496/1903
823	823	2	THE COUNTESS§	Welshpool & Llanfair Railway	BP 3497/1903

§ Name altered to COUNTESS by GWR. Now renamed THE COUNTESS.

POWLESLAND & MASON   0-4-0ST

Built: 1903–06. Survivor sold by GWR 1928 for industrial use.
B.P.: 140 lbf/sq. in.   **Wheel dia.:** 3' 6".   **T.E.:** 11 110 lbf.
Cyls.: 14" x 20" (O).   **Weight:** 24.85 tons.
Valve Gear: Stephenson.

GWR	P&M		
921	6	Snibston Discovery Park	BE 314/1906

CARDIFF RAILWAY   0-4-0ST

Built: 1898. Rebuilt Tyndall Street Works 1916.
B.P.: 160 lbf/sq. in.   **Wheel dia.:** 3' 2½".   **T.E.:** 14 540 lbf.
Cyls.: 14" x 21" (O).   **Weight:** 25.5 tons.
Valve Gear: Kitson.

GWR	Car.R.		
1338	5	Didcot Railway Centre	K 3799/1898

ALEXANDRA DOCKS & RAILWAY COMPANY   0-4-0ST

Built: 1897. Rebuilt Swindon, 1903. Sold by GWR 1932 for industrial use.
B.P.: 120 lbf/sq. in.   **Wheel dia.:** 3' 0".   **T.E.:** 11 110 lbf.
Cyls.: 14" x 20" (O).   **Weight:** 22.5 tons.
Valve Gear: Stephenson.

GWR		AD		
1340	TROJAN	TROJAN	Didcot Railway Centre	AE 1386/1897

1361 CLASS   0-6-0ST

Built: 1910. Churchward design for dock shunting. 5 built (1361–5).
B.P.: 150 lbf/sq. in.   **Wheel dia.:** 3' 8".   **T.E.:** 14 840 lbf.
Cyls.: 16" x 20" (O).   **Weight:** 35.2 tons.
Valve Gear: Allan.

1363	Didcot Railway Centre	Swindon 2377/1910

1366 CLASS   0-6-0PT

Built: 1934. Collett design for dock shunting. Used to work Weymouth Quay boat trains. 6 built. (1366–71).
B.P.: 165 lbf/sq. in.   **Wheel dia.:** 3' 8".   **T.E.:** 16 320 lbf.
Cyls.: 16" x 20" (O).   **Weight:** 35.75 tons.
Valve Gear: Stephenson.

1369	South Devon Railway	Swindon 1934

NORTH PEMBROKESHIRE & FISHGUARD RAILWAY 0-6-0ST

Built: 1878. Absorbed by GWR 1898. Sold to Gwendraeth Valley Railway in 1910. Absorbed by GWR again in 1923 but sold in March of that year to Kidwelly Tinplate Company.
B.P.: 140 lbf/sq. in.   **Wheel dia.:** 4' 0".   **T.E.:** 13 960 lbf.
Cyls.: 16" x 22" (I).   **Weight:** 30.95 tons.
Valve Gear: Stephenson.

GWR	GVR			
1378	2	MARGARET	Scolton Manor Museum	FW 410/1878

1400 CLASS   0-4-2T

Built: 1932–36. Collett design. Push & Pull fitted. Locos renumbered in 1946. 75 built.(1400–74).
B.P.: 165 lbf/sq. in.   **Wheel dia.:** 5' 2", 3' 8".   **T.E.:** 13 900 lbf.
Cyls.: 16" x 24" (I).   **Weight:** 41.3 tons.
Valve Gear: Stephenson.   **Power Class:** Unclassified

1932 No.	1946 No.		
4820	1420	South Devon Railway	Swindon 1933
4842	1442	Tiverton Museum	Swindon 1935
4850	1450	Gloucestershire-Warwickshire Railway	Swindon 1935
4866	1466	Didcot Railway Centre	Swindon 1936

Note: 4850 is receiving attention at The Railway Age, Crewe

1500 CLASS   0-6-0PT

Built: 1949. Hawksworth design. 10 built (1500–09).
B.P.: 200 lbf/sq. in.   **Wheel dia.:** 4' 7½".   **T.E.:** 22 510 lbf.
Cyls.: 17½" x 24" (O).   **Weight:** 58.2 tons.
Valve Gear: Walschaert.   **Power class:** C.   **Restriction:** Red.

1501	Severn Valley Railway	Swindon 1949

1600 CLASS   0-6-0PT

Built: 1949–55. Hawksworth design. 70 built (1600–69).
B.P.: 165 lbf/sq. in.   **Wheel dia.:** 4' 1½".   **T.E.:** 18 510 lbf.
Cyls.: 16½" x 24" (I).   **Weight:** 41.6 tons.
Valve Gear: Stephenson.   **Power class:** A.

1638	Kent & East Sussex Railway	Swindon 1951

2251 CLASS   0-6-0

Built: 1930–48 Collett design. 120 built (2251–99, 2200–50, 3200–19).
B.P.: 200 lbf/sq. in.   **Weight–Loco:** 43.4 tons.   **Wheel dia.:** 5' 2".
Cyls.: 17½" x 24" (I).   **–Tender:** 36.75 tons.   **T.E.:** 20 150 lbf.
Valve Gear: Stephenson.   **Power class:** B.   **Restriction:** Yellow.

3205	South Devon Railway	Swindon 1946

2301 CLASS   0-6-0

Built: 1883–99. Dean design. 280 built (2301–2580).
B.P.: 180 lbf/sq. in.   **Weight–Loco:** 37 tons.   **Wheel dia.:** 5' 2".
Cyls.: 17½" x 24" (I).   **–Tender:** 36.75 tons.   **T.E.:** 18140 lbf.
Valve Gear: Stephenson.   **Power class:** A.

2516	Steam-Museum of the Great Western Railway (N)	Swindon 1557/1897

2800 CLASS   2-8-0

Built: 1903–19. Churchward design for heavy freight. 84 built (2800–83).
B.P.: 225 lbf/sq. in.   **Weight–Loco:** 75.5 tons.   **Wheel dias.:** 3' 2", 4' 7½".
Cyls.: 18½" x 30" (O).   **–Tender:** 43.15 tons.   **T.E.:** 35 380 lbf.
Valve Gear: Stephenson.   **Power class:** E.   **Restriction:** Blue.

2807	Gloucestershire–Warwickshire Railway	Swindon 2102/1905

2818	National Railway Museum	Swindon 2122/1905
2857	Severn Valley Railway	Swindon 2763/1918
2859	Llangollen Railway	Swindon 2765/1918
2861	Vale of Glamorgan Railway	Swindon 2767/1918
2873	South Devon Railway	Swindon 2779/1918
2874	Pontypool & Blaenavon Railway	Swindon 2780/1918

2884 CLASS   2-8-0

Built: 1938–42. Collett development of 2800 Class with side window cabs. 81 built (2884–99, 3800–64).

B.P.: 225 lbf/sq. in. **Weight –Loco:** 76.25 tons. **Wheel dias.:** 3′ 2″, 4′ 7½″.
Cyls.: 18½″ x 30″ (O). **–Tender:** 43.15 tons. **T.E.:** 35 380 lbf.
Valve Gear: Stephenson. **Power class:** E. **Restriction:** Blue.

2885	GWR Preservation Group, Southall	Swindon 1938
3802	Llangollen Railway	Swindon 1938
3803	South Devon Railway	Swindon 1939
3814	North Yorkshire Moors Railway	Swindon 1940
3822	Didcot Railway Centre	Swindon 1940
3845	Swindon & Cricklade Railway	Swindon 1942
3850	West Somerset Railway	Swindon 1942
3855	Pontypool & Blaenavon Railway	Swindon 1942
3862	Northampton & Lamport Railway	Swindon 1942

3200 CLASS   "DUKEDOG"   4-4-0

Built: Rebuilt 1936–39 by Collett using the frames of "Bulldogs" and the boilers of "Dukes". 30 built (9000–29).

B.P.: 180 lbf/sq. in. **Weight –Loco:** 49 tons. **Wheel dias.:** 3′ 8″, 5′ 8″.
Cyls.: 18″ x 26″ (I). **–Tender:** 40 tons. **T.E.:** 18 950 lbf.
Valve Gear: Stephenson. **Power class:** B. **Restriction:** Yellow.

| 3217–9017 | "EARL OF BERKELEY" | Bluebell Railway | Swindon 1938 |

3700 CLASS   CITY   4-4-0

Built: 1903. Churchward design. Reputed to be the first loco to attain 100 m.p.h. when it hauled an "Ocean Mails" special from Plymouth to Paddington in 1904.

B.P.: 200 lbf/sq. in. **Weight –Loco:** 55.3 tons. **Wheel dias.:** 3′ 2″, 6′ 8½″.
Cyls.: 18″ x 26″ (I). **–Tender:** 36.75 tons. **T.E.:** 17 800 lbf.
Valve Gear: Stephenson.

| BR | GWR | | | |
| 3440 | 3717 | CITY OF TRURO | National Railway Museum | Swindon 2000/1903 |

4000 CLASS   STAR   4-6-0

Built: 1906–23. Churchward design for express passenger trains. 73 built (4000–72).
B.P.: 225 lbf/sq. in. **Weight –Loco:** 75.6 tons. **Wheel dias.:** 3′ 2″, 6′ 8½″.
Cyls.: 15″ x 26″ (4). **–Tender:** 40 tons. **T.E.:** 27 800 lbf.
Power class: D. **Restriction:** Red.
Valve Gear: Inside Walschaert with rocking levers for outside valves.

| 4003 | LODE STAR | National Railway Museum | Swindon 2231/1907 |

4073 CLASS   CASTLE   4-6-0

Built: 1923–50. Collett development of Star. 166 built (4073–99, 5000–5099, 7000–37). In addition one Pacific (111) and five Stars (4000/9/16/32/7) were rebuilt as Castles.
B.P.: 225 lbf/sq. in. **Weight –Loco:** 79.85 tons. **Wheel dias.:** 3′ 2″, 6′ 8½″.
Cyls.: 16″ x 26″ (4). **–Tender:** 46.7 tons. **T.E.:** 3630 lbf.
Power class: E. **Restriction:** Red.
Valve Gear: Inside Walschaert with rocking levers for outside valves.

d–Rebuilt with double chimney.   x–Dual (air/vacuum) brakes.

| 4073 | CAERPHILLY CASTLE | Steam-Museum of the Great Western Railway (N) | Swindon 1923 |
| 4079 | PENDENNIS CASTLE | Didcot Railway Centre | Swindon 1924 |

5029x NUNNEY CASTLE	Old Oak Common Depot, London	Swindon 1934
5043d EARL OF MOUNT EDGCUMBE	Tyseley Locomotive Works, Birmingham	Swindon 1936
5051 EARL BATHURST	Didcot Railway Centre	Swindon 1936
5080 DEFIANT	Buckinghamshire Railway Centre	Swindon 1939
7027 THORNBURY CASTLE	The Railway Age, Crewe	Swindon 1949
7029d CLUN CASTLE	Tyseley Locomotive Works, Birmingham	Swindon 1950

5043 was named BARBURY CASTLE to 09/37.
5051 was named DRYSLLWYN CASTLE to 08/37.
5080 was named OGMORE CASTLE to 01/41.

Note: 5080 is on loan from Tyseley Locomotive Works, Birmingham

A pair of GWR 5700 Class 0-6-0 Pannier Tanks Nos. 7760 and 9600 are seen storming away from Stenson Jn. with a Tyseley–Leicester "SHAKESPEARE EXPRESS" excursion on 2 March 2002.

Les Nixon

4200 CLASS 2-8-0T

Built: 1910–23. Churchward design. 105 built (4201–99, 4200, 5200–4).
B.P.: 200 lbf/sq. in.   **Wheel dias.:** 3' 2", 4' 7½".   **T.E.:** 31 450 lbf.
Cyls.: 18½" x 30" (O).   **Weight:** 81.6 tons.
Valve Gear: Stephenson.   **Power class:** E.   **Restriction:** Red.

4247	West Somerset Railway	Swindon 2637/1916
4248	Steam-Museum of the Great Western Railway	Swindon 2638/1916
4253	Pontypool & Blaenavon Railway	Swindon 2643/1917
4270	Swansea Vale Railway	Swindon 2850/1919
4277	North Yorkshire Moors Railway	Swindon 2857/1920

4300 CLASS   2-6-0

Built: 1911–32. Churchward design. 342 built (4300–99 (renumbered from 8300–99 between 1944 and 1948), 6300–99, 7300–21, 7322–41 (renumbered from 9300–19 between 1956 and 1959).
B.P.: 200 (225*) lbf/sq. in.   **Weight –Loco:** 62 (63.85*) tons.   **Wheel dias.:** 3' 2", 5' 8".
Cyls.: 18½" x 30 (O).   **–Tender:** 40 tons.   **T.E.:** 25 670 (28 880*) lbf.
Valve Gear: Stephenson.   **Power class:** D.   **Restriction:** Blue.

8322–5322	Didcot Railway Centre	Swindon 1917
9303*–7325	Steam-Museum of the Great Western Railway	Swindon 1932

4500 CLASS   2-6-2T

Built: 1906–24. Churchward design. (§Built 1927–29. Collett development with larger tanks). 175 built (4500–99, 5500–74).
B.P.: 200 lbf/sq. in.   **Wheel dias.:** 3' 2", 4' 7½", 3' 2".   **T.E.:** 21 250 lbf.
Cyls.: 17" x 24" (O).   **Weight:** 57.9 tons (61 tons§).
Valve Gear: Stephenson.   **Power class:** C.   **Restriction:** Yellow.

4555	"WARRIOR"	Paignton & Dartmouth Railway	Swindon 1924
4561		West Somerset Railway	Swindon 1924
4566		Severn Valley Railway	Swindon 1924
4588§	"TROJAN"	Paignton & Dartmouth Railway	Swindon 1927
5521§		Swindon Railway Workshop, Bream	Swindon 1927
5526§		South Devon Railway	Swindon 1928
5532§		Llangollen Railway	Swindon 1928
5538§		Vale of Glamorgan Railway	Swindon 1928
5539§		Vale of Glamorgan Railway	Swindon 1928
5541§		Dean Forest Railway	Swindon 1928
5542§		West Somerset Railway	Swindon 1928
5552§		Bodmin Steam Railway	Swindon 1928
5553§		West Somerset Railway	Swindon 1928
5572§		Didcot Railway Centre	Swindon 1929

4900 CLASS   HALL   4-6-0

Built: 1928–43. Collett development of Churchward 'Saint' class. 259 in class. (4900 rebuilt from Saint) 4901–99, 5900–99, 6900–58 built as Halls).
B.P.: 225 lbf/sq. in.   **Weight –Loco:** 75 tons.   **Wheel dias.:** 3' 2", 6' 0".
Cyls.: 18½" x 30" (O).   **–Tender:** 46.7 tons.   **T.E.:** 27 270 lbf.
Valve Gear: Stephenson.   **Power class:** D.   **Restriction:** Red.

4920	DUMBLETON HALL	South Devon Railway	Swindon 1929
4930	HAGLEY HALL	Designer Outlet Village, Swindon	Swindon 1929
4936	KINLET HALL	Tyseley Locomotive Works, Birmingham	Swindon 1929
4942	MAINDY HALL	Didcot Railway Centre	Swindon 1929
4953	PITCHFORD HALL	Tyseley Locomotive Works, Birmingham	Swindon 1929
4965	ROOD ASTON HALL	Tyseley Locomotive Works, Birmingham	Swindon 1930
4979	WOOTTON HALL	Helical Technologies, Lytham St. Annes	Swindon 1930
5900	HINDERTON HALL	Didcot Railway Centre	Swindon 1931
5952	COGAN HALL	Oswestry Cycle & Railway Museum	Swindon 1935
5967	BICKMARSH HALL	Pontypool & Blaenavon Railway	Swindon 1937
5972	OLTON HALL	West Coast Railway Company, Carnforth	Swindon 1937

Notes: 4942 may be rebuilt into a Saint.
4965 previously carried the identity 4983 ALBERT HALL.
5972 at present masquerades as "HOGWARTS CASTLE".

5101 CLASS   2-6-2T

Built: 1929–49. Collett development of Churchward 3100 class. 180 built (5101–99, 4100–79).
B.P.: 200 lbf/sq. in.   **Wheel dias.:** 3' 2", 5' 8", 3' 8".   **T.E.:** 24 300 lbf.
Cyls.: 18" x 30" (O).   **Weight:** 78.45 tons.
Valve Gear: Stephenson.   **Power class:** D.   **Restriction:** Yellow.

4110	Heritage Engineering (Swindon)	Swindon 1936
4115	Vale of Glamorgan Railway	Swindon 1936
4121	Tyseley Locomotive Works, Birmingham	Swindon 1937
4141	Llangollen Railway	Swindon 1946
4144	Didcot Railway Centre	Swindon 1946
4150	Severn Valley Railway	Swindon 1947
4160	West Somerset Railway	Swindon 1948
5164	Severn Valley Railway	Swindon 1930
5193	West Somerset Railway	Swindon 1934
5199	Llangollen Railway	Swindon 1934

Note: 5193 is being rebuilt by the West Somerset Railway as a 2-6-0 tender locomotive.

5205 CLASS   2-8-0T

Built: 1923–25/40. Collett development of 4200 class. 60 built (5205–64).
B.P.: 200 lbf/sq. in.   **Wheel dias.:** 3' 2", 4' 7½".   **T.E.:** 33 170 lbf.
Cyls.: 19" x 30" (O).   **Weight:** 82.1 tons.
Valve Gear: Stephenson.   **Power class:** E.   **Restriction:** Red.

5224	West Somerset Railway	Swindon 1925
5227	Vale of Glamorgan Railway	Swindon 1924
5239 "GOLIATH"	Paignton & Dartmouth Railway	Swindon 1924

5600 CLASS   0-6-2T

Built: 1924–28. Collett design. 200 built (5600–99, 6600–99).
B.P.: 200 lbf/sq. in.   **Wheel dias.:** 4' 7½", 3' 8".   **T.E.:** 25 800 lbf.
Cyls.: 18" x 26" (I).   **Weight:** 68 tons.
Valve Gear: Stephenson.   **Power class:** D.   **Restriction:** Red.

5619	Telford Steam Railway	Swindon 1925
5637	East Somerset Railway	Swindon 1925
5643	Lakeside & Haverthwaite Railway	Swindon 1925
5668	Pontypool & Blaenavon Railway	Swindon 1926
6619	North Yorkshire Moors Railway	Swindon 1928
6634	The Railway Age, Crewe	Swindon 1928
6686	Vale of Glamorgan Railway	AW 974/1928
6695	Swanage Railway	AW 983/1928
6697	Didcot Railway Centre	AW 985/1928

Note: 5637 is on loan from the Swindon & Cricklade Railway.

5700 CLASS   0-6-0PT

Built: 1929–49. Collett design. The standard GWR shunter. 863 built (5700–99, 6700–79, 7700–99, 8700–99, 3700–99, 3600–99, 4600–99, 9600–82, 9700–9799. Six of the preserved examples saw use with London Transport following withdrawal by British Railways.
B.P.: 200 lbf/sq. in.   **Wheel dias.:** 4' 7½"   **T.E.:** 22 510 lbf.
Cyls.: 17½" x 24" (I).   **Weight:** 47.5 (49§) tons.   **Power Class:** C.
Valve Gear: Stephenson.   **Restriction:** Blue (Yellow from 1950).

GWR	LTE		
3650		Didcot Railway Centre	Swindon 1939
3738		Didcot Railway Centre	Swindon 1937
4612		Bodmin Steam Railway	Swindon 1942
5764	L95	Severn Valley Railway	Swindon 1929

5775	L89	Keighley & Worth Valley Railway	Swindon 1929
5786	L92	South Devon Railway	Swindon 1930
7714		Severn Valley Railway	KS 4449/1930
7715	L99	Buckinghamshire Railway Centre	KS 4450/1930
7752	L94	Tyseley Locomotive Works, Birmingham	NBL 24040/1930
7754		Llangollen Railway	NBL 24042/1930
7760	L90	Tyseley Locomotive Works, Birmingham	NBL 24048/1930
9600§		Tyseley Locomotive Works, Birmingham	Swindon 1945
9629§		Pontypool & Blaenavon Railway	Swindon 1946
9642§		Dean Forest Railway	Swindon 1946
9681§		Dean Forest Railway	Swindon 1949
9682§		North Norfolk Railway	Swindon 1949

Notes: 9642 is on loan from the Swansea Vale Railway. 9682 is on loan from the GWR Preservation Group.

6000 CLASS   KING   4-6-0

Built: 1927–30. Collett design. 31 built.
B.P.: 250 lbf/sq. in.   **Weight–Loco:** 89 tons.   **Wheel dias.:** 3' 0", 6' 6".
Cyls.: 16¼" x 28" (4).   **–Tender:** 46.7 tons.   **T.E.:** 40 290 lbf.
Power class: Special.   **Restriction:** Double Red.
Valve Gear: Inside Walschaert with rocking levers for outside valves.
x–Dual (air/vacuum) brakes.

6000	KING GEORGE V	Steam-Museum of the Great Western Railway (N)	Swindon 1927
6023	KING EDWARD II	Didcot Railway Centre	Swindon 1930
6024x	KING EDWARD I	Didcot Railway Centre	Swindon 1930

6100 CLASS   2-6-2T

Built: 1931–35. Collett development of 5100. 70 built (6100–69).
B.P.: 225 lbf/sq. in.   **Wheel dias.:** 3' 2", 5' 8", 3' 8".   **T.E.:** 27 340 lbf.
Cyls.: 18" x 30" (O).   **Weight:** 78.45 tons.
Valve Gear: Stephenson.   **Power class:** D.   **Restriction:** Blue.

6106		Didcot Railway Centre	Swindon 1931

6400 CLASS   0-6-0PT

Built: 1932–37. Collett design. Push & Pull fitted. 40 built (6400–39).
B.P.: 165 lbf/sq. in.   **Wheel dias.:** 4' 7½".   **T.E.:** 16 510 lbf.
Cyls.: 16½" x 24" (I).   **Weight:** 45.6 tons.
Valve Gear: Stephenson.   **Power class:** A.   **Restriction:** Yellow.

6412		West Somerset Railway	Swindon 1934
6430		Llangollen Railway	Swindon 1937
6435		Paignton & Dartmouth Railway	Swindon 1937

6959 CLASS   MODIFIED HALL   4-6-0

Built: 1944–49. Hawksworth development of 'Hall'. 71 built (6959–99, 7900–29).
B.P.: 225 lbf/sq. in.   **Weight–Loco:** 75.8 tons.   **Wheel dias.:** 3' 2", 6' 0".
Cyls.: 18½" x 30" (O).   **–Tender:** 47.3 tons.   **T.E.:** 27 270 lbf.
Valve Gear: Stephenson.   **Power class:** D.   **Restriction:** Blue.

6960	RAVENINGHAM HALL	Gloucestershire-Warwickshire Railway	Swindon 1944
6984	OWSDEN HALL	Gloucestershire-Warwickshire Railway	Swindon 1948
6989	WIGHTWICK HALL	Buckinghamshire Railway Centre	Swindon 1948
6990	WITHERSLACK HALL	Great Central Railway	Swindon 1948
6998	BURTON AGNES HALL	Didcot Railway Centre	Swindon 1949
7903	FOREMARKE HALL	Swindon & Cricklade Railway	Swindon 1949
7927	WILLINGTON HALL	Vale of Glamorgan Railway	Swindon 1950

Note: 6990 is receiving attention at Tyseley Locomotive Works.

7200 CLASS
2-8-2T

Built: 1934–50. Collett rebuilds of 4200 and 5205 class 2-8-0Ts. 54 built (7200–53).
B.P.: 200 lbf/sq. in.   **Wheel dias.:** 3′ 2″, 4′ 7½″, 3′ 8″.   **T.E.:** 33 170 lbf.
Cyls.: 19″ x 30″ (O).   **Weight:** 92.6 tons.
Valve Gear: Stephenson.   **Power class:** E.   **Restriction:** Blue.

7200 (rebuilt from 5277)	Heritage Engineering (Swindon)	Swindon 1930 reb. 1934
7202 (rebuilt from 5275)	Didcot Railway Centre	Swindon 1930 reb. 1934
7229 (rebuilt from 5264)	East Lancashire Railway	Swindon 1926 reb. 1935

7800 CLASS   MANOR   4-6-0

Built: 1938–50. Collett design for secondary main lines. 30 built (7800–29).
B.P.: 225 lbf/sq. in.   **Weight–Loco:** 68.9 tons.   **Wheel dias.:** 3′ 0″, 5′ 8″.
Cyls.: 18″ x 30″ (O).   **–Tender:** 40 tons.   **T.E.:** 27 340 lbf.
Valve Gear: Stephenson.   **Power class:** D.   **Restriction:** Blue.

7802	BRADLEY MANOR	Severn Valley Railway	Swindon 1938
7808	COOKHAM MANOR	Didcot Railway Centre	Swindon 1938
7812	ERLESTOKE MANOR	Severn Valley Railway	Swindon 1939
7819	HINTON MANOR	Severn Valley Railway	Swindon 1939
7820	DINMORE MANOR	West Somerset Railway	Swindon 1950
7821	DITCHEAT MANOR	Great Central Railway	Swindon 1950
7822	FOXCOTE MANOR	Llangollen Railway	Swindon 1950
7827	LYDHAM MANOR	Paignton & Dartmouth Railway	Swindon 1950
7828	ODNEY MANOR	West Somerset Railway	Swindon 1950

Note: 7821 is on loan from the Oswestry Cycle & Railway Museum.

9400 CLASS   0-6-0PT

Built: 1947–56. Hawksworth design. 210 built (9400–99, 8400–99, 3400–09).
B.P.: 200 lbf/sq. in.   **Wheel dia.:** 4′ 7½″.   **T.E.:** 22 510 lbf.
Cyls.: 17½″ x 24″ (I).   **Weight:** 55.35 tons.
Valve Gear: Stephenson.   **Power class:** C.   **Restriction:** Red.

9400	Steam-Museum of the Great Western Railway (N)	Swindon 1947
9466	Buckinghamshire Railway Centre	RSH 7617/1952

BURRY PORT & GWENDRAETH VALLEY RAILWAY   0-6-0ST

Built: 1900.   **B.P.:**   **Wheel dias.:** 3′ 6″.
T.E.:   **Cyls.:** 14″ x 20″(O)   **Weight:** 29 tons.

Note: This loco was supplied new to the BPGVR and was sold into industrial service in 1914.

2	PONTYBEREM	Didcot Railway Centre	AE 1421/1900

SANDY & POTTON RAILWAY   0-4-0WT

Built: 1857. The Sandy & Potton Railway became part of the LNWR and the loco worked on the Cromford & High Peak Railway from 1863–1878. The loco was sold to the Wantage Tramway in 1878.
B.P.: 120 lbf/sq. in.   **Wheel dias.:** 3′ 0″   **T.E.:** 5510 lbf.
Cyls.: 9″ x 12″ (O)   **Weight:** 15 tons.

SPR	LNWR	WT		
SHANNON	1863	5	Didcot Railway Centre (N)	GE 1857

SOUTH DEVON RAILWAY   0-4-0WT

Built: 1868. Vertical boilered locomotive.
B.P.:   **Wheel dias.:** 3′ 0″   **T.E.:** lbf.
Cyls.: 9″ x 12″ (V).   **Weight:**   **Gauge:** 7′ 0¼″.

GWR	SDR		
2180	151	TINY	South Devon Railway (N)	Sara 1868

SOUTHERN

1.2. SOUTHERN RAILWAY AND CONSTITUENT COMPANIES' STEAM LOCOMOTIVES

GENERAL

The Southern Railway (SR) was an amalgamation of the London, Brighton and South Coast Railway (LBSCR), the London and South Western Railway (LSWR) and the South Eastern and Chatham Railway (SECR). The latter was formed in 1898 by the amalgamation of the South Eastern Railway (SER) and London, Chatham and Dover Railway (LCDR).

Locomotive Numbering System

On formation of the SR in 1924, all locomotives (including new builds) were given a prefix letter to denote the works which maintained them as follows:

A Ashford Works. All former SECR locomotives plus some D1, L1, U1.
B Brighton Works. All former LBSCR locomotives plus some D1.
E Eastleigh Works. All former LSWR locomotives plus LN, V, Z.

In 1931 locomotives were renumbered. 'E' prefix locomotives merely lost the prefix (except locomotives with an '0' in front of the number to which 3000 was added). 'A' prefix locomotives had 1000 added and 'B' prefix locomotives had 2000 added, e.g. B636 became 2636, E0298 became 3298.

In 1941 Bulleid developed a most curious numbering system for his new locomotives. This consisted of two numbers representing the numbers of leading and trailing axles respectively followed by a letter denoting the number of the driving axles. This was followed by the locomotive serial number. The first pacific was therefore 21C1, and the first Q1 0-6-0 was C1.

In 1948 British Railways added 30000 to all numbers, but the 3xxx series (formerly 0xxx series) were totally renumbered. The Q1s became 33xxx, the MNs 35xxx and the WCs 34xxx. Isle of Wight locomotives had their own number series, denoted by a 'W' prefix. This indicated Ryde Works maintenance and was carried until the end of steam.

In the section which follows, locomotives are listed generally in order of BR numbers. Three old locomotives which were withdrawn before nationalisation are listed at the end of the section.

Classification

The LBSCR originally classified locomotive classes by a letter which denoted the use of the class. A further development was to add a number, to identify different classes of similar use. A rebuild was signified by an 'X' suffix. In its latter years, new classes of different wheel arrangement were given different letters. The SECR gave each class a letter. A number after the letter signified either a new class which was a modification of the original or a rebuild. The SR perpetuated this system. The LSWR had an odd system based on the works order number for the first locomotive of the class to be built. These went A1, B1......Z1, A2......Z2, A3......etc. and did not only apply to locomotives. Locomotives bought from outside contractors were classified by the first number to be delivered, e.g. "0298 Class".

CLASS O2   0-4-4T

Built: 1889–91. Adams LSWR design.
B.P.: 160 lbf/sq. in.   **Wheel dias.:** 4′ 10″   **T.E.:** 17 235 lbf.
Cyls.: 17″ x 24″ (I).   **Weight:** 48.4 tons.
Valve Gear: Stephenson.
Air braked.

BR	SR	LSWR			
W24	E209–W24	209 CALBOURNE	Isle of Wight Steam Railway		Nine Elms 341/1891

CLASS M7   0-4-4T

Built: 1897–1911. Drummond LSWR design. 105 built.
B.P.: 175 lbf/sq. in.   **Wheel dias.:** 5′ 7″, 3′ 7″.   **T.E.:** 19 760 lbf.
Cyls.: 18½″ x 26″ (I).   **Weight:** 60.15 tons.
Valve Gear: Stephenson.
30053 was push and pull fitted and air braked.

BR	SR	LSWR		
30053	E53–53	53	Swanage Railway	Nine Elms 1905
30245	E245–245	245	National Railway Museum	Nine Elms 501/1897

CLASS USA   0-6-0T

Built: 1942–43 by Vulcan Works, Wilkes-Barre, PA, USA for US Army Transportation Corps. 93 built (a further 289 were built by other builders). Thirteen were sold to SR in 1947 becoming 62–74.
B.P.: 210 lbf/sq. in.   **Wheel dia.:** 4′ 6″   **T.E.:** 21 600 lbf.
Cyls.: 16½″ x 24″ (O).   **Weight:** 46.5 tons.
Valve Gear: Walschaert.

BR	SR	USATC			Present
30064	64	1959		Bluebell Railway	VIW 4432/1943
30065	65	1968	"MAUNSELL"	Kent & East Sussex Railway	VIW 4441/1943
30070	70	1960	"WAINWRIGHT"	Kent & East Sussex Railway	VIW 4433/1943
30072	72	1973		Keighley & Worth Valley Railway	VIW 4446/1943

Note: 30065 carried DS237 and 30070 carried DS238 from 1963.

CLASS B4   0-4-0T

Built: 1891–1909. Adams LSWR design for dock shunting (25 built).
B.P.: 140 lbf/sq. in.   **Wheel dia.:** 3′ 9¾″   **T.E.:** 14 650 lbf.
Cyls.: 16″ x 22″ (O).   **Weight:** 33.45 tons.
Valve Gear: Stephenson.

BR	SR			
30096	E96–96	NORMANDY	Bluebell Railway	Nine Elms 396/1893
30102	E102–102	GRANVILLE	Bressingham Steam Museum	Nine Elms 406/1893

CLASS T9   4-4-0

Built: 1889–1924. Drummond LSWR express passenger design. 66 built.
B.P.: 175 lbf/sq. in.   **Weight –Loco:** 51.8 tons.   **Wheel dias.:** 3′ 7″, 6′ 7″.
Cyls.: 19″ x 26″ (I).   **–Tender:** 44.85 tons.   **T.E.:** 17 670 lbf.
Valve Gear: Stephenson.

BR	SR	LSWR		
30120	E120–120	120	Bluebell Railway (N)	Nine Elms 572/1899

CLASS S15 (URIE)   4-6-0

Built: 1920–21. Urie LSWR design. 20 built.
B.P.: 180 lbf/sq. in.   **Weight –Loco:** 79.8 tons.   **Wheel dias.:** 3′ 7″, 5′ 7″.
Cyls.: 21″ x 28″ (O).   **–Tender:** 57.8 tons.   **T.E.:** 28 200 lbf.
Valve Gear: Walschaert.

BR	SR	LSWR		
30499	E499–499	499	Watercress Line	Eastleigh 1920
30506	E506–506	506	Watercress Line	Eastleigh 1920

Note: 30499 is receiving attention at the East Lancashire Railway.

CLASS Q 0-6-0

Built: 1938–39. Maunsell SR design. 20 built (30530–49).
B.P.: 200 lbf/sq. in.   **Weight –Loco:** 49.5 tons.   **Wheel dias.:** 5′ 1″.
Cyls.: 19″ x 26″ (I).   **–Tender:** 40.5 tons.   **T.E.:** 26 160 lbf.
Valve Gear: Stephenson.

BR	SR		
30541	541	Bluebell Railway	Eastleigh 1939

0415 CLASS 4-4-2T

Built: 1882–85. Adams LSWR design. 72 built.
B.P.: 160 lbf/sq. in.   **Wheel dias.:** 3′ 0″, 5′ 7″, 3′ 0″   **T.E.:** 14 920 lbf.
Cyls.: 17½″ x 24″ (O).   **Weight:** 55.25 tons.
Valve Gear: Stephenson.

BR	SR	LSWR		
30583	E0488–3488	488	Bluebell Railway	N 3209/1885

0298 CLASS 2-4-0WT

Built: 1863–75. W. G. Beattie LSWR design. Last used on the Wenford Bridge branch in Cornwall. 85 built. Survivors reboilered in 1921.
B.P.: 160 lbf/sq. in.   **Wheel dias.:** 3′ 7¾″, 5′ 7″.   **T.E.:** 12 160 lbf.
Cyls.: 16½″ x 22″ (O).   **Weight:** 35.75 (36.3§) tons.
Valve Gear: Allan.

BR	SR	LSWR		
30585§	E0314–3314	0314	Buckinghamshire Railway Centre	BP 1414/1874 reb Elh 1921
30587	E0298–3298	0298	Bodmin Steam Railway (N)	BP 1412/1874 reb Elh 1921

CLASS N15   KING ARTHUR 4-6-0

Built: 1925–27. Maunsell SR development of Urie LSWR design. 54 built (30448–457, 30763–806).
B.P.: 200 lbf/sq. in.   **Weight –Loco:** 80.7 tons.   **Wheel dias.:** 3′ 7″, 6′ 7″.
Cyls.: 20½″ x 28″ (O).   **–Tender:** 56.4 tons.   **T.E.:** 25 320 lbf.
Valve Gear: Walschaert.

BR	SR			
30777	777	SIR LAMIEL	Great Central Railway (N)	NBL 23223/1925

CLASS S15 (MAUNSELL) 4-6-0

Built: 1927–36. Maunsell SR development of Urie LSWR design.
B.P.: 200 lbf/sq. in.   **Weight –Loco:** 80.7 (79.25*) tons.   **Wheel dias.:** 3′ 7″, 5′ 7″.
Cyls.: 20½″ x 28″ (O).   **–Tender:** 56.4 tons.   **T.E.:** 29 860 lbf.
Valve Gear: Walschaert.

BR	SR		
30825	825	North Yorkshire Moors Railway	Eastleigh 1927
30828	828	Swanage Railway	Eastleigh 1927
30830	830	North Yorkshire Moors Railway	Eastleigh 1927
30847*	847	Bluebell Railway	Eastleigh 1936

Note: 30825 has been restored using a substantial number of components from 30841.

CLASS LN   LORD NELSON   4-6-0

Built: 1926–29. Maunsell SR design. 16 built (30850–65).
B.P.: 220 lbf/sq. in.   **Weight –Loco:** 83.5 tons.   **Wheel dias.:** 3′ 1″, 6′ 7″.
Cyls.: 16½″ x 26″ (4).   **–Tender:** 56.7 tons.   **T.E.:** 33 510 lbf.
Valve Gear: Walschaert.

BR	*SR*			
30850	E850–850	LORD NELSON	ERPS, Alstom, Eastleigh Works (N)	Eastleigh 1926

CLASS V   SCHOOLS   4-4-0

Built: 1930–35. Maunsell SR design. 40 built (30900–39).
B.P.: 220 lbf/sq. in.   **Weight –Loco:** 67.1 tons.   **Wheel dias.:** 3′ 1″, 6′ 7″.
Cyls.: 16½″ x 26″ (3).   **–Tender:** 42.4 tons.   **T.E.:** 25 130 lbf.
Valve Gear: Walschaert.

BR	*SR*			
30925	925	CHELTENHAM	National Railway Museum	Eastleigh 1934
30926	926	REPTON	North Yorkshire Moors Railway	Eastleigh 1934
30928	928	STOWE	Bluebell Railway	Eastleigh 1934

CLASS P   0-6-0T

Built: 1909–10. Wainwright SECR design. 8 built.
B.P.: 160 lbf/sq. in.   **Wheel dias.:** 3′ 9″.   **T.E.:** 7830 lbf.
Cyls.: 12″ x 18″ (I).   **Weight:** 28.5 tons.
Valve Gear: Stephenson.

Push & pull fitted.

BR	*SR*	*SECR*		
31027	A 27–1027	27	Bluebell Railway	Ashford 1910
31178	A178–1178	178	Bluebell Railway	Ashford 1910
31323	A323–1323	323	Bluebell Railway	Ashford 1910
31556	A556–1556	753	Kent & East Sussex Railway	Ashford 1909

CLASS O1   0-6-0

Built: 1903–15. Wainwright SECR design. 66 built. 59 were rebuilt out of 122 "O" class.
B.P.: 150 lbf/sq. in.   **Weight –Loco:** 41.05 tons.   **Wheel dia.:** 5′ 1″.
Cyls.: 18″ x 26″ (I).   **–Tender:** 25.45 tons.   **T.E.:** 17 610 lbf.
Valve Gear: Stephenson.

BR	*SR*	*SECR*		
31065	A65–1065	65	Bluebell Railway	Ashford 1896 reb. 1908

CLASS H   0-4-4T

Built: 1904–15. Wainwright SECR design. 66 built.
B.P.: 160 lbf/sq. in.   **Wheel dias.:** 5′ 6″, 3′ 7″.   **T.E.:** 17 360 lbf.
Cyls.: 18″ x 26″ (I).   **Weight:** 54.4 tons.
Valve Gear: Stephenson.
Push and Pull fitted. Air brakes.

BR	*SR*	*SECR*		
31263	A263–1263	263	Bluebell Railway	Ashford 1905

CLASS C   0-6-0

Built: 1900–08. Wainwright SECR design. 109 built.
B.P.: 160 lbf/sq. in.   **Weight –Loco:** 43.8 tons.   **Wheel dia.:** 5′ 2″.
Cyls.: 18½″ x 26″ (I).   **–Tender:** 38.25 tons.   **T.E.:** 19 520 lbf.
Valve Gear: Stephenson.

BR	*SR*	*SECR*		
31592–DS239	A592–1592	592	Bluebell Railway	Longhedge 1902

CLASS U   2-6-0

Built: 1928–31. Maunsell SR design. 50 built (31610–39, 31790–809). 31790–809 were converted from class K (River Class) 2-6-4Ts.
B.P.: 200 lbf/sq. in.   **Weight –Loco:** 61.9 (62.55§) tons.   **Wheel dias.:** 3' 1", 6' 0".
Cyls.: 19" x 28" (O).   **–Tender:** 42.4 tons.   **T.E.:** 23 870 lbf.
Valve Gear: Walschaert.

* Formerly class K 2–6–4T A806 RIVER TORRIDGE built Ashford 1926.

BR	SR			
31618	A618–1618		Bluebell Railway	Brighton 1928
31625	A625–1625		Watercress Line	Ashford 1929
31638	A638–1638		Bluebell Railway	Ashford 1931
31806*	A806–1806		Watercress Line	Brighton 1928

CLASS D   4-4-0

Built: 1901–07. Wainwright SECR design. 51 built.
B.P.: 175 lbf/sq. in.   **Weight –Loco:** 50 tons.   **Wheel dias.:** 3' 7", 6' 8".
Cyls.: 19¼" x 26" (I).   **–Tender:** 39.1 tons.   **T.E.:** 17 910 lbf.
Valve Gear: Stephenson.

BR	SR	SECR		
31737	A737–1737	737	National Railway Museum	Ashford 1901

CLASS N   2-6-0

Built: 1917–34. Maunsell SECR design. Some built by SR. 80 built.
B.P.: 200 lbf/sq. in.   **Weight –Loco:** 59.4 tons.   **Wheel dias.:** 3' 1", 5' 6".
Cyls.: 19" x 28" (O).   **–Tender:** 39.25 tons.   **T.E.:** 26 040 lbf.
Valve Gear: Walschaert.

BR	SR	Present		
31874	A874–1874	"5 JAMES"	Watercress Line	Woolwich Arsenal 1925

CLASS E1   0-6-0T

Built: 1874–83. Stroudley LBSCR design. 80 built.
B.P.: 160 lbf/sq. in.   **Wheel dias.:** 4' 6"   **T.E.:** 17 470 lbf.
Cyls.: 17" x 24" (I).   **Weight:** 44.15 tons.
Valve Gear: Stephenson.

BR	SR	LBSCR		
–	B110	110	East Somerset Railway	Brighton 1877

CLASS E4   0-6-2T

Built: 1897–1903. R Billinton LBSCR design. 120 built.
B.P.: 160 lbf/sq. in.   **Wheel dias.:** 5' 0", 4' 0".   **T.E.:** 19 090 lbf.
Cyls.: 18" x 26" (I).   **Weight:** 56.75 tons.
Valve Gear: Stephenson.

BR	SR	LBSCR			
32473	B473–2473	473	BIRCH GROVE	Bluebell Railway	Brighton 1898

CLASSES A1 & A1X   "TERRIER"   0-6-0T

Built: 1872–80 as class A1§. Stroudley LBSCR design. Most rebuilt to A1X from 1911. 50 built. All were built at Brighton.
B.P.: 150 lbf/sq. in.   **Wheel dias.:** 4' 0".   **T.E.:** 10 410 lbf (8890 lbf§†, 7650 lbf*).
Cyls.: 14" (13"†, 12"*) x 20" (I). **Weight:** 28.25 tons.
Valve Gear: Stephenson.

a–air brakes, d–dual brakes.

BR	SR	LBSCR			
32636d†	B636–2636	72	FENCHURCH	Bluebell Railway	1872
32640a	W11–2640	40	NEWPORT	Isle of Wight Steam Railway	1878
32646a	W2–W8	46–646	FRESHWATER	Isle of Wight Steam Railway	1876

32650d*	B650–W9	50–650	WHITECHAPEL	Kent & East Sussex Railway	1876
DS680a*	A751–680S	54–654	WADDON	Canadian Railroad Historical Museum	1875
32655	B655–2655	55–655	STEPNEY	Bluebell Railway	1875
32662a*	B66–2662	62–662	MARTELLO	Bressingham Steam Museum	1875
32670		70	POPLAR	Kent & East Sussex Railway	1872
32678d	B678–W4–W14	78–678	KNOWLE	Kent & East Sussex Railway	1880
a	380S	82–682	BOXHILL	National Railway Museum	1880

Notes:

32640 was also named BRIGHTON.
32646 was sold to the LSWR and became 734. It has also been named NEWINGTON.
32650 became 515S (departmental) and was named FISHBOURNE when on the Isle of Wight. It is now named "SUTTON".
DS680 was sold to the SECR and became their 75.
32678 was named BEMBRIDGE when on the Isle of Wight.
32640 was originally Isle of Wight Central Railway No. 11
32646 was originally Freshwater Yarmouth and Newport Railway No. 2.

CLASS Q1   0-6-0

Built: 1942. Bulleid SR "Austerity" design. 40 built (33001–40).
B.P.: 230 lbf/sq. in.   **Weight –Loco:** 51.25 tons.   **Wheel dia.:** 5' 1".
Cyls.: 19" x 26" (I).   **–Tender:** 38 tons.   **T.E.:** 30 080 lbf.
Valve Gear: Stephenson.

BR	*SR*			
33001	C1		Bluebell Railway (N)	Brighton 1942

CLASSES WC & BB   4-6-2
WEST COUNTRY and BATTLE OF BRITAIN

Built: 1945–51. Bulleid SR design with "air smoothed" casing, thermic syphons and Boxpox driving wheels. 110 built (34001–110). All built at Brighton.
B.P.: 250 lbf/sq. in.   **Weight –Loco:** 86 (91.65*) tons.
Cyls.: 16³/₈" x 24" (3).   **–Tender:** 42.7, 47.9 or 47.75 tons.
Wheel dias.: 3' 1", 6' 2", 3' 1".   **T.E.:** 27 720 lbf.
Valve Gear: Bulleid chain driven (Walschaert*).

* Rebuilt at Eastleigh by Jarvis 1957–61 with the removal of the air-smoothed casing.
x Dual (air/vacuum) brakes.

BR	*SR*			
34007	21C107	WADEBRIDGE	Bodmin Steam Railway	1945
34010*	21C110	SIDMOUTH	Hope Farm, Sellindge	1945 reb 1959
34016*	21C116	BODMIN	Watercress Line	1945 reb 1958
34023	21C123	BLACKMORE VALE	Bluebell Railway	1946
34027*x	21C127	TAW VALLEY	Severn Valley Railway	1946 reb 1957
34028*	21C128	EDDYSTONE	Swanage Railway	1946 reb 1958
34039*	21C139	BOSCASTLE	Great Central Railway	1946 reb 1959
34046*	21C146	BRAUNTON	West Somerset Railway	1946 reb 1959
34051	21C151	WINSTON CHURCHILL	National Railway Museum	1946
34053*	21C153	SIR KEITH PARK	Hope Farm, Sellindge	1947 reb 1958
34058*	21C158	SIR FREDERICK PILE	Avon Valley Railway	1947 reb 1960
34059*	21C159	SIR ARCHIBALD SINCLAIR	Bluebell Railway	1947 reb 1960
34067	21C167	TANGMERE	Watercress Line	1947
34070	21C170	MANSTON	Hope Farm, Sellindge	1947
34072		257 SQUADRON	Swanage Railway	1948
34073		249 SQUADRON	Watercress Line	1948
34081		92 SQUADRON	Nene Valley Railway	1948
34092		CITY OF WELLS	Keighley & Worth Valley Railway	1949
34101		HARTLAND	North Yorkshire Moors Railway	1950 reb 1960
34105		SWANAGE	Watercress Line	1950

Notes:

34010 will be restored as "34109 SIR TRAFFORD LEIGH–MALLORY"
34023 was named BLACKMOOR VALE to 4/50.
34067 is receiving attention at the East Lancashire Railway.
34092 was named WELLS to 3/50.

CLASS MN   MERCHANT NAVY   4-6-2

Built: 1941–49. Bulleid SR design with air smoothed casing and similar features to 'WC' and 'BB'. All rebuilt 1956–59 by Jarvis to more conventional appearance. 30 built (35001–30). All locomotives were built and rebuilt at Eastleigh.
B.P.: 250 lbf/sq. in.   **Weight –Loco:** 97.9 tons.   **Wheel dias.:** 3' 1", 6' 2", 3' 7".
Cyls.: 18" x 24" (3).   **–Tender:** 47.8 tons.   **T.E.:** 33 490 lbf.
Valve Gear: Walschaert.

§ Sectioned.
x Dual (air/vacuum) brakes.

BR	SR			
35005	21C5	CANADIAN PACIFIC	Watercress Line	1941 reb 1959
35006	21C6	PENINSULAR & ORIENTAL S.N. Co.	Gloucestershire–Warwickshire Rly	1941 reb 1959
35009	21C9	SHAW SAVILL	Designer Outlet Village, Swindon	1942 reb 1957
35010	21C10	BLUE STAR	Colne Valley Railway	1942 reb 1957
35011	21C11	GENERAL STEAM NAVIGATION	HLPG, Binbrook Trading Estate	1944 reb 1959
35018	21C18	BRITISH INDIA LINE	Watercress Line	1945 reb 1956
35022		HOLLAND AMERICA LINE	Hope Farm, Sellindge	1948 reb 1956
35025		BROCKLEBANK LINE	Great Central Railway	1948 reb 1956
35027		PORT LINE	Swanage Railway	1948 reb 1957
35028x		CLAN LINE	MNLPS, Stewarts Lane, London	1948 reb 1959
35029§		ELLERMAN LINES	National Railway Museum	1949 reb 1959

CLASS T3   4-4-0

Built: 1982–93. Adams LSWR design. 20 built
B.P.: 175 lbf/sq. in.   **Weight –Loco:** 48.55 tons.   **Wheel dias.:** 3' 7", 6' 7".
Cyls.: 19" x 26" (O).   **–Tender:** 33.2 tons.   **T.E.:** 17 670 lbf.
Valve Gear: Stephenson.

SR	LSWR			
E563–563	563		National Railway Museum	Nine Elms 380/1893

CLASS B1   "GLADSTONES"   0-4-2

Built: 1882–91. Stroudley LBSCR design. 49 built.
B.P.: 150 lbf/sq. in.   **Weight –Loco:** 38.7 tons.   **Wheel dias.:** 6' 6", 4' 6".
Cyls.: 18¼" x 26" (I).   **–Tender:** 29.35 tons.   **T.E.:** 14 160 lbf.
Valve Gear: Stephenson. Air brakes.

SR	LBSCR			
B618	214–618	GLADSTONE	National Railway Museum	Brighton 1882

CANTERBURY & WHITSTABLE RAILWAY   0-4-0

Built: 1830. Robert Stephenson & Company design.
B.P.: 40 lbf/sq. in.   **Weight –Loco:** 6.25 tons   **Wheel dias.:** 4' 0".
Cyls.: 10½" x 18" (O).   **–Tender:**   **T.E.:** 2680 lbf.

INVICTA	Canterbury Heritage Centre	RS 24/1830

1.3. LONDON MIDLAND & SCOTTISH RAILWAY & CONSTITUENT COMPANIES' STEAM LOCOMOTIVES

GENERAL

The LMS was formed in 1923 by the amalgamation of the Midland Railway, London and North Western Railway (LNWR), Caledonian Railway (CR), Glasgow and South Western Railway (GSWR) and Highland Railway (HR), plus a few smaller railways. Prior to this the North London Railway (NLR) and the Lancashire and Yorkshire Railway (L&Y) had been absorbed by the LNWR and the London, Tilbury and Southend Railway (LTSR) and been absorbed by the Midland Railway.

Numbering System

Originally number series were allocated to divisions as follows:

1– 4999	Midland Division (Midland and North Staffordshire Railway).
5000– 9999	Western Division 'A' (LNWR).
10000–13999	Western Division 'B' (L & Y).
14000–17999	Northern Division (Scottish Railways).

From 1934 onwards, all LMS standard locomotives and new builds were numbered in the range from 1–9999, and any locomotives which would have had their numbers duplicated had 20000 added to their original number.

At nationalisation 40000 was added to all LMS numbers except that locomotives which were renumbered in the 2xxxx series were further renumbered generally in the 58xxx series. In the following section locomotives are listed in order of BR number or in the position of the BR number they would have carried if they had lasted into BR days, except for very old locomotives which are listed at the end of the section.

Classification System

LMS locomotives did not generally have unique class designations but were referred to by their power classification which varied from 0 to 8 followed by the letters 'P' for a passenger locomotive and 'F' for a freight locomotive. Mixed traffic locomotives had no suffix letter, but BR used the description 'MT' to denote these.

CLASS 4P   COMPOUND   4-4-0

Built: 1902–03. Johnson Midland design, rebuilt by Deeley 1914–19 to a similar design to the Deeley compounds which were built 1905–09. A further similar batch was built by the LMS in 1924–32. 240 built (41000–41199, 40900–40939).

B.P.: 200 lb/sq. in.   **Weight–Loco:** 61.7 tons.   **Wheel dias.:** 3′ 6½″, 7′ 0″.
T.E.: 23 205 lbf.   **–Tender:** 45.9 tons.
Cyls.: One high pressure. 19″ x 26″ (I).
    Two low pressure. 21″ x 26″ (O).
Valve Gear: Stephenson.

BR   LMS   MR
41000 1000 1000 (2361 pre-1907)   National Railway Museum   Derby 1902 reb 1914

CLASS 2MT   2-6-2T

Built: 1946–52. Ivatt LMS design. 130 built (41200–41329).
B.P.: 200 lb/sq. in.   **Wheel dias.:** 3′ 0″, 5′ 0″, 3′ 0″. **T.E.:** 18 510 (17 410*) lbf.
Cyls.: 16½″ (16″*) x 24″ (O).   **Weight:** 65.2 (63.25*) tons.
Valve Gear: Walschaert.

41241*	Keighley & Worth Valley Railway	Crewe 1949
41298	Buckinghamshire Railway Centre	Crewe 1951
41312	Watercress Line	Crewe 1952
41313	Buckinghamshire Railway Centre	Crewe 1952

CLASS 1F   0-6-0T

Built: 1874–92. Johnson Midland design. Rebuilt with Belpaire boiler. 262 built.
B.P.: 150 lb/sq. in.   **Wheel dias.:** 4′ 6½″.   **T.E.:** 16 230 lbf.
Cyls.: 17″ x 24″ (I).   **Weight:** 45.45 tons.
Valve Gear: Stephenson.

BR   LMS   MR
41708 1708 1708   Avon Valley Railway   Derby 1880

LTS 79 CLASS (3P)   4-4-2T

Built: 1909. Whitelegg LTSR design. 4 built.
B.P.: 170 lb/sq. in.   **Wheel dias.:** 3′, 6″, 6′ 6″, 3′ 6″. **T.E.:** 17 390 lbf.
Cyls.: 19″ x 26″ (O).   **Weight:** 69.35 tons.
Valve Gear: Stephenson.

BR   LMS   MR   LTSR
41966 2148 2177 80 THUNDERSLEY   Bressingham Steam Museum (N)   RS 3367/1909

CLASS 4MT   2-6-4T

Built: 1945–51. Fairburn modification of Stanier design (built 1936–43). This in turn was a development of a Fowler design built 1927–34. 383 built (Stanier & Fairburn). (42030–299/425–494/537–699).
B.P.: 200 lb/sq. in.   **Wheel dias.:** 3′, 3½″, 5′ 9″, 3′ 3½″. **T.E.:** 24 670 lbf.
Cyls.: 19¾″ x 26″ (O).   **Weight:** 85.25 tons.
Valve Gear: Walschaert.

42073	Lakeside & Haverthwaite Railway	Brighton 1950
42085	Lakeside & Haverthwaite Railway	Brighton 1951

CLASS 4MT   2-6-4T

Built: 1934. Stanier LMS 3-cylinder design for LTS line. 37 built (42500–36).
B.P.: 200 lb/sq. in.   **Wheel dias.:** 3′, 3½″, 5′ 9″, 3′ 3½″. **T.E.:** 24 600 lbf.
Cyls.: 16″ x 26″ (3).   **Weight:** 92.5 tons.
Valve Gear: Walschaert.

BR   LMS
42500 2500   National Railway Museum   Derby 1934

Stanier Class 5MT 4-6-0 No. 45407 has been masquerading as No. 45157 "GLASGOW HIGHLANDER" for some time now. Here it is seen near Ramsbottom on a Bury–Rawtenstall train (with No. 75014 assisting at the rear!) on 27 January 2001.

Les Nixon

CLASS 5MT   "CRAB"   2-6-0

Built: 1926–32. Hughes LMS design. 245 built (42700–944).
B.P.: 180 lb/sq. in.   **Weight–Loco:** 66 tons.   **Wheel dias.:** 3′ 6½″, 5′ 6″.
Cyls.: 21″ x 26″ (O).   **–Tender:** 42.2 (41.5*) tons. **T.E.:** 26 580 lbf.
Valve Gear: Walschaert.

BR	LMS		
42700	13000–2700	Barrow Hill Roundhouse (N)	Horwich 1926
42765*	13065–2765	East Lancashire Railway	Crewe 5757/1927
42859	13159–2859	HLPG, Binbrook Trading Estate	Crewe 5981/1930

CLASS 5MT   2-6-0

Built: 1933–34. Stanier LMS design. 40 built (42945–84).
B.P.: 225 lb/sq. in.   **Weight–Loco:** 69.1 tons.   **Wheel dias.:** 3′ 3½″, 5′ 6″.
Cyls.: 18″ x 28″ (O).   **–Tender:** 42.2 tons.   **T.E.:** 26 290 lbf.
Valve Gear: Walschaert.

BR	LMS		
42968	13268–2968	Severn Valley Railway	Crewe 1934

CLASS 4MT   2-6-0

Built: 1947–52. Ivatt design. 162 built (43000–161).
B.P.: 225 lb/sq. in.   **Weight–Loco:** 59.1 tons.   **Wheel dias.:** 3′ 0″, 5′ 3″.
Cyls.: 17½″ x 26″ (O).   **–Tender:** 40.3 tons.   **T.E.:** 24 170 lbf.
Valve Gear: Walschaert.

43106	Severn Valley Railway	Darlington 2148/1951

CLASS 4F   0-6-0

Built: 1911–41. Fowler Midland design. Locomotives from 44027 onwards were LMS design with higher sided tenders. The preserved Midland locomotive has an LMS tender. 772 built (43835–44606).
B.P.: 175 lb/sq. in.   **Weight–Loco:** 48.75 tons.   **Wheel dias.:** 5′ 3″.
Cyls.: 20″ x 26″ (I).   **–Tender:** 41.2 tons.   **T.E.:** 24 560 lbf.
Valve Gear: Stephenson.

BR	LMS	MR		
43924	3924	3924	Keighley & Worth Valley Railway	Derby 1920
44027	4027		Midland Railway Centre (N)	Derby 1924
44123	4123		Avon Valley Railway	Crewe 5658/1925
44422	4422		Churnet Valley Railway	Derby 1927

CLASS 5MT   "BLACK 5"   4-6-0

Built: 1934–50. Stanier design. 842 built (45000–45499 then 44999–44658 in descending order).
B.P.: 225 lb/sq. in.   **Weight–Loco:** 72.1 (75.3*) tons.   **Wheel dias.:** 3′ 3½″, 6′ 0″
Cyls.: 18½″ x 28″ (O).   **–Tender:** 53.65 (53.8*) tons. **T.E.:** 25 450 lbf.
Valve Gear: Walschaert (Outside Stephenson*).

x–Dual (air/vacuum) brakes.

BR	LMS			
44767*	4767	"GEORGE STEPHENSON"	North Yorkshire Moors Railway	Crewe 1947
44806	4806	"MAGPIE"	Llangollen Railway	Derby 1944
44871	4871	"SOVEREIGN"	East Lancashire Railway	Crewe 1945
44901	4901		Vale of Glamorgan Railway	Crewe 1945
44932	4932		Midland Railway Centre	Horwich 1945
45000	5000		National Railway Museum	Crewe 216/1935
45025	5025		Strathspey Railway	VF 4570/1934
45110	5110	"RAF BIGGIN HILL"	Severn Valley Railway	VF 4653/1935
45163	5163		Colne Valley Railway	AW 1204/1935
45212	5212		North Yorkshire Moors Railway	AW 1253/1935
45231	5231		Great Central Railway	AW 1286/1936
45293	5293		Colne Valley Railway	AW 1348/1936

45305	5305		Great Central Railway	AW 1360/1937
45337	5337		North Yorkshire Moors Railway	AW 1392/1937
45379	5379		Watercress Line	AW 1434/1937
45407x	5407		East Lancashire Railway	AW 1462/1937
45428	5428	"ERIC TREACY"	North Yorkshire Moors Railway	AW 1483/1937
45491	5491		Midland Railway Centre	Derby 1943

CLASS 6P (Formerly 5XP)   JUBILEE   4-6-0

Built: 1934–36. Stanier taper boiler development of Patriot class. 191 built (45552–45742).
B.P.: 225 lb/sq. in.   **Weight–Loco:** 79.55 tons.   **Wheel dias.:** 3′ 3½″, 6′ 9″.
Cyls.: 17″ x 26″ (3).   **–Tender:** 53.65 tons.   **T.E.:** 26 610 lbf.
Valve Gear: Walschaert.
* Fitted with double chimney.

BR	LMS			
45593	5593	KOLHAPUR	Barrow Hill Roundhouse	NBL 24151/1934
45596	5596*	BAHAMAS	Keighley & Worth Valley Railway	NBL 24154/1935
45690	5690	LEANDER	East Lancashire Railway	Crewe 288/1936
45699	5699	GALATEA	West Coast Railway Company, Carnforth	Crewe 297/1936

CLASS 7P (Formerly 6P)   ROYAL SCOT   4-6-0

Built: 1927–30. Fowler parallel design. All rebuilt 1943–55 with taper boilers and curved smoke deflectors. 71 built (46100–70).
B.P.: 250 lb/sq. in.   **Weight–Loco:** 83 tons.   **Wheel dias.:** 3′ 3½″, 6′ 9″.
Cyls.: 18″ x 26″ (3).   **–Tender:** 54.65 tons.   **T.E.:** 33 150 lbf.
Valve Gear: Walschaert.

BR	LMS			
46100	6100	ROYAL SCOT	Bressingham Steam Museum(N)	Derby 1930 reb Crewe 1947
46115	6115	SCOTS GUARDSMAN	The Railway Age, Crewe	NBL 23610/1927 reb Crewe 1950

Notes:

6100 was built as 6152 THE KING'S DRAGOON GUARDSMAN. This loco swapped identities permanently with 6100 ROYAL SCOT in 1933 for a tour of the USA.

CLASS 8P (Formerly 7P)   PRINCESS ROYAL   4-6-2

Built: 1933–35. Stanier design. 13 built (46200–12).
B.P.: 250 lb/sq. in.   **Weight**   **–Loco:** 105.5 tons. **W h e e l dias.:** 3′ 0″, 6′ 9″, 3′ 9″.
Cyls.: 16¼″ x 28″ (4).   **–Tender:** 54.65 tons.   **T.E.:** 40 290 lbf.
Valve Gear: Walschaert.

x–Dual (air/vacuum) brakes.

BR	LMS			
46201x	6201	PRINCESS ELIZABETH	East Lancashire Railway	Crewe 107/1933
46203	6203	PRINCESS MARGARET ROSE	Midland Railway Centre	Crewe 253/1935

CLASS 8P (Formerly 7P)   CORONATION   4-6-2

Built: 1937–48. Stanier design. 24 of this class were built streamlined but had the casing removed later. Certain locomotives were built with single chimneys, but all finished up with double chimneys. The tenders were fitted with steam driven coal-pushers. 38 built (46220–57).
B.P.: 250 lb/sq. in.   **Weight–Loco:** 105.25 tons.   **Wheel dias.:** 3′ 0″, 6′ 9″, 3′ 9″.
Cyls.: 16½″ x 28″ (4).   **–Tender:** 56.35 tons.   **T.E.:** 40 000 lbf.
Valve Gear: Walschaert.

d–Formerly streamlined. Built with double chimney. Casing removed.
n–Never streamlined. Built with single chimney. Dual air/vacuum brakes.
s–Formerly streamlined. Built with single chimney. Casing removed.

BR	LMS			
46229 s	6229	DUCHESS OF HAMILTON	National Railway Museum	Crewe 1938
46233 n	6233	DUCHESS OF SUTHERLAND	Midland Railway Centre	Crewe 1938
46235 d	6235	CITY OF BIRMINGHAM	Birmingham Museum of Sc. & I.	Crewe 1939

CLASS 2MT   2-6-0

Built: 1946–53. Ivatt design. 128 built (46400–527).
B.P.: 200 lb/sq. in.   **Weight–Loco:** 47.1 (48.45*) tons.   **Wheel dias.:** 3' 0", 5' 0".
Cyls.: 16" (16½"*) x 24" (O).   **–Tender:** 37.15 tons.   **T.E.:** 17 410 (18 510*) lbf.
Valve Gear: Walschaert.

46428		East Lancashire Railway	Crewe 1948
46441		East Lancashire Railway	Crewe 1950
46443		Severn Valley Railway	Crewe 1950
46447		Buckinghamshire Railway Centre	Crewe 1950
46464		Caledonian Railway	Crewe 1950
46512*	"E.V. COOPER ENGINEER"	Strathspey Railway	Swindon 1952
46521*		Great Central Railway	Swindon 1953

CLASS 3F   "JINTY"   0-6-0T

Built: 1924–31. Fowler LMS development of his own Midland design. 422 built (47260–47681).
B.P.: 160 lb/sq. in.   **Wheel dia.:** 4' 7".   **T.E.:** 20 830 lbf.
Cyls.: 18" x 26" (I).   **Weight:** 49.5 tons.
Valve Gear: Stephenson.

BR	LMS		
47279	7119–7279	Keighley & Worth Valley Railway	VF 3736/1924
47298	7138–7298	Llangollen Railway	HE 1463/1924
47324	16407–7324	East Lancashire Railway	NBL 23403/1926
47327	16410–7327	Midland Railway Centre	NBL 23406/1926
47357	16440–7357	Midland Railway Centre	NBL 23436/1926
47383	16466–7383	Severn Valley Railway	VF 3954/1926
47406	16489–7406	Great Central Railway	VF 3977/1926
47445	16528–7445	Midland Railway Centre	HE 1529/1927
47493	16576–7493	Spa Valley Railway	VF 4195/1928
47564	16647–7564	Midland Railway Centre	HE 1580/1928

Note: 47564 was latterly used as a stationary boiler numbered 2022.

CLASS 8F   2-8-0

Built: 1934–46. Stanier design. 331 built (8000–8225, 8301–8399, 8490–5). A further 521 were built to Ministry of Supply (208) Railway Executive Committee (245) and LNER (68) orders. Many of these operated on Britain's Railways with 228 being shipped overseas during the war. Postwar many were taken into LMS/BR stock including some returned from overseas
B.P.: 225 lb/sq. in.   **Weight–Loco:** 72.1 tons.   **Wheel dias.:** 3' 3½", ,4' 8½".
Cyls.: 18½" x 28" (O).   **–Tender:** 53.65 tons.   **T.E.:** 32 440 lbf.
Valve Gear: Walschaert.
Turkish locos have air brakes.

*–Number allocated but never carried.
§–Became Persian Railways 41.109. WD number was 70307 in 1944 and 500 in 1952.

BR	LMS	WD	TCDD/IRR		
48151	8151			West Coast Railway Company, Carnforth	Crewe 1942
48173	8173			Avon Valley Railway	Crewe 1943
	8266*	340	45168		
	8267*	341	45166		
	8274*	348	45160	Gloucestershire-Warwickshire Railway	NBL 24648/1940
	8279*	353	45165	Izmir Alsancak Station, Turkey	NBL 24653/1940
	8283*	357	45153		
		522	45161	Camlik Museum, Turkey	NBL 24670/1941
		547	1429	IRR, Baghdad, Iraq	NBL 24740/1941
		554	45170		
48305	8305			Churnet Valley Railway	Crewe 1943
48431	8431			Keighley & Worth Valley Railway	Swindon 1944
48518	8518			Vale of Glamorgan Railway	Doncaster 1966/1944
48624	8624			Peak Railway	Ashford 1943
48773	8233	307§		Severn Valley Railway	NBL 24607/1940

CLASS 7F   0-8-0

Built: 1921–22. Beames development of 1912 Bowen-Cooke LNWR design. 60 built (49395–454). In addition many 1912 locos were rebuilt to similar condition.
B.P.: 175 lb/sq. in.   **Weight–Loco:** 62 tons.   **Wheel dia.:** 4′ 5½″.
Cyls.: 20½″ x 24″ (I).   **–Tender:** 40.75 tons.   **T.E.:** 28 040 lbf.
Valve Gear: Joy.

BR	LMS	LNWR		
49395	9395	485	The Railway Age, Crewe (N)	Crewe 5662/1921

L & Y CLASS 5   2-4-2T

Built: 1889–1909. Aspinall L & Y design (2P) 210 built.
B.P.: 180 lb/sq. in.   **Wheel dias.:** 3′ 7⅛″, 5′ 7⅝″, 3′ 7⅛″.
Cyls.: 18″ x 26″ (I).   **Weight:** 55.45 tons.   **T.E.:** 18 990 lbf.
Valve Gear: Joy.

BR	LMS	L&Y		
50621	10621	1008	National Railway Museum	Horwich 1/1889

L & Y CLASS 21   "PUG"   0-4-0ST

Built: 1891–1910. Aspinall L & Y design. (0F). 57 built.
B.P.: 160 lb/sq. in.   **Wheel dia.:** 3′ 0¾″.   **T.E.:** 11 370 lbf.
Cyls.: 13″ x 18″ (O).   **Weight:** 21.25 tons.
Valve Gear: Stephenson.

BR	LMS	L&Y		
51218	11218	68	Keighley & Worth Valley Railway	Horwich 811/1901
	11243	19	Keighley & Worth Valley Railway	Horwich 1097/1910

L & Y CLASS 23   0-6-0ST

Built: 1891–1900. Aspinall rebuild of Barton Wright L & Y 0-6-0. 230 built.
B.P.: 140 lb/sq. in.   **Wheel dia.:** 4′ 5⅞″.   **T.E.:** 17 590 lbf.
Cyls.: 17½″ x 26″ (I).   **Weight:** 43.85 tons.
Valve Gear: Joy.

BR	LMS	L&Y		
	11456	752	Keighley & WV Railway	BP 1989/1881 reb. Hor. 1896

L & Y CLASS 25   0-6-0

Built: 1876–87. Barton Wright L & Y design (2F) 280 built.
B.P.: 140 lb/sq. in.   **Weight–Loco:** 39.05 tons.   **Wheel dia.:** 4′ 5⅞″.
Cyls.: 17½″ x 26″ (I).   **–Tender:** 28.5 tons.   **T.E.:** 17 590 lbf.
Valve Gear: Joy.

BR	LMS	L&Y		
52044	12044	957	Keighley & Worth Valley Railway	BP 2840/1887

L & Y CLASS 27   0-6-0

Built: 1889–1917. Aspinall L & Y design (3F). 448 built.
B.P.: 180 lb/sq. in.   **Weight–Loco:** 44.3 tons.   **Wheel dia.:** 5″ 0⅞″.
Cyls.: 18″ x 26″ (I).   **–Tender:** 26.1 tons.   **T.E.:** 21 170 lbf.
Valve Gear: Joy.

BR	LMS		
52322	12322 1300	East Lancashire Railway	Horwich 420/1896

CLASS 7F 2-8-0

Built: 1914–25. Fowler design for Somerset & Dorset Joint Railway (Midland and LSWR jointly owned). 11 built (53800–10).
B.P.: 190 lb/sq. in.   **Weight–Loco:** 64.75 tons.   **Wheel dias.:** 3' 3½", 4' 7½".
Cyls.: 21" x 28" (O).   **–Tender:** 26.1 tons.   **T.E.:** 35 950 lbf.
Valve Gear: Walschaert.

BR	LMS	S&DJR			
53808	9678–13808		88	West Somerset Railway	RS 3894/1925
53809	9679–13809		89	Midland Railway Centre	RS 3895/1925

Note: 53809 often carries the name "BEAUMONT".

CALEDONIAN RAILWAY   4–2–2

Built: 1886. Drummond design (1P). 1 built.
B.P.: 160 lb/sq. in.   **Weight–Loco:** 41.35 tons.   **Wheel dias.:** 3' 6", 7' 0", 4' 6".
Cyls.: 18" x 26" (I).   **–Tender:** 35.4 tons.   **T.E.:** 13 640 lbf.
Valve Gear: Stephenson.

BR	LMS	CR		
	14010	123	Glasgow Museum of Transport	N 3553/1886

CALEDONIAN RAILWAY 439 CLASS   0-4-4T

Built: 1900–14. McIntosh design (2P). 68 built.
B.P.: 160 lb/sq. in.   **Wheel dias.:** 5' 9", 3' 2".   **T.E.:** 16 600 lbf.
Cyls.: 18" x 26" (I).   **Weight:** 53.95 tons.
Valve Gear: Stephenson.
Dual brakes.

BR	LMS	CR		
55189	15189	419	Bo'ness & Kinneil Railway	St. Rollox 1908

GSWR 322 CLASS   0-6-0T

Built: 1917. Drummond design. (3F). 3 built.
B.P.: 160 lb/sq. in.   **Wheel dia.:** 4' 2".   **T.E.:** 17 290 lbf.
Cyls.: 17" x 22" (O).   **Weight:** 40 tons.
Valve Gear: Walschaert.

BR	LMS	GSWR		
	16379	9	Glasgow Museum of Transport	NBL 21521/1917

CALEDONIAN RAILWAY 812 CLASS   0-6-0

Built: 1899–1900. McIntosh design (3F). 96 built (57550–645).
B.P.: 160 lb/sq. in.   **Weight–Loco:** 45.7 tons.   **Wheel dia.:** 5' 0".
Cyls.: 18½" x 26" (I).   **–Tender:** 37.9 tons.   **T.E.:** 20 170 lbf.
Valve Gear: Stephenson.
Air brakes.

BR	LMS	CR		
57566	17566	828	Strathspey Railway	St. Rollox 1899

HIGHLAND RAILWAY   "JONES GOODS"   4-6-0

Built: 1894. Jones design (4F). 15 built.
B.P.: 175 lb/sq. in.   **Weight–Loco:** 56 tons.   **Wheel dias.:** 3' 3", 5' 3".
Cyls.: 20" x 26" (O).   **–Tender:** 38.35 tons.   **T.E.:** 24 560 lbf.
Valve Gear: Stephenson.

BR	LMS	HR		
	17916	103	Glasgow Museum of Transport	SS 4022/1894

NORTH LONDON RAILWAY 75 CLASS   0-6-0T

Built: 1881–1905. Park design. (2F). 15 built.
B.P.: 160 lb/sq. in.   **Wheel dia.:** 4′ 4″.   **T.E.:** 18 140 lbf.
Cyls.: 17″ x 24″ (O).   **Weight:** 45.55 tons.
Valve Gear: Stephenson.

| *BR* | *LMS* | *LNWR* | *NLR* | | |
| 58850 | 7505–27505 | 2650 | 116 | Barrow Hill Roundhouse | Bow 181/1881 |

Note: On loan from Bluebell Railway

LNWR COAL TANK   0-6-2T

Built: 1881–1896. Webb design. 300 built.
B.P.: 150 lb/sq. in.   **Wheel dias.:** 4′ 5½″, 3′ 9″.   **T.E.:** 16 530 lbf.
Cyls.: 17″ x 24″ (I).   **Weight:** 43.75 tons.
Valve Gear: Stephenson.

| *BR* | *LMS* | *LNWR* | | |
| 58926 | 7799 | 1054 | Keighley & Worth Valley Railway | Crewe 2979/1888 |

MIDLAND 156 CLASS   2-4-0

Built: 1866–68. Kirtley design (1P). 23 built.
B.P.: 140 lb/sq. in.   **Weight–Loco:** 41.25 tons.   **Wheel dias.:** 4′ 3″, 6′ 3″.
Cyls.: 18″ x 24″ (I).   **–Tender:** 34.85 tons.   **T.E.:** 12 340 lbf.
Valve Gear: Stephenson.

| *LMS* | *MR* | | |
| 2–20002 | 158–158A | Midland Railway Centre (N) | Derby 1866 |

MIDLAND 115 CLASS   "SPINNER"   4–2–2

Built: 1887–1900. Johnson design. 95 built.
B.P.: 170 lb/sq. in.   **Weight–Loco:** 43.95 tons.   **Wheel dias.:** 3′ 10″, 7′ 9½″, 4′ 4½″.
Cyls.: 19″ x 26″ (I).   **–Tender:** 21.55 tons.   **T.E.:** 15 280 lbf.
Valve Gear: Stephenson.

| *LMS* | *MR* | | |
| 673 | 118–673 | National Railway Museum | Derby 1897 |

NORTH STAFFS RAILWAY New L CLASS   0-6-2T

Built: 1903–23. Hookham design. 34 built.
B.P.: 175 lb/sq. in.   **Wheel dias.:** 5′ 0″, 4′ 0″.   **T.E.:** 22 060 lbf.
Cyls.: 18½″ x 26″ (I).   **Weight:** 64.95 tons.
Valve Gear: Stephenson.

| *LMS* | *NSR* | | |
| 2271 | 2 | Churnet Valley Railway (N) | Stoke 1923 |

Note: Although built in 1923, this loco carried an NSR number, since the NSR was not taken over by the LMS until late 1923.

LNWR   PRECEDENT   2-4-0

Built: 1874–82. Webb design. 166 built.
B.P.: 150 lb/sq. in.   **Weight–Loco:** 35.6 tons.   **Wheel dias.:** 3′ 9″, 6′ 9″.
Cyls.: 17″ x 24″ (I).   **–Tender:** 25 tons.   **T.E.:** 10 920 lbf.
Valve Gear: Allan.

| *LMS* | *LNWR* | | | |
| 5031 | 790 | HARDWICKE | National Railway Museum | Crewe 3286/1892 |

LNWR 2–2–2

Built: 1847. Trevithick design rebuilt by Ramsbottom in 1858.
B.P.: 140 lb/sq. in. **Weight–Loco:** 29.9 tons. **Wheel dias.:** 3′ 6″, 8′ 6″, 3′ 6″.
Cyls.: 17¼″ x 24″ (O). **–Tender:** 25 tons. **T.E.:** 8330 lbf.
Valve Gear: Stephenson.

LNWR
173–3020 CORNWALL The Railway Age, Crewe (N) Crewe 35/1847

LNWR 0-4-0ST

Built: 1865. Ramsbottom design.
B.P.: 120 lb/sq. in. **Wheel dia.:** 4′ 0″. **T.E.:** 8330 lbf.
Cyls.: 14″ x 20″ (I). **Weight:** 22.75 tons.

LNWR
1439–1985–3042 East Lancashire Railway (N) Crewe 842/1865

GRAND JUNCTION RAILWAY 2–2–2

Built: 1845. Trevithick design.
B.P.: 120 lb/sq. in. **Weight–Loco:** 20.4 tons. **Wheel dias.:** 3′ 6″, 6′ 0″, 3′ 6″.
Cyls.: 15″ x 20″ (O). **–Tender:** 16.4 tons. **T.E.:** 6375 lbf.
Valve Gear: Allan.

LNWR   *GJR*
49   49–1868 COLUMBINE Science Museum, London (N) Crewe 25/1845

FURNESS RAILWAY 0-4-0

Built: 1846.
B.P.: 110 lb/sq. in. **Weight–Loco:** 20 tons. **Wheel dia.:** 4′ 9″.
Cyls.: 14″ x 24″ (I). **–Tender:** 13 tons. **T.E.:** 7720 lbf.
Valve Gear: Stephenson.

3   COPPERNOB National Railway Museum BCK 1846

FURNESS RAILWAY 0-4-0

Built: 1863 as 0-4-0. Sold in 1870 to Barrow Steelworks and numbered 7. Rebuilt 1915 as 0-4-0ST. Restored to original condition 1999.
B.P.: 120 lb/sq. in. **Wheel dia.:** 4′10″ **T.E.:** 10140 lbf.
Cyls.: 15½″ x 24″(I) **Weight:**

FR
20   Lakeside & Haverthwaite Railway SS 1435/1863

FURNESS RAILWAY 0-4-0ST

Built: 1865 as 0-4-0. Sold in 1873 to Barrow Steelworks and numbered 17. Rebuilt 1921 as 0-4-0ST.
B.P.: 120 lb/sq. in. **Wheel dia.:** 4′3″ **T.E.:** 11532 lbf.
Cyls.: 15½″ x 24″(I) **Weight:**

FR   *Present*
25   6 West Coast Railway Company, Carnforth SS 1585/1865

LIVERPOOL & MANCHESTER RAILWAY 0–2–2

Built: 1829 for the Rainhill trials.
B.P.: 50 lb/sq. in. **Weight–Loco:** 4.25 tons. **Wheel dias.:** 4′ 8½″, 2′ 6″.
Cyls.: 8″ x 17″ (O). **–Tender:** 5.2 tons. **T.E.:** 820 lbf.

ROCKET   Science Museum (London) (N) RS 1/1829

LIVERPOOL & MANCHESTER RAILWAY 0-4-0

Built: 1829 for the Rainhill trials.
B.P.: 50 lb/sq. in.   **Weight–Loco:** 4.25 tons.   **Wheel dias.:** 4' 6".
Cyls.: 7" x 18" (O).   **–Tender:** 5.2 tons.   **T.E.:** 690 lbf.

SANS PAREIL   National Railway Museum   Hack 1829

LIVERPOOL & MANCHESTER RAILWAY 0–4–2

Built: 1838–9. Four built. The survivor was the star of the film "The Titfield Thunderbolt"
B.P.: 50 lb/sq. in.   **Weight–Loco:** 14.45 tons.   **Wheel dias.:** 5' 0", 3' 3".
Cyls.: 14" x 24" (I).   **–Tender:**   **T.E.:** 3330 lbf.

L&M   *LNWR*
57   116   LION   Greater Manchester Museum of Science & Industry   TKL 1838

Note: On loan from Liverpool Museum.

MERSEY RAILWAY 0–6–4T

Built: 1885. Withdrawn 1903 on electrification. No. 5 was sold to Coppice colliery in Derbyshire.
B.P.: 150 lb/sq. in.   **Wheel dias.:** 4' 7", 3' 0".   **T.E.:** 26 600 lbf.
Cyls.: 21" x 26" (I).   **Weight:** 67.85 tons.
Valve Gear: Stephenson.

1   THE MAJOR   Rail Transport Museum, Thirlemere, NSW, Australia   BP 2601/1885
5   CECIL RAIKES   Museum of Liverpool Life   BP 2605/1885

LNWR 0-4-0STT

Built: 1865 for Crewe Works internal system.
B.P.:   **Wheel dias.:** 1' 4¼".   **T.E.:** lbf.
Cyls.: 5½" x 6" (I)   **Weight:**   **Gauge:** 1' 6".

PET   National Railway Museum   Crewe 6/1865

L & YR 0-4-0STT

Built: 1887 for Horwich Works internal system.
B.P.: 170 lb/sq. in.   **Wheel dias.:** 1" 4¼".   **T.E.:** 1330 lbf.
Cyls.: 5" x 6" (O).   **Weight:** 3.55 tons.   **Gauge:** 1' 6".
Valve Gear: Joy.

WREN   National Railway Museum   BP 2825/1887

1.4. LONDON & NORTH EASTERN RAILWAY AND CONSTITUENT COMPANIES' STEAM LOCOMOTIVES

GENERAL

The LNER was formed in 1923 by the amalgamation of the Great Northern Railway (GNR). North Eastern Railway (NER), Great Eastern Railway (GER), Great Central Railway (GCR), North British Railway (NBR) and Great North of Scotland Railway (GNSR). Prior to this the Hull and Barnsley Railway (H & B) had been absorbed by the NER in 1922.

Locomotive Numbering System

Initially pre grouping locomotive numbers were retained, but in September 1923 suffix letters started to be applied depending upon the works which repaired the locomotives. In 1924 loco-motives were renumbered in blocks as follows: NER locomotives remained unaltered, GNR lo-comotives had 3000 added, GCR 5000, GNSR 6800, GER 7000 and NBR 9000. New locomotives filled in gaps between existing numbers. By 1943 the numbering of new locomotives had be-come so haphazard that it was decided to completely renumber locomotives so that locomo-tives of a particular class were all contained in the same block of numbers. On nationalisation in 1948, 60000 was added to LNER numbers.

Classification System

The LNER gave each class a unique code consisting of a letter denoting the wheel arrangement and a number denoting the individual class within the wheel arrangement. Route availability (RA) was denoted by a number, the higher the number the more restricted the route availability.

LNER Class LNER Y7 0-4-0T No. 68088 is seen top-and tailing a service train with Ivatt Class 2MT 2-6-2T No. 41312 at Barrow Hill Roundhouse's steam gala on 13 July 2002. GWR pannier tank No. 7754 can be seen alongside.
Robert Pritchard

CLASS A4   4-6-2

Built: 1935–38. Gresley steamlined design. "MALLARD" attained the world speed record for a steam locomotive of 126.4 mph in 1938 and is still unbeaten. 35 built (2509–12, 4462–9/82–500/900–3).
B.P.: 250 lb/sq. in.   **Weight–Loco:** 102.95 tons.   **Wheel dias.:** 3' 2", 6' 8", 3' 8".
Cyls.: 18½" x 26" (3).   **–Tender:** 64.15 tons.   **T.E.:** 35 450 lbf.
Valve Gear: Walschaert with derived motion for inside cylinder.
RA: 9.

x–Dual (air/vacuum) brakes.

BR	LNER				
60007	4498–7	SIR NIGEL GRESLEY	North Yorkshire Moors Railway	Doncaster	1863/1937
60008	4496–8	DWIGHT D. EISENHOWER	National RR Museum, USA	Doncaster	1861/1937
60009x	4488–9	UNION OF SOUTH AFRICA	Severn Valley Railway	Doncaster	1853/1937
60010	4489–10	DOMINION OF CANADA	Canadian RR Historical Museum	Doncaster	1854/1937
60019	4464–19	BITTERN	Watercress Line	Doncaster	1866/1937
60022	4468–22	MALLARD	National Railway Museum	Doncaster	1870/1937

CLASS A3   4-6-2

Built: 1922–35. Gresley design (Originally class A1–later altered to A10). 79 built. (60035–113). Rebuilt 1959 with Kylchap blastpipe, double chimney and German-style smoke deflectors. Restored to original state on preservation in 1963, but restored to rebuilt state in 1993.
B.P.: 220 lb/sq. in.   **Weight–Loco:** 96.25 tons.   **Wheel dias.:** 3' 2", 6' 8", 3' 8".
Cyls.: 19" x 26" (3).   **–Tender:** 62.4 tons.   **T.E.:** 32 910 lbf.
Valve Gear: Walschaert with derived motion for inside cylinder.
RA: 9.   Air braked.

BR	LNER			
60103	1472–4472–502–103	FLYING SCOTSMAN	FSR, Southall Depot	Doncaster 1564/1923

CLASS A2   4-6-2

Built: 1944–48. Thompson design, later developed by Peppercorn. 40 built (60500–39).
B.P.: 250 lb/sq. in.   **Weight–Loco:** 101 tons.   **Wheel dias.:** 3' 2", 6' 2", 3' 8".
Cyls.: 19" x 26" (3).   **–Tender:** 60.35 tons.   **T.E.:** 40 430 lbf.
Valve Gear: Walschaert.   **RA:** 9.

60532		BLUE PETER	North Yorkshire Moors Railway	Doncaster 2023/1948

CLASS V2   2-6-2

Built: 1936–44. Gresley design for express passenger and freight. 184 built (60800–983).
B.P.: 220 lb/sq. in.   **Weight–Loco:** 93.1 tons.   **Wheel dias.:** 3' 2", 6' 2", 3' 8".
Cyls.: 18½" x 26" (3).   **–Tender:** 52 tons.   **T.E.:** 33 730 lbf.
Valve Gear: Walschaert with derived motion for inside cylinder.
RA: 9.

BR	LNER			
60800	4771–800	GREEN ARROW	National Railway Museum	Doncaster 1837/1936

CLASS B1   4-6-0

Built: 1942–51. Thompson design. 410 built (61000–409).
B.P.: 225 lb/sq. in.   **Weight–Loco:** 71.15 tons.   **Wheel dias.:** 3' 2", 6' 2".
Cyls.: 20" x 26" (O).   **–Tender:** 52 tons.   **T.E.:** 26 880 lbf.
Valve Gear: Walschaert.   **RA:** 5.

BR	LNER	Present		
61264	1264		Great Central Railway	NBL 26165/1947
61306		1306 "MAYFLOWER"	Nene Valley Railway	NBL 26207/1948

Notes: The original MAYFLOWER was 61379. 61264 also carried Departmental 29.

CLASS B12   4-6-0

Built: 1911–28. Holden GER design. 80 built (8500–5/7–80). GER class S69.
B.P.: 180 lb/sq. in.   **Weight–Loco:** 69.5 tons.   **Wheel dias.:** 3′ 3″, 6′ 6″.
Cyls.: 20″ x 28″ (I).   **–Tender:** 39.3 tons.   **T.E.:** 21 970 lbf.
Valve Gear: Stephenson.   **RA:** 5.   Dual brakes.

BR   LNER   GER
61572   8572   1572   North Norfolk Railway   BP 6488/1928

CLASS K4   2-6-0

Built: 1937–38. Gresley design for West Highland line. 6 built (61993–8).
B.P.: 200 lb/sq. in.   **Weight–Loco:** 68.4 tons.   **Wheel dias.:** 3′ 2″, 5′ 2″.
Cyls.: 18½″ x 26″ (3).   **–Tender:** 44.2 tons.   **T.E.:** 36 600 lbf.
Valve Gear: Walschaert with derived motion for inside cylinder.
RA: 6.

BR   LNER
61994   3442–1994   THE GREAT MARQUESS   Severn Valley Railway   Darlington 1761/1938

CLASS K1   2-6-0

Built: 1949–50. Peppercorn design. 70 built (62001–70).
B.P.: 225 lb/sq. in.   **Weight–Loco:** 66 tons.   **Wheel dias.:** 3′ 2″, 5′ 2″.
Cyls.: 20″ x 26″ (O).   **–Tender:** 52.2 tons.   **T.E.:** 32 080 lbf.
Valve Gear: Walschaert.   **RA:** 6.

BR   Present
62005   2005   North Yorkshire Moors Railway   NBL 26609/1949

CLASS D40   4-4-0

Built: 1889–1921. Pickersgill GNSR class F. 20 built.
B.P.: 165 lb/sq. in.   **Weight–Loco:** 48.65 tons.   **Wheel dias.:** 3′ 9½″, 6′ 1″.
Cyls.: 18″ x 26″ (I).   **–Tender:** 37.4 tons.   **T.E.:** 16 180 lbf.
Valve Gear: Stephenson.   **RA:** 4.

BR   LNER   GNSR
62277   6849–2277   49   GORDON HIGHLANDER   Glasgow Museum of Transport   NBL 22563/1920

CLASS D34   GLEN   4-4-0

Built: 1913–20. Reid NBR class K. 32 built.
B.P.: 165 lb/sq. in.   **Weight–Loco:** 57.2 tons.   **Wheel dias.:** 3′ 6″, 6′ 0″.
Cyls.: 20″ x 26″ (I).   **–Tender:** 46.65 tons.   **T.E.:** 22 100 lbf.
Valve Gear: Stephenson.   **RA:** 6.

BR   LNER   NBR
62469   9256–2469   256   GLEN DOUGLAS   Bo'ness & Kinneil Railway   Cowlairs 1913

CLASS D11   IMPROVED DIRECTOR   4-4-0

Built: 1919–22. Robinson GCR class 11F. 11 built (62660–70). 24 similar locomotives were built by the LNER.
B.P.: 180 lb/sq. in.   **Weight–Loco:** 61.15 tons.   **Wheel dias.:** 3′ 6″, 6′ 9″.
Cyls.: 20″ x 26″ (I).   **–Tender:** 48.3 tons.   **T.E.:** 19 640 lbf.
Valve Gear: Stephenson.   **RA:** 6.

BR   LNER   GCR
62660   5506–2660   506   BUTLER HENDERSON   National Railway Museum   Gorton 1919

Ex-Great Central Railway Class O4 No. 63601 passes Quorn with a demonstration freight on 28 July 2001.

CLASS D49   4-4-0

Built: 1927. Gresley design. 76 built (62700–75).

B.P.: 180 lb/sq. in.	**Weight–Loco:** 66 tons.	**Wheel dias.:** 3′ 1¼″, 6′ 8″.
Cyls.: 17″ x 26″ (3).	**–Tender:** 52 tons.	**T.E.:** 21 560 lbf.
Valve Gear: Walschaert.	**RA:** 8.	

BR   *LNER*
62712 246–2712   MORAYSHIRE   Bo'ness & Kinneil Railway Darlington 1391/1928

CLASS E4   2-4-0

Built: 1891–1902. Holden GER class T26. 100 built.

B.P.: 160 lb/sq. in.	**Weight–Loco:** 40.3 tons.	**Wheel dias.:** 4′ 0″, 5′ 8″.
Cyls.: 17½″ x 24″ (I).	**–Tender:** 30.65 tons.	**T.E.:** 14 700 lbf.
Valve Gear: Stephenson.	**RA:** 2.	Air brakes.

BR   *LNER*   *GER*
62785 7490–7802–2785 490   Bressingham Steam Museum (N) Stratford 836/1894

CLASS C1   4-4-2

Built: 1902–10. Ivatt GNR class C1. 94 built.

B.P.: 170 lb/sq. in.	**Weight–Loco:** 69.6 tons.	**Wheel dias.:** 3′ 8″, 6′ 8″, 3′ 8″.
Cyls.: 20″ x 24″ (O).	**–Tender:** 43.1 tons.	**T.E.:** 17 340 lbf.
Valve Gear: Stephenson.	**RA:** 7.	

BR   *LNER*   *GNR*
      3251–2800 251   National Railway Museum   Doncaster 991/1902

CLASS Q6   0-8-0

Built: 1913–21. Raven NER class T2. 120 built (63340–459).

B.P.: 180 lb/sq. in.	**Weight–Loco:** 65.9 tons.	**Wheel dia.:** 4′ 7¼″.
Cyls.: 20″ x 26″ (O).	**–Tender:** 44.1 tons.	**T.E.:** 28 800 lbf.
Valve Gear: Stephenson.	**RA:** 6.	

BR   *LNER*   *NER*
63395 2238–3395 2238   NELPG, Hopetown, Darlington   Darlington 1918

CLASS Q7   0-8-0

Built: 1919–24. Raven NER class T3. 15 built (63460–74).

B.P.: 180 lb/sq. in.	**Weight–Loco:** 71.6 tons.	**Wheel dia.:** 4′ 7¼″.
Cyls.: 18½″ x 26″ (3).	**–Tender:** 44.1 tons.	**T.E.:** 36 960 lbf.
Valve Gear: Stephenson.	**RA:** 7.	

BR   *LNER*   *NER*
63460 901–3460 901   North Yorkshire Moors Railway (N) Darlington 1919

CLASS O4   2-8-0

Built: 1911–20. Robinson GCR class 8K 70 built. A further 521 were built, being ordered by the railway operating department (ROD). These saw service on British and overseas railways during and after the first world war. Some subsequently passed to British railway administrations whilst others were sold abroad.

B.P.: 180 lb/sq. in.	**Weight–Loco:** 73.2 tons.	**Wheel dias.:** 3′ 6″, 4′ 8″.
Cyls.: 21″ x 26″ (O).	**–Tender:** 48.3 tons.	**T.E.:** 31 330 lbf.
Valve Gear: Stephenson.	**RA:** 6.	

BR   *LNER*   *GCR*
63601 5102–3509–3601 102   Great Central Railway (N)   Gorton 1911

ROD
1984 Dorrigo, Northern New South Wales, Australia   NBL 22042/1918
2003 Dorrigo, Northern New South Wales, Australia   Gorton 1918
2004 Richmond Vale Steam Centre, Kurri-Kurri, NSW, Australia   Gorton 1918

CLASS J21   0-6-0

Built: 1886–95. Worsdell NER class C. 201 built.
B.P.: 160 lb/sq. in.   **Weight–Loco:** 43.75 tons.   **Wheel dia.:** 5' 1¼".
Cyls.: 19" x 24" (I).   **–Tender:** 36.95 tons.   **T.E.:** 19 240 lbf.
Valve Gear: Stephenson.   **RA:** 3.

BR	LNER	NER		
65033	876–5033	876	North of England Open Air Museum Gateshead	1889

CLASS J36   0-6-0

Built: 1889–1900. Holmes NBR class C. 168 built.
B.P.: 165 lb/sq. in.   **Weight–Loco:** 41.95 tons.   **Wheel dia.:** 5' 0".
Cyls.: 18" x 26" (I).   **–Tender:** 33.5 tons.   **T.E.:** 20 240 lbf.
Valve Gear: Stephenson.   **RA:** 3.

BR	LNER	NBR		
65243	9673–5243	673 MAUDE	Bo'ness & Kinneil Railway	N 4392/1891

CLASS J15   0-6-0

Built: 1883–1913. Worsdell GER class Y14. 189 built.
B.P.: 160 lb/sq. in.   **Weight–Loco:** 37.1 tons.   **Wheel dia.:** 4' 11".
Cyls.: 17½" x 24" (I).   **–Tender:** 30.65 tons.   **T.E.:** 16 940 lbf.
Valve Gear: Stephenson.   **RA:** 1.   Dual brakes.

BR	LNER	GER		
65462	7564–5462	564	North Norfolk Railway	Stratford 1912

CLASS J17   0-6-0

Built: 1900–11. Holden GER class G58. 90 built (65500–89).
B.P.: 180 lb/sq. in.   **Weight–Loco:** 45.4 tons.   **Wheel dia.:** 4' 11".
Cyls.: 19" x 26" (I).   **–Tender:** 38.25 tons.   **T.E.:** 24 340 lbf.
Valve Gear: Stephenson.   **RA:** 4.   Air brakes.

BR	LNER	GER		
65567	8217–5567	1217	National Railway Museum	Stratford 1905

CLASS J27   0-6-0

Built: 1906–23. Worsdell NER class P3. 115 built.
B.P.: 180 lb/sq. in.   **Weight–Loco:** 47 tons.   **Wheel dia.:** 4' 7¼".
Cyls.: 18½" x 26" (I).   **–Tender:** 37.6 tons.   **T.E.:** 24 640 lbf.
Valve Gear: Stephenson.   **RA:** 5.

BR	LNER		
65894	2392–5894	North Yorkshire Moors Railway	Darlington 1923

CLASS J94. 68077/8 (LNER 8077/8) – see War Department Steam Locomotives.

CLASS Y5   0-4-0ST

Built: 1874–1903. Neilson & Company design for GER (class 209). 8 built. Survivor sold in 1917.
B.P.: 140 lb/sq. in.   **Wheel dia.:** 3' 7".   **T.E.:** 7970 lbf.
Cyls.: 12" x 20" (O).   **Weight:** 21.2 tons.
Valve Gear: Stephenson.   **RA:** 1.

GER		
229	North Woolwich Station Museum	N 2119/1876

CLASS Y7 0-4-0T

Built: 1888–1923. Worsdell NER class H. 24 built.
B.P.: 160 lb/sq. in.   **Wheel dia.:** 4' 0".   **T.E.:** 11 140 lbf.
Cyls.: 14" x 20" (I).   **Weight:** 22.7 tons.
Valve Gear: Joy.   **RA:** 1.
* No train brakes.

BR	LNER	NER		
68088*	985–8088		Nottingham Heritage Centre	Darlington 1205/1923
	1310	1310	Middleton Railway	Gateshead 38/1891

CLASS Y9 0-4-0ST

Built: 1882–99. Drummond NBR class G. 35 built.
B.P.: 130 lb/sq. in.   **Wheel dia.:** 3' 8".   **T.E.:** 9840 lbf.
Cyls.: 14" x 20" (I).   **Weight:** 27.8 tons.
Valve Gear: Stephenson.   **RA:** 2.

BR	LNER	NBR	
68095	9042–8095	42	Bo'ness & Kinneil Railway	Cowlairs 1887

CLASS Y1 4wT

Built: 1925–33. Sentinel geared loco. 24 built.
B.P.: 275 lb/sq. in.   **Wheel dia.:** 2' 6".   **T.E.:** 7260 lbf.
Cyls.: 6¾" x 9" (I).   **Weight:** 19.8 tons.
Valve Gear: Rotary cam.   **RA:** 1.

BR	LNER		
68153	59–8153	Middleton Railway	S 8837/1933

Also carried DEPARTMENTAL LOCOMOTIVE No. 54.

CLASS J69 0-6-0T

Built: 1890–1904. holden GER class S56. 126 locomotives (including many rebuilt from J67).
B.P.: 180 lb/sq. in.   **Wheel dia.:** 4' 0".   **T.E.:** 19 090 lbf.
Cyls.: 16½" x 22" (I).   **Weight:** 42.45 tons.
Valve Gear: Stephenson.   **RA:** 3.   Air brakes.

BR	LNER	GER	
68633	7087–8633	87	National Railway Museum	Stratford 1249/1904

CLASS J52 0-6-0ST

Built: 1897–1902. Ivatt GNR class J13. Many rebuilt from Stirling locomotives (built 1892–97).
B.P.: 170 lb/sq. in.   **Wheel dia.:** 4' 8".   **T.E.:** 21 740 lbf.
Cyls.: 18" x 26" (I).   **Weight:** 51.7 tons.
Valve Gear: Stephenson.   **RA:** 5.

BR	LNER	GNR	
68846	4247–8846	1247	National Railway Museum	SS 4492/1899

CLASS J72 0-6-0T

Built: 1898–1925. Worsdell NER class E1. Further batch built 1949–51 by BR. 113 built.
B.P.: 140 lb/sq. in.   **Wheel dia.:** 4' 1¼".   **T.E.:** 16 760 lbf.
Cyls.: 17" x 24" (I).   **Weight:** 38.6 tons.
Valve Gear: Stephenson.   **RA:** 5.

69023–Departmental No. 59   North Yorkshire Moors Railway Darlington 2151/1951

CLASS N2 $\qquad$ 0-6-2T

Built: 1920–29. Gresley GNR class N2. 107 built (69490–69596).
B.P.: 170 lb/sq. in. $\qquad$ **Wheel dia.:** 5′ 8″, 3′ 8″. $\qquad$ **T.E.:** 19 950 lbf.
Cyls.: 19″ x 26″ (I). $\qquad$ **Weight:** 70.25 tons.
Valve Gear: Stephenson. $\qquad$ **RA:** 6.

BR	*LNER*	*GNR*		
69523	4744–9523	1744	Great Central Railway	NBL 22600/1921

CLASS N7 $\qquad$ 0-6-2T

Built: 1915–28. Hill GER class L77. 134 built (69600–69733).
B.P.: 180 lb/sq. in. $\qquad$ **Wheel dias.:** 4′ 10″, 3′ 9″. $\qquad$ **T.E.:** 20 510 lbf.
Cyls.: 18″ x 24″ (I). $\qquad$ **Weight:** 61.8 tons.
Valve Gear: Walschaert (inside). $\qquad$ **RA:** 5. $\qquad$ Dual brakes.

BR	*LNER*	*GER*			
69621	999E–7999–9621	999	"A.J. HILL"	North Norfolk Railway	Stratford 1924

CLASS X1 $\qquad$ 2-2-4T

Built: 1869 by NER as 2–2–2WT. Rebuilt 1892 to 4–2–2T and rebuilt as 2–cyl compound 2–2–4T and used for pulling inspections saloons. (NER class 66).
B.P.: 175 lb/sq. in. $\qquad$ **Wheel dias.:** 3′ 7″, 5′ 7¾″, 3′ 1¼″. $\quad$ **T.E.:** 6390 lbf.
Cyls.: 13″ x 24″ (hp) + 18½″ x 20″ (lp) (I). $\qquad$ **Weight:** 44.95 tons.
Valve Gear: Stephenson.

LNER	*NER*			
66	1478–66	AEROLITE	National Railway Museum	Gateshead 1869

NER 901 CLASS $\qquad$ 2-4-0

Built: 1872–82. Fletcher design. 55 built.
B.P.: 160 lb/sq. in. $\qquad$ **Weight–Loco:** 39.7 tons. $\qquad$ **Wheel dias.:** 4′ 6″, 7′ 6″.
Cyls.: 18″ x 24″ (I). $\qquad\qquad$ **–Tender:** 29.9 tons. $\qquad$ **T.E.:** 12 590 lbf.
Valve Gear: Stephenson.

LNER	*NER*		
910	910	Darlington North Road Museum (N)	Gateshead 1875

NER 1001 CLASS $\qquad$ 0-6-0

Built: 1864–75. Bouch design for Stockton and Darlington Railway.
B.P.: 130 lb/sq. in. $\qquad$ **Weight–Loco:** 35 tons. $\qquad$ **Wheel dia.:** 5′ 0½″.
Cyls.: 17″ x 26″ (I). $\qquad\qquad$ **–Tender:** 18 tons. $\qquad$ **T.E.:** 13 720 lbf.
Valve Gear: Stephenson.

LNER	*NER*		
1275	1275	National Railway Museum	Darlington 708/1874

CLASS E5 $\qquad$ 2-4-0

Built: 1885. Tennant NER 1463 class. 20 built.
B.P.: 160 lb/sq. in. $\qquad$ **Weight–Loco:** 42.1 tons. $\qquad$ **Wheel dias.:** 4′ 6″, 7′ 0″.
Cyls.: 18″ x 24″ (I). $\qquad\qquad$ **–Tender:** 32.1 tons. $\qquad$ **T.E.:** 12 590 lbf.
Valve Gear: Stephenson.

LNER	*NER*		
1463	1463	Darlington North Road Museum (N)	Darlington 1885

CLASS D17 — 4-4-0

Built: 1893–7. Worsdell NER class M1 (later class M). 20 built.
B.P.: 160 lb/sq. in. **Weight–Loco:** 52 tons. **Wheel dias.:** 3′ 7¼″, 7′ 1¼″.
Cyls.: 19″ x 26″ (I). **–Tender:** 41 tons. **T.E.:** 14 970 lbf.
Valve Gear: Stephenson. **RA:** 6.

LNER   *NER*
1621   1621   National Railway Museum   Gateshead 1893

CLASS C2 — "KLONDYKE" — 4-4-2

Built: 1898–1903. H. A. Ivatt GNR class C1. 22 built.
B.P.: 170 lb/sq. in. **Weight–Loco:** 62 tons. **Wheel dias.:** 3′ 8″, 6′ 8″, 3′ 8″.
Cyls.: 19″ x 24″ (O). **–Tender:** 42.1 tons. **T.E.:** 15 650 lbf.
Valve Gear: Stephenson. **RA:** 4.

LNER   *GNR*
3990   990   HENRY OAKLEY   Bressingham Steam Museum   Doncaster 769/1898

GNR — 4-2-2

Built: 1870–95. Stirling design.
B.P.: 140 lb/sq. in. **Weight–Loco:** 38.5 tons. **Wheel dias.:** 3′ 10″, 8′ 1″, 4′ 1″.
Cyls.: 18″ x 28″ (O). **–Tender:** 30 tons. **T.E.:** 11 130 lbf.
Valve Gear: Stephenson.

1   National Railway Museum   Doncaster 50/1870

STOCKTON & DARLINGTON RAILWAY — 0-4-0

Built: 1825–6. George Stephenson design. 6 built.
B.P.: 50 lb/sq. in. **Weight–Loco:** 6.5 tons. **Wheel dia.:** 3′ 11″.
Cyls.: 9½″ x 24″ (O). **–Tender:** **T.E.:** 2050 lbf.

1   LOCOMOTION   Darlington North Road Museum (N)   RS1/1825

STOCKTON & DARLINGTON RAILWAY — 0-6-0

Built: 1845.
B.P.: 75 lb/sq. in. **Weight–Loco:** 6.5 tons. **Wheel dia.:** 4′ 0″.
Cyls.: 14½″ x 24″ (O). **–Tender:** **T.E.:** 6700 lbf.

25   DERWENT   Darlington North Road Museum (N)   Kitching 1845

1.5. BRITISH RAILWAYS STANDARD STEAM LOCOMOTIVES

GENERAL

From 1951 onwards BR produced a series of standard steam locomotives under the jurisdiction of R.A. Riddles. Examples of most classes have been preserved, the exceptions being the Class 6MT "Clan" Pacifics, the Class 3MT 2-6-0s (77000 series), the Class 3MT 2-6-2Ts (82000 series) and the Class 2MT 2-6-2Ts (84000 series). Attempts are being made, however, to rectify two of the omissions. The Bluebell Railway are rebuilding a Class 2MT 2-6-0 for which they have no tender into a Class 2MT 2-6-2T. It will be numbered 84030, following on from the production series. Another group have started to build a "Clan" from scratch. Ten Clans were built, numbered 72000–09 and were all given names of Scottish Clans. Another 15 were ordered, but the order was cancelled and they were never built. The first five of these were to be for the Southern Region and were to be named HENGIST, HORSA, CANUTE, WILDFIRE and FIREBRAND respectively. The new locomotive will therefore be known as 72010 HENGIST.

Numbering System

Tender engines were numbered in the 70000 series and tank engines in the 80000 series, the exceptions being the class 9F 2-10-0s which were numbered in the 92000 series.

Classification System

British Railways standard steam locomotives were referred to by power classification like LMS locomotives. All locomotives were classed as "MT" denoting "mixed traffic" except for 71000 and the Class 9F 2-10-0s. The latter were, however, often used on passenger trains on summer Saturdays.

CLASS 7MT   BRITANNIA   4-6-2

Built: 1951–54. 55 built (70000–54).
B.P.: 250 lb/sq. in.   **Weight–Loco:** 94 tons.   **Wheel dias.:** 3' 0", 6' 2", 3' 3½".
Cyls.: 20" x 28" (O).   **–Tender:** 49.15 tons.   **T.E.:** 32 160 lbf.
Valve Gear: Walschaert.   **RA:** 7

x–Dual (air/vacuum) brakes.

| 70000x | BRITANNIA | The Railway Age, Crewe | Crewe 1951 |
| 70013 | OLIVER CROMWELL | Bressingham Steam Museum (N) | Crewe 1951 |

CLASS 8P   4-6-2

Built: 1954. 1 built.
B.P.: 250 lb/sq. in.   **Weight–Loco:** 101.25 tons.   **Wheel dias.:** 3' 0", 6' 2", 3' 3½".
Cyls.: 18" x 28" (3).   **–Tender:** 53.7 tons.   **T.E.:** 39 080 lbf.
Valve Gear: British Caprotti (outside). **RA:** 8.

| 71000 | DUKE OF GLOUCESTER | East Lancashire Railway | Crewe 1954 |

CLASS 5MT   4-6-0

Built: 1951–57. 172 built (73000–171).
B.P.: 225 lb/sq. in.   **Weight–Loco:** 76 tons.   **Wheel dias.:** 3' 0", 6' 2".
Cyls.: 19" x 28" (O).   **–Tender:** 49.15 tons.   **T.E.:** 26 120 lbf.
Valve Gear: Walschaert (*outside British Caprotti).   **RA:** 5.
73050 has dual brakes.

73050	"CITY OF PETERBOROUGH"	Nene Valley Railway	Derby 1954
73082	CAMELOT	Bluebell Railway	Derby 1955
73096		Watercress Line	Derby 1955
73129 *		Midland Railway Centre	Derby 1956
73156		Great Central Railway	Doncaster 1956

CLASS 4MT   4-6-0

Built: 1951–57. 80 built (75000–79).
B.P.: 225 lb/sq. in.   **Weight–Loco:** 67.9 tons.   **Wheel dias.:** 3' 0", 5' 8".
Cyls.: 18" x 28" (O).   **–Tender:** 42.15 tons.   **T.E.:** 25 520 lbf.
Valve Gear: Walschaert.   **RA:** 4.

* Fitted with double chimney.

75014		North Yorkshire Moors Railway	Swindon 1951
75027		Bluebell Railway	Swindon 1954
75029	"THE GREEN KNIGHT"	North Yorkshire Moors Railway	Swindon 1954
75069 *		Severn Valley Railway	Swindon 1955
75078 *		Keighley & Worth Valley Railway	Swindon 1956
75079 *		Plym Valley Railway	Swindon 1956

CLASS 4MT   2-6-0

Built: 1952–57. 115 built (76000–114).
B.P.: 225 lb/sq. in.   **Weight–Loco:** 59.75 tons.   **Wheel dias.:** 3' 0", 5' 3".
Cyls.: 17½" x 26" (O).   **–Tender:** 42.15 tons.   **T.E.:** 24 170 lbf.
Valve Gear: Walschaert.   **RA:** 4.

x–Dual (air/vacuum) brakes.

76017		Watercress Line	Horwich 1953
76077		Gloucestershire–Warwickshire Railway	Horwich 1956
76079x		East Lancashire Railway	Horwich 1957
76084		Ian Storey Engineering, Hepscott	Horwich 1957

CLASS 2MT   2-6-0

Built: 1952–56. 65 built (78000–64). These locomotives were almost identical to the Ivatt LMS Class 2MT 2-6-0s (46400–46527).
B.P.: 200 lb/sq. in.   **Weight–Loco:** 49.25 tons.   **Wheel dias.:** 3′ 0″, 5′ 0″.
Cyls.: 16½″ x 24″ (O).   **–Tender:** 36.85 tons.   **T.E.:** 18 510 lbf.
Valve Gear: Walschaert.   **RA:** 4.

78018	Darlington North Road Goods Shed	Darlington 1954
78019	Great Central Railway	Darlington 1954
78022	Keighley & Worth Valley Railway	Darlington 1954

CLASS 4MT   2-6-4T

Built: 1951–57. 155 built (80000–154).
B.P.: 225 lb/sq. in.   **Wheel dias:.** 3′ 0″, 5′ 8″, 3′ 0″. **T.E.:** 25 520 lbf.
Cyls.: 18″ x 28″ (O).   **Weight:** 86.65 tons.
Valve Gear: Walschaert.   **RA:** 4.

80002	Keighley & Worth Valley Railway	Derby 1952
80064	Bluebell Railway	Brighton 1953
80072	Llangollen Railway	Brighton 1953
80078	Swanage Railway	Brighton 1954
80079	Severn Valley Railway	Brighton 1954
80080	Midland Railway Centre	Brighton 1954
80097	East Lancashire Railway	Brighton 1954
80098	Churnet Valley Railway	Brighton 1954
80100	Bluebell Railway	Brighton 1955
80104	Swanage Railway	Brighton 1955
80105	Bo'ness & Kinneil Railway	Brighton 1955
80135	North Yorkshire Moors Railway	Brighton 1956
80136	West Somerset Railway	Brighton 1956
80150	Vale of Glamorgan Railway	Brighton 1956
80151	Bluebell Railway	Brighton 1957

Notes: 80098 is on loan from the Midland Railway Centre.
       80136 is on loan from the Churnet Valley Railway.

CLASS 2MT   2-6-2T

This class of 30 locos (84000–29) were built 1953–57 and were almost identical to the Ivatt LMS Class 2MT 2-6-2Ts (41200–41329). The locomotive mentioned here was built in 1956 as Class 2MT 2-6-0 No. 78059 and is undergoing conversion.
B.P.: 200 lb/sq. in.   **Wheel dias:.** 3′ 0″, 5′ 0″, 3′ 0″. **T.E.:** 18 510 lbf.
Cyls.: 16½″ x 24″ (O).   **Weight:**   . tons.
Valve Gear: Walschaert.   **RA:** 4.

84030	Bluebell Railway	Darlington 1956 reb. Bluebell

CLASS 9F   2-10-0

Built: 1954–60. 251 built (92000–250). 92220 was the last steam locomotive to be built for British Railways.
B.P.: 250 lb/sq. in.   **Weight–Loco:** 86.7 tons.   **Wheel dias.:** 3′ 0″, 5′ 0″.
Cyls.: 20″ x 28″ (O).   **–Tender:** 52.5 tons.   **T.E.:** 39 670 lbf.
Valve Gear: Walschaert.   **RA:** 4.

* Fitted with single chimney. All other surviving members of the class have double chimneys.

92134 *		The Railway Age, Crewe	Crewe 1957
92203	"BLACK PRINCE"	Swindon Railway Workshop, Bream	Swindon 1959
92207	"MORNING STAR"	East Lancashire Railway	Swindon 1959
92212		Watercress Line	Swindon 1959
92214		Midland Railway Centre	Swindon 1959
92219		Midland Railway Centre	Swindon 1960
92220	EVENING STAR	National Railway Museum	Swindon 1960
92240		Bluebell Railway	Crewe 1958
92245		Vale of Glamorgan Railway	Crewe 1958

1.6. BRITISH RAILWAYS DEPARTMENTAL STEAM LOCOMOTIVES

BEESTON CREOSOTE WORKS — 0-4-0ST

Built: 1911 for Judkins Ltd., Tuttle Hill Granite Quarries, Nuneaton. Sold to British Railways for use on Beeston Creosote Works internal system in 1956.

B.P.:   **Wheel dias.:**   **T.E.:**
Cyls.:   **Weight:**   **Gauge:** 3' 0".
Valve Gear: Joy.

ED 10   F&W Saunders & Son, Huntingdon   WB 1889/1911

1.7. METROPOLITAN RAILWAY STEAM LOCOMOTIVES

The Metropolitan railway was a constituent of the present day London Underground Ltd., it being the only constituent company of LUL from which steam locomotives survive.

CLASS A — 4-4-0T

Built: 1866 by Beyer Peacock.
B.P.: 120 lb/sq. in   **Wheel dias.:** 3' 0", 5' 9"   **T.E.:** 12 680 lbf.
Cyls.: 17¼" x 24" (O)   **Weight:** 42.15 tons.
Valve Gear: Stephenson.

23–L45   London Transport Museum   BP 710/1866

BRILL BRANCH — 4w WT

Built: 1872 by Aveling & Porter for use on Brill branch (Wotton Tramway).
B.P.:   **Wheel dias.:** 3' 0" "   **T.E.:** .
Cyls.: 7¾" x 10"   **Weight:**
Valve Gear: Stephenson.

–   London Transport Museum   AP 807/1872

CLASS E — 0-4-4T

Built: 1898 at Neasden. 7 built.
B.P.: 150 lb/sq. in   **Wheel dias.:** 5' 6", 3' 9½"   **T.E.:** 15 420 lbf.
Cyls.: 17¼" x 26" (I)   **Weight:** 54.5 tons.
Valve Gear: Stephenson.

1–L44   Buckinghamshire Railway Centre   Neasden 3/1898

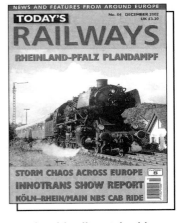

▲ 1400 Class 0-4-2T No. 1420 runs down the Dart Valley near Hood Bridge with the 14.10 Buckfastleigh–Totnes service on 8 April 2000.

▼ 1500 Class pannier tank No. 1501 climbs Eardington Bank on the Severn Valley Railway with the 13.45 Bridgnorth–Kidderminster on 17 February 2001. **John Chalcraft (2)**

4200 Class No. 4277 is seen hauling a demonstration goods train in the Dee Valley on the Llangollen Railway, near Glyndyfrdwy, on 5 April 2000.
Hugh Ballantyne

▲ 4073 Class 4-6-0 No. 5029 "NUNNEY CASTLE" is seen at Gloucester on 28 September 2001 on a returning railtour from Newport to Bristol. **Stephen Widdowson**

▼ 6000 Class 4-6-0 No. 6024 "KING EDWARD I" storms away from Leamington Spa with a Birmingham–London Paddington railtour on 13 April 2002. **Paul Chancellor**

▲ 7800 Class 4-6-0 No. 7822 "FOXCOTE MANOR" passes Carrog station on the Llangollen Railway with a goods charter on 11 April 2002. **Doug Birmingham**

▼ 5700 Class 0-6-0PT No. 9600 hurries past the old station at Kingskerswell with the 16.40 Paignton–Newton Abbot "Newton Antelope" shuttle organised by Past Time Railtours on 13 May 2000. **John Chalcraft**

▲ Isle of Wight Steam Railway Class O2 0-4-4T No. W24 "CALBOURNE" is seen near Whitfield Farm Crossing with a Smallbrook Jn.–Havenstreet service on 24 July 2001. **Chris Booth**

▼ Class S15 4-6-0 No. 828 climbs past New Barn Farm with the 13.20 Swanage–Norchard service on 14 September 2002. **John Chalcraft**

▲ The Bluebell Railway's E4 0-6-2T No. 473 "BIRCH GROVE" is seen near Treemans with the 13.30 Horsted Keynes–Sheffield Park service **Alan Barnes**

▼ Class A1X "Terrier" 0-6-0-Ts No. 55 "STEPNEY" and No. 8 pass Deacons on the Isle of Wight Steam Railway with the 17.06 Smallbrook Jn.–Havenstreet service on 28 July 2001. **John Chalcraft**

▲ Unrebuilt Battle of Britain Pacific No. 34072 "357 SQUADRON" ambles downgrade towards Corfe Castle with a Swanage–Norden service on 14 September 2002.

▼ Rebuilt Merchant Navy Pacific No. 35005 "CANADIAN PACIFIC" passes Dundas Aqueduct as it heads south along the Limpley Stoke Valley with the 15.58 Bristol–London Victoria "Daylight Trains" excursion on 26 June 2002. **John Chalcraft (2)**

◀ Class 2MT 2-6-2T
No. 41312 leaves Rothley on
the Great Central Railway
with the 09.15 Loughborough
Central–Leicester North on
30 December 2001.
Keith Satterly

▼ Fairburn Class 4MT 2-6-4T
No. 42073 approaches Newby
Bridge on the Lakeside
and Haverthwaite Railway.
21 August 2002.
Tom Heavyside

▲ Class 4F No. 44422 and GWR 1400 Class No. 1420 are seen side by side at Barrow Hill shed during a photographers night-shoot on 14 July 2000.

▼ Stanier Class 5 4-6-0 No. 45110 heads accross Oldbury Viaduct on the Severn Valley Railway with the 17.05 Bridgnorth–Kidderminster on 27 August 2001. **Hugh Ballantyne (2)**

"PRINCESS ROYAL" Pacific No. 46201 "PRINCESS ELIZABETH" is seen on the climb to Shap summit with Pathfinders "Cumbrian Mountain Express" Railtour of 20 April 2002.

John Calton

▲ Ivatt Class 2MT 2-6-0 No. 46441 is seen with a demonstration freight train at Burrs on the East Lancashire Railway on 28 October 2001. **Andrew Rapacz**

▼ Class 3F "Jinty" 0-6-0T No. 47298 is seen at Garthydwr on the Llangollen Railway with a freight charter. 4 February 2001. **Doug Brimingham**

▼ Caledonian Railway 439 Class 0-4-4T No. 419 is seen at Bo'ness with its first solo run after an extensive overhaul in 2001. **Alex Hogg**

▲ Class A4 No. 60009 "UNION OF SOUTH AFRICA" is seen passing Hellifield on 30 March 2002 with a Carlisle bound railtour. **Les Nixon**

▼ The legendary Class A3 No. 4472 "FLYING SCOTSMAN" is seens here departing Worcester with a Didcot bound railtour on 13 October 2001. **John Calton**

▲ V2 2-6-2 No. 60800 "GREEN ARROW" passes Helwith Bridge with a Hellifield–Carlisle Railtour on 28 December 2001. **Keith Satterly**

▼ B1 4-6-0 No. 61264 provides a fine sight as it storms out of Fort William with the West Coast Railway Company's "Jacobite" train to Mallaig on 21 July 2001. **Dick Crane**

▲ Ex-Great Eastern Railway Class B12 4-6-0 No. 61572 leaves Weybourne on the North Norfolk Railway with a Sheringham–Holt service on 1 September 2002. **Mervyn Turvey**

▼ Ex-Great Eastern Railway Class J15 0-6-0 No. 65462 (disguised as No. 65447) works a special freight train at the Mid-Suffolk Railway on 19 July 2002. **Alan Barnes**

Class K1 2-6-0 No. 62005 heads up the bank to County March summit on the West Highland line with a 30742 Charters railtour with WCRC stock on 30 September 2001.
Mervyn Turvey

1.8. BRITISH MILITARY STEAM LOCOMOTIVES
1.8.1. WAR DEPARTMENT LOCOMOTIVES

GENERAL

During the Second World War the War Department (WD) acquired and utilised a considerable number of steam locomotives. Upon the cessation of hostilities many of these locomotives were sold for further service both to industrial users and other railway administrations. The bulk of WD steam locomotives preserved date from this period. By 1952 many of the large wartime fleet of steam locomotives had been disposed of and those remaining were renumbered into a new series. From 1st April 1964 the WD became the Army Department of the Ministry of Defence with consequent renumbering taking place in 1968. Also included in this section are the steam locomotives built to WD designs for industrial users.

CLASS WD　　　　　AUSTERITY　　　　　2-10-0

Built: 1943–45 by North British. 150 built. Many sold to overseas railways. 25 sold to British Railways in 1948 and numbered 90750–74.

B.P.: 225 lb/sq. in.	**Weight–Loco:** 78.3 tons.	**Wheel dias.:** 3' 2", 4' 8½".
Cyls.: 19" x 28" (O).	**–Tender:** 55.5 tons	**T.E.:** 34 210 lbf.

Valve Gear: Walschaert.
g Hellenic Railways (Greece) numbers.
n NS (Netherlands Railways) number.

WD	AD/Overseas				
3651–73651	600	GORDON	Severn Valley Railway	NBL 25437/1943
3652–73652	Lb951 g	"90775"	Great Central Railway	NBL 25438/1943
3656–73656	Lb955 g		Thessaloniki Depot, Greece (S)	NBL 25442/1943
3672–73672	Lb960 g	"DAME VERA LYNN"	North Yorkshire Moors Railway	NBL 25458/1944
3674–73674	Lb961 g		Achame Station, Athens, Greece	NBL 25460/1944
3677–73677	Lb962 g		Thessaloniki Depot, Greece	NBL 25463/1944
3682–73682	Lb964 g		Thessaloniki Depot, Greece	NBL 25468/1944
3684–73684	Lb966 g		Thessaloniki Depot, Greece (S)	NBL 25470/1944
3755–73755	5085 n	LONGMOOR	National Railway Museum, Utrecht	NBL 25541/1945

CLASS WD　　　　　AUSTERITY　　　　　2-8-0

Built: 1943–45 by North British & Vulcan Foundry. 935 built. Many sold to overseas railways. 200 were sold to LNER in 1946. These became LNER Nos. 3000–3199 and BR 90000–100, 90422–520. A further 533 were sold to British Railways in 1948 and numbered 90101–421, 90521–732.

B.P.: 225 lb/sq. in.	**Weight–Loco:** 70.25 tons.	**Wheel dias.:** 3' 2", 4' 8½".
Cyls.: 19" x 28" (O).	**–Tender:** 55.5 tons.	**T.E.:** 34 210 lbf.

Valve Gear: Walschaert.

This locomotive was purchased from the Swedish State Railways (SJ), it previously having seen service with Netherlands Railways (NS). It is being restored to BR condition.

SJ	NS	WD	Present		
4464	1931	79257	90733	Keighley & Worth Valley Railway	VF 5200/1945

CLASS 50550　　　　　　　　　　　0-6-0ST

Built: 1941–42. Eight locomotives were built to this design, all being intended for Stewarts and Lloyd Minerals. Only one was delivered with three being taken over by WD becoming 65–67. The other four went to other industrial users and two of these survive.

B.P.: 170 lb/sq. in.	**Wheel dia.:** 4' 5".	**T.E.:** 22 150 lbf.
Cyls.: 18" x 26" (I).	**Weight:** 48.35 tons.	

Valve Gear: Stephenson.

No. 24-RRM 7	Rutland Railway Museum	HE 2411/1941
GUNBY	Gwili Railway	HE 2413/1942

WD	Present		
66-70066	S112 SPITFIRE	Embsay & Bolton Abbey Railway	HE 2414/1942

Note: This loco is receiving attention at Bryn Engineering, Pemberton, near Wigan.

CLASS WD　　　AUSTERITY　　　0-6-0ST

Built: 1943–1953 for Ministry of Supply and War Department. 391 built. 75 bought by LNER and classified J94. Many others passed to industrial users. The design of this class was derived from the '50550' class of Hunslet locomotives (see above).

B.P.: 170 lb/sq. in.　　**Wheel dia.:** 4' 3".　　**T.E.:** 23 870 lbf.
Cyls.: 18" x 26" (I).　　**Weight:** 48.25 tons.
Valve Gear: Stephenson.　　**RA:** 5.

§ Oil fired.
x Dual (air/vacuum) brakes.
† Rebuilt as 0-6-0 tender locomotive. Weights unknown.

BR	LNER	WD		
68078	8078	71463	Hope Farm, Sellindge	AB 2212/1946
68077	8077	71466	Keighley & Worth Valley Railway	AB 2215/1946

WD/AD	Present		
71480	Unnumbered	Shropshire Locomotive Collection	RSH 7289/1945
71499	Unnumbered	Bryn Engineering, Pemberton	HC 1776/1944
71505–118	BRUSSELS§	Keighley & Worth Valley Railway	HC 1782/1945
71515	68005	Embsay & Bolton Abbey Railway	RSH 7169/1944
71516	WELSH GUARDSMAN	Gwili Railway	RSH 7170/1944
71529–165	No. 15	Telford Steam Railway	AB 2183/1945
75006		Nene Valley Railway	HE 2855/1943
75008	SWIFTSURE	Bodmin Steam Railway	HE 2857/1943
75015	48	Strathspey Railway	HE 2864/1943
75019–168	COAL PRODUCTS No.6	Rutland Railway Museum	HE 2868/1943
			rebuilt HE 3883/1962
75030		Caledonian Railway	HE 2879/1943
75031–101	No. 17	Bo'ness & Kinneil Railway	HE 2880/1943
75041–107†	BARBARA	Watercress Line	HE 2890/1943
			rebuilt HE 3882/1962
75050	No. 27	Hope Farm, Sellindge	RSH 7086/1943
75061	No. 9	Strathspey Railway	RSH 7097/1943
75062	49	Tanfield Railway	RSH 7098/1943
75080	NS 8811	Stoom Stichting Nederland, Rotterdam	HC 1737/1943
75091	ROBERT No. 7	The Railway Age, Crewe	HC 1752/1943
75105	Unnumbered	Ribble Steam Railway	HE 3155/1944
75113–132	SAPPER	South Devon Railway	HE 3163/1944
			rebuilt HE 3885/1964
75115	JULIA V	Van Raak, Tilburg, Netherlands	HE 3165/1944
75118–134	WHELDALE	Embsay & Bolton Abbey Railway	HE 3168/1944
75130	ANTWERP	North Yorkshire Moors Railway	HE 3180/1944
75133–138	Unnumbered	Peak Railway, Darley Dale	HE 3183/1944
75141–139 x	68006	Dartmoor Railways, Okehampton	HE 3192/1944
			rebuilt HE 3888/1964
75142–140	68012 BLACKIE	Lavender Line, Isfield	HE 3193/1944
			rebuilt HE 3887/1964
75158–144	THE DUKE 68012	Peak Railway	WB 2746/1944
75161	No. 6	Caledonian Railway	WB 2749/1944
75170	CEFN COED	Cefn Coed Colliery Museum	WB 2758/1946
75171–147	No. 16	Caledonian Railway	WB 2759/1944
75178		Bodmin Steam Railway	WB 2766/1945
75186–150	WARRINGTON 68006	Peak Railway	RSH 7136/1944
			rebuilt HE 3892/1969
75189–152	No. 8	Pontypool & Blaenavon Railway	RSH 7139/1944
			rebuilt HE 3880/1962
75254–175	No. 7	Bo'ness & Kinneil Railway	WB 2777/1945
75256	20 TANFIELD	Tanfield Railway	WB 2779/1945
75282–181	HAULWEN No. 2	Gwili Railway	VF 5272/1945

			rebuilt HE 3879/1961
75300	3.55	Tunisville, Tunisia	VF 5290/1945
75319	72	Colne Valley Railway	VF 5309/1945
190–90		Colne Valley Railway	HE 3790/1952
191–91	HOLMAN F. STEPHENS	Kent & East Sussex Railway	HE 3791/1952
192–92	WAGGONER	Museum of Army Transport	HE 3792/1953
193–93	SHROPSHIRE	Ribble Steam Railway	HE 3793/1953
194–94	CUMBRIA	Lakeside & Haverthwaite Railway	HE 3794/1953
196	68011 ERROL LONSDALE	South Devon Railway	HE 3796/1953
197	NORTHIAM	Kent & East Sussex Railway	HE 3797/1953
198–98	ROYAL ENGINEER	Isle of Wight Steam Railway	HE 3798/1953
200	ROLVENDEN	Kent & East Sussex Railway	HE 3800/1953

Notes: 75115 carries worksplate 3164/1944 and 196 carries worksplate 3799/1953.

In addition to the 391 locomotives built for the Ministry of Supply and the War Department, a further 93 were built for industrial users, those that survive being:

No. 60	Strathspey Railway	HE 3686/1949
WHISTON	Foxfield Railway	HE 3694/1950
IR	Ribble Steam Railway	HE 3696/1950
11 REPULSE	Lakeside & Haverthwaite Railway	HE 3698/1950
NORMA	Oswestry Cycle & Railway Museum	HE 3770/1952
8 SIR ROBERT PEEL	Embsay & Bolton Abbey Railway	HE 3776/1952
"68030"	Churnet Valley Railway	HE 3777/1952
THOMAS 1	Watercress Line	HE 3781/1952
No. 69	Embsay & Bolton Abbey Railway	HE 3785/1953
MONCKTON No.1	Embsay & Bolton Abbey Railway	HE 3788/1953
WILBERT	Dean Forest Railway	HE 3806/1953
3809	North Norfolk Railway	HE 3809/1954
GLENDOWER	South Devon Railway	HE 3810/1954
68019	Bo'ness & Kinneil Railway	HE 3818/1954
WARRIOR	Dean Forest Railway	HE 3823/1954
LNER 8009	North Norfolk Railway	HE 3825/1954
Unnumbered	Swansea Vale Railway	HE 3829/1955
No. 5	Bo'ness & Kinneil Railway	HE 3837/1955
WIMBLEBURY	Foxfield Railway	HE 3839/1956
PAMELA	Vale of Glamorgan Railway	HE 3840/1956
Unnumbered	Appleby-Frodingham RPS, Scunthorpe	HE 3846/1956
JUNO	Buckinghamshire Railway Centre	HE 3850/1958
CADLEY HILL No. 1	Snibston Discovery Park	HE 3851/1962
65	Rutland Railway Museum	HE 3889/1964
66	Buckinghamshire Railway Centre	HE 3890/1964

Note: 8 SIR ROBERT PEEL is receiving attention at Bryn Engineering, Pemberton, near Wigan.

SHROPSHIRE & MONTGOMERY RLY   0-4-2WT

Built: 1893 by Alfred Dodman & Company for William Birkitt. Sold to Shropshire & Montgomery Railway in 1911 when it was rebuilt from 2-2-2WT.
B.P.: ? lbf/sq. in.   **Wheel dias.:** 2' 3", 2'3".   **T.E.:** lbf.
Cyls.: 4" x 9" (I).   **Weight:** 5.5 tons.
Note: This locomotive together with three others (LNWR coal engines) became BR (WR) stock in 1950 when this line was nationalised. The locomotives were then withdrawn.

1	GAZELLE	Kent & East Sussex Railway	Dodman 1893

WOOLMER INSTRUCTIONAL RAILWAY   0-6-0ST

Built: 1910. Used at Woolmer Instructional Railway and Longmoor Military Railway.
B.P.:   **Wheel dias.:** 3' 3"   **T.E.:**
Cyls.: 14" x 20" (O).   **Weight:** 30 tons.
WD

010–70074	WOOLMER	Museum of Army Transport	AE 1572/1910

MINISTRY OF SUPPLY   0-4-0ST

Built: 1946. Used at various establishments. Sold for industrial use in 1957.
B.P.: 160 lb/sq. in.   **Wheel dias.:** 3' 0"   **T.E.:**   6800 lbf.
Cyls.: 10" x 16" (O).   **Weight:** 20 tons.

1   MILLOM   Buckinghamshire Railway Centre   HC 1742/1946

WOOLWICH ARSENAL   0-4-0ST

Built: 1915. Used at Woolwich Arsenal Military Railway. To Royal Aircraft Establishment,
Farnborough 1955.
B.P.: 160 lb/sq. in.   **Wheel dias.:** 3' 6"   **T.E.:**   13965 lbf.
Cyls.: 14" x 22".   **Weight:** 27.5 tons.

INVINCIBLE   Isle of Wight Steam Railway   HL 3135/1915

WOOLWICH ARSENAL   0-4-0ST

Built: 1914.   Full details not available.

LION   Lincolnshire Wolds Railway   P 1351/1914

WOOLWICH ARSENAL   0-4-0T

Built: 1916   **Gauge:** 1' 6"
Full details not available.

WOOLWICH   "BWR No. 1"   Bicton Woodland Railway   AE 1748/1916

MINISTRY OF MUNITIONS   0-6-0ST

Built: 1918 for Sulphide Corporation, London. Requisitioned by the Ministry of Munutions and
sent to Persia. Subsequently sold for industrial use.
B.P.: 160 lb/sq. in.   **Wheel dias.:** 3' 7"   **T.E.:**   19430 lbf.
Cyls.: 16" x 24".   **Weight:** 39.5 tons.

AJAX   Isle of Wight Steam Railway   AB 1605/1918

ROYAL ORDNANCE   0-4-0ST

Built: 1941.
Full details not available.

No. 1   Tyseley Locomotive Works, Birmingham P 2004/1941
HERBERT   Cadeby Light Railway   P 2012/1941

For other ex-WD steam locos see LMS Class 8F.

1.8.2. AIR MINISTRY STEAM LOCOMOTIVES

RAF KENLEY   0-6-0ST

Built: 1882 for Perry & Company., Wombourn, Staffordshire. Sold to Air Ministry for use at RAF
Kenley, Surrey.
Full details not available.

111   ALDWYTH   Leeds Industrial Museum   MW 865/1882

CALSHOT   0-4-0WT

Built: 1918.
Full details not available.

?   "No. 6 DOUGLAS"   Tallyllyn Railway   AB 1431/1918

KINGSNORTH AIRSHIP STATION   0-4-0ST

Built: 1915. Used at Kingsnorth Airship Station and Royal Aircraft Establishment, Farnborough.
B.P.:   **Wheel dia.:** 3' 0".   **T.E.:**
Cyls.: 10" x 18" (O).   **Weight:** 16 tons.

125   LORD FISHER   East Somerset Railway   AB 1398/1915

1.8.3. ADMIRALTY STEAM LOCOMOTIVES

ROSYTH DOCKYARD   0-4-0ST

Built: 1914.
Full details not available.

No.1   Gwili Railway   AB 1385/191

Note: Currently receiving attention at the Swansea Vale Railway.

CHATHAM DOCKYARD   0-4-0ST

Built: 1936
Full details not available.

SINGAPORE   Rutland Railway Museum   HL 3865/1936

CHATHAM (DEVONPORT§) DOCKYARD   0-4-0ST

Built: 1945 – 46.
B.P.: 160 lb/sq. in.   **Wheel dias.**: 3′ 2″   **T.E.**:   12000 lbf.
Cyls.: 12″ x 20″.   **Weight**: 25 tonnes.

VICTORY   8   Colne Valley Railway   AB 2199/1945
INVICTA   Stratford & Broadway Railway   AB 2220/1946
No. 2§   Dean Forest Railway   AB 2221/1946

CHATHAM DOCKYARD   0-4-0ST

Built: 1941.
Full details not available.

AJAX   Chatham Dockyard Historic Trust   RSHN 7042/1941

Note: This loco is currently receiving attention at Heritage Engineering (Swindon).

DEVONPORT DOCKYARD   0-4-0ST

Built: 1950.
Full details not available.

No. 19   Bodmin Steam Railway   WB 2962/1950

WD "AUSTERITY" 0-6-0ST No. 198 "ROYAL ENGINEER" runs round its train at Smallbrook Jn. on the
Isle of Wight Steam Railway before hauling the 11.00 to Wootton on 14 August 2002.   **Alan Yearsley**

1.9. UNITED STATES ARMY TRANSPORTATION CORPS STEAM LOCOMOTIVES

CLASS S160   2-8-0

Built: 1942–45 by various American builders. It is estimated that 2120 were built. Many saw use on Britain's railways during the second world war. Post war many were sold to overseas railway administrations. Only those currently in Great Britain are shown here.

B.P.: 225 lb/sq. in.   **Weight–Loco:** 73 tons.   **Wheel dias.:** 3' 2", 4' 9".
Cyls.: 19" x 26" (O).   **–Tender:** 52.1 tons.   **T.E.:** 31490 lbf.
Valve Gear: Walschaert.
§ PKP (Polish Railways)   ‡ Chinese State Railways
★ Hungarian Railways
f FS (Italian Railways). Passed to Hellenic Railways (Greece) and numbered 575. Carries name "FRANKLYN D. ROOSEVELT".

USATC	Overseas Railway		
1631	411.388 ★	Ribble Steam Railway	AL 70284/1942
2253	Ty203-288§	North Yorkshire Moors Railway	BLW 69496/1943
3278	736-073 f	Watercress Line	AL 71533/1944
5197	KD6.463 ‡	Churnet Valley Railway	Lima 8856/1945
5820	Ty203-474§	Keighley & Worth Valley Railway	Lima 8758/1945
6046	411.144 ★	Churnet Valley Railway	BLW 72080/1945
?	?	East Lancashire Railway	BLW?
?	?	East Lancashire Railway	?

1.10 REPLICA STEAM LOCOMOTIVES
GENERAL

Details are included of locomotives which would have been included in the foregoing had the locomotive they replicate survived. Locomotives are listed under the heading of the Railway/ Manufacturer they replicate.

STOCKTON & DARLINGTON RAILWAY   0-4-0

Built: 1975.
B.P.: 50 lb/sq. in.   **Weight–Loco:** 6.5 tons.   **Wheel dias.:** 3' 11"
Cyls.: 9½" x 24" (O).   **–Tender:**   **T.E.:** 1960 lbf.

LOCOMOTION	North of England Open Air Museum	Loco. Ent.No. 1/1975

LIVERPOOL & MANCHESTER RAILWAY   0-2-2

Built: 1934/79.
B.P.: 50 lb/sq. in.   **Weight–Loco:** 4.5 tons.   **Wheel dias.:** 4' 8½", 2'6".
Cyls.: 8" x 17" (O).   **–Tender:** 5.2 tons.   **T.E.:** 820 lbf.

ROCKET	National Railway Museum	RS 4089/1934
ROCKET	National Railway Museum	Loco. Ent.No. 2/1979

LIVERPOOL & MANCHESTER RAILWAY   0-2-2

Built: 1979.
B.P.: 50 lb/sq. in.   **Weight–Loco:** 4.5 tons.   **Wheel dias.:** 4' 6"
Cyls.: 7" x 18" (O).   **–Tender:** 5.2 tons.   **T.E.:** 690 lbf.

SANS PAREIL	Timothy Hackworth Museum	Shildon/1980

LIVERPOOL & MANCHESTER RAILWAY   2-2-0

Built: 1992.
B.P.:   **Weight–Loco:**   **Wheel dias.:**
Cyls.:   **–Tender:**   **T.E.:**

PLANET   Greater Manchester Museum of Science & Industry   Manch 1992

BRAITHWAITE & ERICCSON & COMPANY   0-4-0

Built: 1929 (using parts from 1829 original)/1980.
B.P.:   **Weight–Loco:**   **Wheel dias.:**
Cyls.:   **–Tender:**   **T.E.:**

NOVELTY   Greater Manchester Museum of Science & Industry(N)   Science Museum 1929
NOVELTY   Swedish Railway Museum, Gayle, Sweden   Loco. Ent. 1980

Note: The 1980 locomotive is to be displayed at The National Railway Museum during 2003.

GREAT WESTERN RAILWAY   3000 CLASS   4-2-2

Built: 1983 as a non working replica without a tender.
B.P.: 160 lb/sq. in.   **Weight–Loco:** 44.2 tons.   **Wheel dias.:** 4'7", 7'8½", 4'7".
Cyls.: 20" x 24".   **T.E.:** 14,115 lbf.

3041   THE QUEEN   Madame Tussauds, Windsor   Carn 1983

GREAT WESTERN RAILWAY   2-2-2

Built: 1925 (using parts from 1837 original).   **Gauge:** 7' 0¼".
B.P.: 90 lb/sq. in.   **Weight–Loco:** 23.35 tons.   **Wheel dias.:** 4'0", 7'0",4'0".
Cyls.: 16" x 16"   **–Tender:** 6.5 tons.   **T.E.:**

NORTH STAR   Steam – Museum of the Great Western Railway (N)   Swindon 1925

GREAT WESTERN RAILWAY   2-2-2

Under construction at Didcot Railway Centre.   **Gauge:** 7' 0¼".
B.P.: 50 lb/sq. in.   **Weight–Loco:** 23.35 tons   **Wheel dias.:** 4'0", 7'0", 4'0".
Cyls.: 15" x 18".   **–Tender:** 6.5 tons   **T.E.**

FIRE FLY   Didcot Railway Centre   Not yet completed

GREAT WESTERN RAILWAY   4-2-2

Built: 1985.   **Gauge:** 7' 0¼".
B.P.:   **Weight–Loco:** 35.5 tons   **Wheel dias.:** 4'6", 8'0", 4'6".
Cyls.: 18" x 24".   **–Tender:**   **T.E.**

IRON DUKE   National Railway Museum   Resco 1985

LONDON & NORTH WESTERN RAILWAY   4-2-2

Built: 1991 (Under construction at Tyseley Locomotive Works§).
B.P.:   **Weight–Loco:**   **Wheel dias.:**
Cyls.: (I).   **–Tender:**   **T.E.**

1009   WOLVERTON   Milton Keynes Central Station   MF 1991
10??§   Tyseley Locomotive Works, Birmingham   Not yet completed

LONDON BRIGHTON & SOUTH COAST RLY CLASS C2X   0-6-0T

Built:
B.P.: 170 lb/sq.in   **Weight:** 45.25 t   **Wheel dia.:** 5'0"
Cyls.: 17½ x 26"   **T.E.:** 19 170 lbf

32521   Elham Valley Museum, Folkestone   ?

2. DIESEL LOCOMOTIVES
GENERAL

It was not until the mid-1950s that diesel locomotives appeared in great numbers. However, during the 1930s, particularly on the LMS with diesel shunting locomotives, several small building programmes were authorised. A few locomotives survive from this period along with several others built post war. During the Second World War a large proportion of LMS locomotives were transferred to the war department whom also authorised the construction of further orders. Many of these were shipped across the Channel and were subsequently lost in action. It is, however, possible some still remain undiscovered by the authors. Notification of these would be gratefully appreciated.

From the mid-1950s the re-equipment of the railway network began in earnest and vast numbers of new, mainly diesel locomotives were constructed by British Railways and private contractors, many early examples of which are still in service.

NOTES
Wheel Arrangement

The Whyte notation is used for diesel shunters with coupled driving wheels (see steam section). For other shunting and main-line diesel and electric locomotives, the system whereby the number of driven axles on a bogie or frame is denoted by a letter (A = 1, B = 2, C = 3 etc) and the number of undriven axles is denoted by a number is used. The letter "o" after a letter indicates that each axle is individually powered and a + sign indicates that the bogies are intercoupled.

Dimensions

SI units are generally used. Imperial units are sometimes given in parentheses.

Tractive Effort

Continuous and maximum tractive efforts are generally quoted for vehicles with electric transmission.

Brakes

Locomotives are assumed to have train vacuum brakes unless otherwise stated.

Numbering Systems

Prior to nationalisation each railway company allocated locomotive numbers in accordance with its own policy. However, after nationalisation in 1948 a common system was devised and internal combustion locomotives were allocated five figure numbers in the series 10000–19999.

Diesel locomotives built prior to nationalisation or to pre-nationalisation designs are arranged generally in order of the 1948 numbers with those withdrawn before 1948 listed at the beginning of each section. In 1957 a new numbering scheme was introduced for locomotives built to British Railways specifications and details of this are given in the introduction to the British Railways section.

2.1. LONDON MIDLAND & SCOTTISH RAILWAY

DIESEL MECHANICAL   0-4-0

Built: 1934 by English Electric at Preston Works for Drewry Car Company.
Engine: Allan 8RS18 of 119 kW (160 h.p.) at 1200 r.p.m. (Now fitted with a Gardner 6L3 of 114 kW (153 h.p.).
Transmission: Mechanical. Wilson four-speed gearbox driving a rear jackshaft.
Max. T.E.: 50 kN (15300 lbf).   **Weight:** 25.8 tonnes.
Max. Speed: 12 m.p.h.   **Wheel Dia:** 914 mm.
No train brakes.

LMS	WD		AD				
7050	224–70224–846	240	"RORKE'S DRIFT"	Museum of Army Transport	DC 2047/EE 847/1934		

DIESEL MECHANICAL   0-6-0

Built: 1932 by Hunslet Engine Company (taken into stock 1933).
Engine: MAN 112 kW (150 h.p.) at 900 r.p.m. (Now fitted with a Maclaren/Ricardo 98 kW engine).
Transmission: Mechanical. Hunslet constant mesh four-speed gearbox.
Max. T.E.: 33 kN.   **Weight:** 21.7 tonnes.
Max. Speed: 30 m.p.h.   **Wheel Dia:** 914 mm.
Built without train brakes, but vacuum brakes now fitted.

7401–7051	"JOHN ALCOCK"	Middleton Railway	HE 1697/1933

DIESEL ELECTRIC   0-6-0

Built: 1935 by English Electric. 11 built, 3 taken over by BR as 12000–2 (LMS 7074/6/9).
Scrapped 1956–62. Others sold to WD for use in France.
Engine: English Electric 6K of 261 kW (350 h.p.) at 675 r.p.m.
Transmission: Electric. Two axle-hung traction motors with a single reduction drive.
Power at Rail:
Max. T.E.: 147 kN (33000 lbf).   **Weight:** 52 tonnes.
Max Speed: 30 m.p.h.   **Wheel Dia:** 1232 mm.
No train brakes.

LMS	WD			
7069	18	Gloucestershire-Warwickshire Railway	DK 1935	

DIESEL ELECTRIC   0-6-0

Built: 1939–42 at Derby. 40 built, 30 taken over by BR as 12003–32 (LMS 7080–99, 7110–9).
Scrapped 1964–7. Others sold to WD for use in Italy and Egypt.
Engine: English Electric 6KT of 261 kW (350 h.p.) at 680 r.p.m.
Transmission: Electric. One traction motor with jackshaft drive.
Power at Rail:
Max. T.E.: 147 kN (33000 lbf).   **Weight:** 56 tonnes.
Max Speed: 20 m.p.h.   **Wheel Dia:** 1295 mm.
Built without train brakes, but air brakes now fitted.

LMS	WD	FS	Present		
7103	52–70052	700.001	Unnumbered	Piedmont Rail Museum, Torino, Italy	Derby 1941
7106	55–70055	700.003	Unnumbered	LFI, Arezzostia Pescaiola, Italy	Derby 1941

BR CLASS 11   DIESEL ELECTRIC   0-6-0

Built: 1945–53. LMS design. 120 built. The first order for 20 was for the WD, 14 being delivered as 260–8/70269–73, the balance passing to the LMS as 7120–7125 (BR 12033–38). 260–8 were renumbered 70260–8 and 70260–9 were sold to the NS (Netherlands Railways) in 1946.
Engine: English Electric 6KT of 261 kW (350 h.p.) at 680 r.p.m.
Transmission: Electric. Two EE 506 axle hung traction motors.
Power at Rail: 183 kW (245 h.p.).

Max. T.E.: 156 kN (35000 lbf). **Weight:** 56 tonnes.
Cont. T.E.: 49.4 kN (11100 lbf) at 8.8 m.p.h. **Wheel Dia:** 1372 mm.
Max. Speed: 20 m.p.h.
No train brakes except 70272, 12099 and 12131 which have since been fitted with vacuum brakes and 12083 which has since been fitted with air brakes.

BR	WD	AD	Present		
	70269		508§	National Railway Museum, Utrecht, Netherlands	Derby 1944
	70272–878	601	7120	Lakeside & Haverthwaite Railway	Derby 1944
12049				Watercress Line	Derby 1948
12052			MP228	Caledonian Railway	Derby 1949
12061			4	Gwili Railway	Derby 1949
12077				Midland Railway Centre	Derby 1950
12083				Battlefield Railway	Derby 1950
12088				Crouch Mining, Widdington Disposal Point	Derby 1951
12093			MP229	Caledonian Railway	Derby 1951
12098				European Metal Recycling, Kingsbury	Derby 1952
12099				Severn Valley Railway	Derby 1952
12131				North Norfolk Railway	Darlington 1952

§ NS number.

Note: Three further locomotives were built to this design by EE for ICI in 1948. One of these remains masquerading as an ex-BR locomotive. This is:

12139 Redcar   North Yorkshire Moors Railway   EE1553/1948

2.2. SOUTHERN RAILWAY
BR CLASS 12   DIESEL ELECTRIC   0-6-0

Built: 1949–52. Based on pre-war LMS design. 26 built.
Engine: English Electric 6KT of 350 h.p. at 680 r.p.m.
Transmission: Electric. Two EE 506A axle-hung traction motors.
Power at Rail: 163 kW (218 h.p.).
Max. T.E.: 107 kN (24000 lbf). **Weight:** 45 tonnes.
Cont. T.E.: 36 kN (8000 lbf) at 10.2 m.p.h. **Wheel Dia:** 1370 mm.
Max. Speed: 27 m.p.h.
No train brakes.

15224   Spa Valley Railway   Ashford 1949

2.3. BRITISH RAILWAYS
Numbering System

In 1957 British Railways introduced a new numbering system which applied to all diesel locomotives except those built to pre-nationalisation designs. Each locomotive was allocated a number of up to four digits prefixed with a 'D'. Diesel electric shunters already built numbered in the 13xxx series had the '1' replaced by a 'D'. Diesel mechanical shunters already built numbered in the11xxx series were allocated numbers in the D2xxx series.

When all steam locomotives had been withdrawn, the prefix letter was officially eliminated from the number of diesel locomotives, although it continued to be carried on many of them. For this reason, no attempt is made to distinguish between those locomotives which did or did not have the 'D' prefix removed. Similarly, in preservation, no distinction is made between locomotives which do or do not carry a 'D' prefix at present.

Locomotives in this section are listed in order of their 1957 numbers with experimental and departmental locomotives listed at the end.

With the introduction of modern communications each class was allocated a two digit class number followed by a three digit serial number. These started to be applied in 1972 and several locomotives have carried more than one number in this scheme.

Classification System

It was not until the British Railways organisation was set up that some semblance of order was introduced. This broadly took the following form:

Type	Engine Horsepower	Number Range
1	800–1000	D 8000–D 8999
2	1001–1499	D 5000–D 6499
3	1500–1999	D 6500–D 7999
4	2000–2999	D 1–D 1999
5	3000 +	D 9000–D 9499
Shunting	150/300	D 2000–D 2999
Shunting	350/400	D 3000–D 4999
Shunting	650	D 9500–D 9999
A.C. Electric		E 1000–E 4999
D.C. Electric		E 5000–E 6999

Note: Locomotives which have recently been preserved, but have not yet moved from the Railtrack network are shown with the location left blank.

BR Green Class 40 No. D345 is seen at Little Burrs on the East Lancashire Railway on 6 July 2002 with a Ramsbottom–Bury service. **Les Nixon**

CLASS 44   PEAK   1Co-Co1

Built: 1959–60. 10 Built.
Engine: Sulzer 12LDA28A of 1720 kW (2300 h.p.) at 750 r.p.m.
Transmission: Electric. Six Crompton Parkinson C171B1 axle-hung traction motors.
Power at Rail: 1342 kW (1800 h.p.).
Max. T.E.: 222 kN (50000 lbf).   **Weight:** 135 tonnes.
Cont. T.E.: 129.kN (29100 lbf) at 23.2 m.p.h.   **Wheel Dias:** 914/1143 mm.
Max. Speed: 90 m.p.h.
Train Heating: Built with steam but facility removed in 1962.

D 4–44004	GREAT GABLE	Nottingham Heritage Centre	Derby 1959
D 8–44008	PENYGHENT	Peak Railway	Derby 1959

Note: D 4 is on loan from the Midland Railway Centre.

CLASS 45   1Co-Co1

Built: 1960–63. 127 built.
Engine: Sulzer 12LDA28B of 1860 kW (2500 h.p.) at 750 r.p.m.
Transmission: Electric. Six Crompton Parkinson C172A1 axle-hung traction motors.
Power at Rail: 1491 kW (2000 h.p.).
Max. T.E.: 245 kN (55000 lbf).
Weight: 135 tonnes. (138 tonnes D14, D53 and D100)
Cont. T.E.: 133 kN (30000 lbf) at 25 m.p.h.   **Wheel Dias:** 914/1143 mm.
Max. Speed: 90 m.p.h.   Dual braked.
Train Heating: Built with steam but subsequently replaced with electric except D14, D53 and D100.

D 14–45015		Battlefield Railway	Derby 1960
D 22–45132		Watercress Line	Derby 1961
D 40–45133		Midland Railway Centre	Derby 1961
D 53–45041	ROYAL TANK REGIMENT	Midland Railway Centre	Crewe 1962
D 61–45112	THE ROYAL ARMY ORDNANCE CORPS	Fragonset Railways, Derby	Crewe 1962
D 67–45118	THE ROYAL ARTILLERYMAN	Northampton & Lamport Railway	Crewe 1962
D 86–45105		Barrow Hill Roundhouse	Crewe 1961
D 99–45135	3rd CARABINIER	East Lancashire Railway	Crewe 1961
D 100–45060	SHERWOOD FORESTER	Barrow Hill Roundhouse	Crewe 1961
D 120–45108		The Railway Age, Crewe	Crewe 1961
D 123–45125		Great Central Railway	Crewe 1961
D 135–45149	"PHAETON"	Gloucestershire-Warwickshire Railway	Crewe 1961

CLASS 46   1Co-Co1

Built: 1961–63. 56 built.
Engine: Sulzer 12LDA28B of 1860 kW (2500 h.p.) at 750 r.p.m.
Transmission: Electric. Six Brush TM73-68 MkIII axle-hung traction motors.
Power at Rail: 1460 kW (1960 h.p.).
Max. T.E.: 245 kN (55000 lbf).   **Weight:** 141 tonnes.
Cont. T.E.: 141 kN (31600 lbf) at 22.3 m.p.h.   **Wheel Dias:** 914/1143 mm.
Max. Speed: 90 m.p.h.   Dual braked.
Train Heating: Steam.

D 147–46010		Llangollen Railway	Derby 1961
D 172–46035-97403	IXION	The Railway Age, Crewe	Derby 1962
D 182–46045-97404		Midland Railway Centre	Derby 1962

CLASS 40   1Co-Co1

Built: 1958–62 at Vulcan Foundry & Robert Stephenson & Hawthorn. 200 built.
Engine: English Electric 16SVT MkII of 1480 kW (2000 h.p.) at 850 r.p.m.
Transmission: Electric. Six EE 526/5D axle-hung traction motors.
Power at Rail: 1156 kW (1550 h.p.).
Max. T.E.: 231 kN (52000 lbf).   **Weight:** 132 tonnes.
Cont. T.E.: 137 kN (30900 lbf) at 18.8 m.p.h.   **Wheel Dias:** 914/1143 mm.
Max. Speed: 90 m.p.h.   Dual braked except D 306.

Train Heating: Steam.

D 200–40122		National Railway Museum	EE/VF 2367/D395	1958
D 212–40012–97407	AUREOL	Midland Railway Centre	EE/VF 2667/D429	1959
D 213–40013	ANDANIA	Midland Railway Centre	EE/VF 2668/D430	1959
D 306–40106	"ATLANTIC CONVEYOR"	Nene Valley Railway	EE/RSH 2726/8136	1960
D 318–40118–97408		Tyseley Locomotive Works	EE/RSH 2853/8148	1961
D 335–40135–97406		East Lancashire Railway	EE/VF 3081/D631	1961
D 345–40145		East Lancashire Railway	EE/VF 3091/D641	1961

CLASS 50   Co-Co

Built: 1967–68 at Vulcan Foundry. 50 built.
Engine: English Electric 16CVST of 2010 kW (2700 h.p.) at 850 r.p.m.
Transmission: Electric. Six EE 538/5A axle-hung traction motors.
Power at Rail: 1540 kW (2070 h.p.).
Max. T.E.: 216 kN (48500 lbf).   **Weight:** 117 tonnes.
Cont. T.E.: 147 kN (33000 lbf) at 18.8 m.p.h.   **Wheel Dia:** 1092 mm.
Max. Speed: 100 m.p.h.   Dual braked.
Train Heating: Electric.

D 400–50050	Fearless	Tyseley Locomotive Works	EE/VF 3770/D1141 1967
D 402–50002	Superb	Barrow Hill Roundhouse	EE/VF 3772/D1143 1967
D 407–50007	SIR EDWARD ELGAR	Midland Railway Centre	EE/VF 3777/D1148 1968
D 408–50008	Thunderer	The Railway Age, Crewe	EE/VF 3778/D1149 1968
D 415–50015	Valiant	East Lancashire Railway	EE/VF 3785/D1156 1968
D 417–50017	Royal Oak	Tyseley Locomotive Works	EE/VF 3787/D1158 1968
D 419–50019	Ramillies	Mid-Norfolk Railway	EE/VF 3789/D1160 1968
D 421–50021	Rodney	Tyseley Locomotive Works	EE/VF 3791/D1162 1968
D 423–50023	Howe	Barrow Hill Roundhouse	EF/VF 3793/D1164 1968
D 426–50026	Indomitable	MoD DSDA Bicester Military Rly.	EE/VF 3796/D1167 1968
D 427–50027	Lion	North Yorkshire Moors Railway	EE/VF 3797/D1168 1968
D 429–50029	Renown	Peak Railway	EE/VF 3799/D1170 1968
D 430–50030	Repulse	Peak Railway	EE/VF 3800/D1171 1968
D 431–50031	Hood	Severn Valley Railway	EE/VF 3801/D1172 1968
D 433–50033	Glorious	National Railway Museum	EE/VF 3803/D1174 1968
D 435–50035	Ark Royal	Severn Valley Railway	EE/VF 3805/D1176 1968
D 440–50040	Centurion	Coventry Railway Centre	EE/VF 3810/D1181 1968
D 442–50042	Triumph	Bodmin Steam Railway	EE/VF 3812/D1183 1968
D 444–50044	Exeter	Severn Valley Railway	EE/VF 3814/D1185 1968
D 449–50049–50149	Defiance	Severn Valley Railway	EE/VF 3819/D1190 1968

Note: 50007 was previously named 'Hercules' and 50040 was previously named 'Leviathan'.

CLASS 42   WARSHIP   B-B

Built: 1958–61. 38 Built.
Engines: Two Maybach MD650 of 821 kW (1100 h.p.) at 1530 r.p.m.
Transmission: Hydraulic. Mekydro K 104U.
Max. T.E.: 223 kN (52400 lbf).   **Weight:** 80 tonnes.
Cont. T.E.: 209 kN (46900 lbf) at 11.5 m.p.h.   **Wheel Dia:** 1033 mm.
Max. Speed: 90 m.p.h.   **Train Heating:** Steam.

D 821	GREYHOUND	Severn Valley Railway	Swindon 1960
D 832	ONSLAUGHT	East Lancashire Railway	Swindon 1961

CLASS 52   WESTERN   C-C

Built: 1961–64. 74 built.
Engines: Two Maybach MD655 of 1007 kW (1350 h.p.) at 1500 r.p.m.
Transmission: Hydraulic. Voith L630rV.
Max. T.E.: 297.3 kN (66770 lbf).   **Weight:** 111 tonnes.
Cont. T.E.: 201.2 kN (45200 lbf) at 14.5 m.p.h.   **Wheel Dia:** 1092 mm.
Max. Speed: 90 m.p.h.   **Train Heating:** Steam.
Dual braked.

D 1010§	WESTERN CAMPAIGNER	West Somerset Railway	Swindon 1962
D 1013	WESTERN RANGER	Severn Valley Railway	Swindon 1962
D 1015	WESTERN CHAMPION	Severn Valley Railway	Swindon 1963
D 1023	WESTERN FUSILIER	National Railway Museum	Swindon 1963
D 1041	WESTERN PRINCE	East Lancashire Railway	Crewe 1962
D 1048	WESTERN LADY	Midland Railway Centre	Crewe 1962
D 1062	WESTERN COURIER	Severn Valley Railway	Crewe 1963

§ Masquerades as D 1035 WESTERN YEOMAN.

CLASS 47 Co-Co

Built: 1963–67. 512 built.
Engine: Sulzer 12LDA28C of 1920 kW (2580 h.p.) at 750 r.p.m.
Transmission: Electric. Six Brush TG 160-60 axle-hung traction motors.
Power at Rail: 1550 kW (2080 h.p.).
Max. T.E.: 245 kN (55000 lbf). (267 kN (60000 lbf)§). **Weight:** 119–121 tonnes.
Cont. T.E.: 133 kN (33000 lbf) at 26 m.p.h.   **Wheel Dias:** 1143 mm.
Max. Speed: 95 m.p.h.   Dual braked.
Train Heating: Built with Steam/Electric (§ steam only). Electric heating fitted & steam heating removed on D 1566 in 1973 and on D 1970 in 1986.

D 1705 was built with a Sulzer 12LVA24 engine but replaced with a 12LDA28C in 1972.

D 1500–47401	North Eastern	Midland Railway Centre	BE 342/1962
D 1501–47402	Gateshead	East Lancashire Railway	BE 343/1962
D 1516–47417		Midland Railway Centre	BE 358/1963
D 1566–47449§		Llangollen Railway	Crewe 1964
D 1693–47105§		Gloucestershire-Warwickshire Railway	BE 455/1964
D 1705–47117§		Great Central Railway	BE 467/1965
D 1842–47192§		The Railway Age, Crewe	Crewe 1965
D 1970–47269–47643§		Bo'ness & Kinneil Railway	Crewe 1965

Notes: 47401 also carried the name 'Star of the East' for a time.

CLASS 03 0-6-0

Built: 1957–62. 230 built.
Engine: Gardner 8L3 of 152 kW (204 h.p.) at 1200 r.p.m. Replaced with VM V12 (300 - 350 h.p.) on D 2128 and D 2134.
Transmission: Mechanical. Wilson CA5 epicyclic gearbox.
Max. T.E.: 68 kN (15300 lbf).   **Weight:** 31 tonnes.
Wheel Dia: 1092 mm.   **Max. Speed:** 28 m.p.h.
x Dual braked   a Air brakes only

§ modified with cut down cab for working on Burry Port & Gwendraeth Valley Line.

BR	Present		
11205–D 2018–03018		Lavender Line, Isfield	Swindon 1958
11206–D 2019	1	Stabilimento ISA, Ospitaletto, Brescia, Italy	Swindon 1958
11207–D 2020–03020		Lavender Line, Isfield	Swindon 1958
11209–D 2022–03022		Swindon & Cricklade Railway	Swindon 1958
11210–D 2023		Kent & East Sussex Railway	Swindon 1958
11211–D 2024	No. 4	Kent & East Sussex Railway	Swindon 1958
D 2027–03027		Peak Railway	Swindon 1958
D 2032	2	Stabilimento ISA, Ospitaletto, Brescia, Italy	Swindon 1958
D 2033	Profilatinave 2	Siderurgica, Montirone, Brescia, Italy	Swindon 1958
D 2036	Profilatinave 1	Siderurgica, Montirone, Brescia, Italy	Swindon 1959
D 2037–03037		Lavender Line, Isfield	Swindon 1959
D 2041		Colne Valley Railway	Swindon 1959
D 2046	Unnumbered	Petroplus International, Waterston	Doncaster 1958
D 2051		North Norfolk Railway	Doncaster 1959
D 2059–03059x		Isle of Wight Steam Railway	Doncaster 1959
D 2062–03062		East Lancashire Railway	Doncaster 1959
D 2063–03063x		North Norfolk Railway	Doncaster 1959
D 2066–03066x		Barrow Hill Roundhouse	Doncaster 1959
D 2069–03069		Gloucestershire-Warwickshire Railway	Doncaster 1959

D 2072–03072		Lakeside & Haverthwaite Railway	Doncaster 1959
D 2073–03073x		The Railway Age, Crewe	Doncaster 1959
D 2078–03078x		Stephenson Railway Museum	Doncaster 1959
D 2079–03079		Derwent Valley Light Railway	Doncaster 1960
D 2081–03081		Genappe Sugar Works, Belgium	Doncaster 1960
D 2084–03084x		Peak Railway	Doncaster 1959
D 2089–03089x		Mangapps Farm, Burnham-on-Crouch	Doncaster 1960
D 2090–03090		National Railway Museum	Doncaster 1960
D 2094–03094x		Barrow Hill Roundhouse	Doncaster 1960
D 2099–03099		Peak Railway	Doncaster 1960
D 2112–03112x		Port of Boston Authority, Boston Docks	Doncaster 1960
D 2113–03113	Unnumbered	Peak Railway	Doncaster 1960
D 2117	LHR No. 8	Lakeside & Haverthwaite Railway	Swindon 1959
D 2118		Rutland Railway Museum	Swindon 1959
D 2119–03119§	"LINDA"	West Somerset Railway	Swindon 1959
D 2120–03120§		Fawley Hill Railway	Swindon 1959
D 2128–03128a		Dean Forest Railway	Swindon 1960
D 2133		West Somerset Railway	Swindon 1960
D 2134–03134a		Royal Deeside Railway	Swindon 1960
D 2138		Midland Railway Centre	Swindon 1960
D 2139	No. 1	Peak Railway	Swindon 1960
D 2141–03141§		Dean Forest Railway	Swindon 1960
D 2144–03144x	"WESTERN WAGGONER"	MoD DSDA Bicester Military Railway	Swindon 1960
D 2145–03145§		Long Coppice, Moreton-on-Lugg	Swindon 1960
D 2148		Ribble Steam Railway	Swindon 1960
D 2152–03152§	Unnumbered	Swindon & Cricklade Railway	Swindon 1960
D 2158–03158x		Peak Railway	Swindon 1960
D 2162–03162x		Llangollen Railway	Swindon 1960
D 2170–03170x		Battlefield Railway	Swindon 1960
D 2178	2	Gwili Railway	Swindon 1962
D 2180–03180x		Battlefield Railway	Swindon 1962
D 2182		Gloucestershire-Warwickshire Railway	Swindon 1962
D 2184		Colne Valley Railway	Swindon 1962
D 2189–03189		Ribble Steam Railway	Swindon 1961
D 2192	"ARDENT"	Paignton & Dartmouth Railway	Swindon 1961
D 2196–03196x		West Coast Railway Company, Carnforth	Swindon 1961
D 2197–03197x		Lavender Line, Isfield	Swindon 1961
D 2199		Hanson Aggregates, Machen Quarry, Near Newport	Swindon 1961
Dept 92–D 2371–03371x		Rowden Mill Station, Herefordshire	Swindon 1958
D 2381		West Coast Railway Company, Carnforth	Swindon 1961
D 2399–03399x		Mangapps Farm, Burnham-on-Crouch	Doncaster 1961

Notes: D 2199 is on loan from the Peak Railway.

CLASS 04   0-6-0

Built: 1952–62. Drewry design built by Vulcan Foundry & Robert Stephenson & Hawthorn. 140 built.
Engine: Gardner 8L3 of 152 kW (204 h.p.) at 1200 r.p.m.
Transmission: Mechanical. Wilson CA5 epicyclic gearbox
Max. T.E.: 69.7 kN (15650 lbf).   **Weight:** 32 tonnes.
Wheel Dia: 1067 mm.   **Max. Speed:** 28 m.p.h.

BR	Present		
11103–D 2203		Embsay & Bolton Abbey Railway	DC/VF 2400/D145/1952
11106–D 2205		West Somerset Railway	DC/VF 2486/D212/1953
11108–D 2207		North Yorkshire Moors Railway	DC/VF 2482/D208/1953
11122–D 2216	3	Stabilimento ISA, Ospitaletto, Brescia, Italy	DC/VF 2539/D265/1955
11135–D 2229	No. 5	Peak Railway	DC/VF 2552/D278/1955
11215–D 2245		Battlefield Railway	DC/RSH 2577/7864/1956
11216–D 2246		South Devon Railway	DC/RSH 2578/7865/1956
D 2271		West Somerset Railway	DC/RSH 2615/7913/1958
D 2272	"ALFIE"	Lavender Line, Isfield	DC/RSH 2616/7914/1958

D 2279		East Anglian Railway Museum	DC/RSH 2656/8097/1960
D 2280	No. 2	North Norfolk Railway	DC/RSH 2657/8098/1960
D 2284		Peak Railway	DC/RSH 2661/8102/1960
D 2289		Acciaierie, Lonato, Italy	DC/RSH 2669/8122/1960
D 2298		Buckinghamshire Railway Centre	DC/RSH 2679/8157/1960
D 2302		Rutland Railway Museum	DC/RSH 2683/8161/1960
D 2310		Battlefield Railway	DC/RSH 2691/8169/1960
D 2324	Unnumbered	Lavender Line, Isfield	DC/RSH 2705/8183/1961
D 2325		Mangapps Farm, Burnham-on-Crouch	DC/RSH 2706/8184/1961
D 2334	NCB 33 NO. 4	Churnet Valley Railway	DC/RSH 2715/8193/1961
D 2337	"DOROTHY"	Peak Railway	DC/RSH 2718/8196/1961

Notes: A locomotive of similar appearance built for industrial use to an earlier specification masquerades as a BR locomotive. This is:-

11104		Mangapps Farm, Burnham-on-Crouch	DC/VF 2252/D78/1948

CLASS 06   0-4-0

Built: 1958–60 by Andrew Barclay, Kilmarnock. 35 built.
Engine: Gardner 8L3 of 152 kW (204 h.p.) at 1200 r.p.m.
Transmission: Mechanical. Wilson CA5 epicyclic gearbox.
Max. T.E.: 88 kN (19800 lbf).   **Weight:** 37 tonnes.
Wheel Dia: 1092 mm.   **Max. Speed:** 23 m.p.h.

D 2420–06003–97804	Barrow Hill Roundhouse	AB 435/1959

UNCLASSIFIED   HUDSWELL-CLARKE   0-6-0

Built: 1955–61. 20 built.
Engine: Gardner 8L3 of 152 kW (204 h.p.) at 1200 r.p.m.
Transmission: Mechanical. SSS powerflow double synchro.
Max. T.E.: 85.7 kN (19245 lbf).   **Weight:** 34 tonnes.
Cont. T.E.: 76 kN (17069 lbf) at 3.72 m.p.h.   **Wheel Dia:** 1067 mm.
Max. Speed: 25 m.p.h.

D 2511	Keighley & Worth Valley Railway	HC D 1202/1961

CLASS 05   0-6-0

Built: 1955–61. 69 built.
Engine: Gardner 8L3 of 152 kW (204 h.p.) at 1200 r.p.m.
Transmission: Mechanical. Hunslet gearbox.
Max. T.E.: 64.6 kN (14500 lbf).   **Weight:** 31 tonnes.
Wheel Dia: 1121 (1016*) mm.   **Max. Speed:** 18 m.p.h.

BR	Present		
11140*–D 2554–05001–97803		Isle of Wight Steam Railway	HE 4870/1956
D 2578	2 "CIDER QUEEN"	Long Coppice, Moreton-on-Lugg	HE 5460/1958
			rebuilt HE 6999/1968
D 2587		Lavender Line, Isfield	HE 5636/1959
			rebuilt HE 7180/1969
D 2595		Ribble Steam Railway	HE 5644/1960
			rebuilt HE 7179/1969

UNCLASSIFIED   NORTH BRITISH   0-4-0

Built: 1957–61. 73 built.
Engine: M.A.N. W6V 17.5/22A of 168 kW (225 h.p.) at 1100 r.p.m.
Transmission: Mechanical. Voith L33YU.
Max. T.E.: 89.4 kN (20080 lbf).   **Weight:** 28 tonnes.
Cont. T.E.: 53.4 kN (12000 lbf) at 4 m.p.h.   **Wheel Dia:** 1067 mm.
Max. Speed: 15 m.p.h.

D 2767	Bo'ness & Kinneil Railway	NBL 28020/1960
D 2774	Strathspey Railway	NBL 28027/1960

CLASS 02   0-4-0

Built: 1960–61. 20 built.
Engine: Rolls Royce C6NFL of 127 kW (170 h.p.) at 1800 r.p.m.
Transmission: Hydraulic. Rolls Royce CF 10000. (§ electric).
Max. T.E.: 66.8 kN (15000 lbf).   **Weight:** 28.6 tonnes.
Cont. T.E.: 61 kN (13700 lbf) at 1.4 m.p.h.   **Wheel Dia:** 1067 mm.
Max. Speed: 30 m.p.h.

BR	Present		
D 2853–02003	"PETER"	Rutland Railway Museum	YE 2812/1960
D 2854		Peak Railway	YE 2813/1960
D 2858	Unnumbered	Midland Railway Centre	YE 2817/1960
D 2860		National Railway Museum	YE 2843/1961
D 2866	Unnumbered	Peak Railway	YE 2849/1961
D 2867	"DIANNE"	Battlefield Railway	YE 2850/1961
D 2868	"SAM"	Lavender Line, Isfield	YE 2851/1961

Notes: Locomotives of similar design built for industrial use with minor detail differences and no train brakes masquerade as BR locomotives. These are:-

D 2870	Ribble Steam Railway	YE 2677/1960
02101§	Gwili Railway	YE 2779/1960

CLASS 01   0-4-0

Built: 1956. 4 built.
Engine: Gardner 6L3 of 114 kW (153 h.p.) at 1200 r.p.m.
Transmission: Mechanical. Wilson SE4 epicyclic
Max. T.E.: 56.8 kN (12750 lbf).   **Weight:** 25.5 tonnes.
Wheel Dia: 965 mm.   **Max. Speed:** 14 m.p.h.
No train brakes.

11503–D 2953	Peak Railway	AB 395/1956
11506–D 2956	East Lancashire Railway	AB 398/1956

CLASS 07   0-6-0

Built: 1962. 14 built.
Engine: Paxman 6RPHL Mk III of 205 kW (275 h.p.) at 1360 r.p.m.
Transmission: Electric. One AEI RTB 6652 traction motor.
Power at Rail: 142 kW (190 h.p.).
Max. T.E.: 126 kN (28240 lbf).   **Weight:** 43.6 tonnes.
Cont. T.E.: 71 kN (15950 lbf) at 4.38 m.p.h.   **Wheel Dia:** 1067 mm.
Max. Speed: 20 m.p.h.   x-Dual braked.

BR	Present		
D 2989–07005x	Unnumbered	Barrow Hill Roundhouse	RH 480690/1962
D 2991		ERPS, Alstom, Eastleigh Works	RH 480692/1962
D 2994–07010		Avon Valley Railway	RH 480695/1962
D 2995–07011x	"CLEVELAND"	St. Leonards Railway Engineering	RH 480696/1962
D 2996–07012		Lavender Line, Isfield	RH 480697/1962
D 2997–07013x	Unnumbered	Barrow Hill Roundhouse	RH 480698/1962

CLASS 08   0-6-0

Built: 1952–62. Built at Derby, Darlington, Crewe, Horwich & Doncaster. 996 built.
Engine: English Electric 6KT of 298 kW (400 h.p.) at 680 r.p.m.
Transmission: Electric. Two EE 506 axle-hung traction motors.
Power at Rail: 194 kW (260 h.p.).
Max. T.E.: 156 kN (35000 lbf).   **Weight:** 50 tonnes.
Cont. T.E.: 49.4 kN (11100 lbf) at 8.8 m.p.h.   **Wheel Dia:** 1372 mm.
Max. Speed: 15 m.p.h.

x-Dual braked.   a-Air braked only.

BR	Present			
13000–D 3000		Barrow Hill Roundhouse	Derby	1952
13002–D 3002		Plym Valley Railway	Derby	1952
13014–D 3014	"VOLUNTEER"	Paignton & Dartmouth Railway	Derby	1952
13018–D 3018–08011		Chinnor & Princes Risborough Railway	Derby	1953
13019–D 3019		Battlefield Railway	Derby	1953
13022–D 3022–08015		Severn Valley Railway	Derby	1953
13023–D 3023–08016		Peak Railway	Derby	1953
13029–D 3029–08021		Tyseley Locomotive Works, Birmingham	Derby	1953
13030–D 3030–08022	"LION"	Cholsey & Wallingford Railway	Derby	1953
13044–D 3044–08032	33 "MENDIP"	Foster Yeoman, Merehead Stone Terminal	Derby	1954
13047–D 3047	105	Lamco, Nimba, Liberia	Derby	1954
13059–D 3059–08046	"Brechin City"	Caledonian Railway	Derby	1954
13067–D 3067–08054	210277	Tilcon, Swinden Quarry, Grassington	Darlington	1953
13074–D 3074–08060	"UNICORN"	Cholsey & Wallingford Railway	Darlington	1953
13079–D 3079–08064		National Railway Museum	Darlington	1954
13092–D 3092	101	Lamco, Nimba, Liberia	Derby	1954
13094–D 3094	102	Lamco, Nimba, Liberia	Derby	1954
13098–D 3098	103	Lamco, Nimba, Liberia	Derby	1955
13100–D 3100	104	Lamco, Nimba, Liberia	Derby	1955
13101–D 3101		Great Central Railway	Derby	1955
13167–D 3167–08102		Lincolnshire Wolds Railway	Derby	1955
13174–D 3174–08108		Kent & East Sussex Railway	Derby	1955
13179–D 3179–08113		RMS Locotec, Dewsbury	Derby	1955
13180–D 3180–08114		Nottingham Heritage Centre, Ruddington	Derby	1955
13190–D 3190–08123	"George Mason"	Cholsey & Wallingford Railway	Derby	1955
13201–D 3201–08133		Severn Valley Railway	Derby	1955
13232–D 3232–08164		East Lancashire Railway	Darlington	1956
13236–D 3236–08168		Alstom, Asfordby Test Track	Darlington	1956
13255–D 3255		Brighton Railway Museum	Derby	1956
13261–D 3261		Swindon & Cricklade Railway	Derby	1956
13265–D 3265–08195	"MARK"	Llangollen Railway	Derby	1956
13272–D 3272–08202		The Potter Group, Knowsley, Merseyside	Derby	1956
13290–D 3290–08220	Unnumbered	West Coast Railway Company, Carnforth	Derby	1956
13308–D 3308–08238		Dean Forest Railway	Darlington	1956
13309–D 3309–08239		European Metal Recycling, Kingsbury	Darlington	1956
13336–D 3336–08266		Keighley & Worth Valley Railway	Darlington	1957
D 3358–08288	Unnumbered	Watercress Line	Derby	1957
13366–D 3366–08296	001	Hanson Aggregates, Whatley Quarry	Derby	1957
D 3390–08320	"SUSAN" P400D	Imerys, Blackpool Dries	Derby	1957
D 3415–08345		Deanside Transit, Hillington, Glasgow	Derby	1958
D 3420–08350		Churnet Valley Railway	Crewe	1957
D 3429–08359		Tyseley Locomotive Works, Birmingham	Crewe	1958
D 3462–08377		West Somerset Railway	Darlington	1957
D 3503–08388 a		UK Rail Shunter Hire, Manchester	Derby	1958
D 3505–08390 a		Barrow Hill Roundhouse	Derby	1958
D 3513–08398	"ANNABEL"	Imerys, Rocks Dries	Derby	1958
D 3534–08419 a		Bombardier Transportation, Doncaster Works	Derby	1958
D 3538–08423 a		Faber-Prest Ports, Flixborough Wharf, Scunthorpe	Derby	1958
D 3551–08436		Hayes Chemicals, Sandbach, Cheshire	Derby	1958
D 3558–08443	H011	Bo'ness and Kinneil Railway	Derby	1958
D 3559–08444		Bodmin Steam Railway	Derby	1958
D 3560–08445 a		East Lancashire Railway	Derby	1958
D 3562–08447 a		Deanside Transit, Hillington, Glasgow	Derby	1958
D 3586–08471		Severn Valley Railway	Crewe	1958
D 3588–08473		Dean Forest Railway	Crewe	1958
D 3591–08476		Swanage Railway	Crewe	1958
D 3594–08479		East Lancashire Railway	Horwich	1958
D 3605–08490		Strathspey Railway	Horwich	1958
D 3657–08502 a		ETOL, Wilton Works, Middlesbrough	Doncaster	1958
D 3658–08503 a		ETOL, Wilton Works, Middlesbrough	Doncaster	1958
D 3679–08517 a		Wabtec Rail, Doncatser	Darlington	1958
D 3723–08556		North Yorkshire Moors Railway	Darlington	1959
D 3757–08590 x		Midland Railway Centre	Crewe	1959

D 3761–08594 x		Wabtec Rail, Doncaster	Crewe 1959
D 3765–08598		The Potter Group, Selby	Derby 1959
D 3767–08600 a		A.V. Dawson, Middlesbrough	Derby 1959
D 3769–08602	004	Bombardier Transportation, Derby Carriage Works	Derby 1959
D 3771–08604 x	604	Didcot Railway Centre	Derby 1959
D 3782–08615 x		Hanson Aggregates, Whatley Quarry	Derby 1959
D 3789–08622 x		RMS Locotec, Dewsbury	Derby 1959
D 3792–08625 x		Fire Service College, Moreton-in-Marsh	Derby 1959
D 3801–08634 x		West Coast Railway Company, Carnforth	Derby 1959
D 3817–08650 x	55	Foster Yeoman, Isle of Grain	Horwich 1959
D 3819–08652 x	66	Foster Yeoman, Merehead Stone Terminal	Horwich 1959
D 3835–08668 x		Wabtec Rail, Doncaster	Crewe 1960
D 3845–08678 a	678 "ULVERSTONIAN"	West Coast Railway Company, Carnforth	Horwich 1959
D 3859–08692 x		West Coast Railway Company, Carnforth	Horwich 1959
D 3866–08699 x	Unnumbered	Bombardier Transportation, Crewe Works	Horwich 1960
D 3867–08700 a		West Coast Railway Company, Carnforth	Horwich 1960
D 3871–08704 x		Port of Boston Authority, Boston Docks	Horwich 1960
D 3874–08707 a		West Coast Railway Company, Carnforth	Crewe 1960
D 3896–08728 a		Deanside Transit, Hillington, Glasgow	Crewe 1960
D 3902–08734 x		Dean Forest Railway	Crewe 1960
D 3904–08736 a		Deanside Transit, Hillington, Glasgow	Crewe 1960
D 3932–08764 x	003 "FLORENCE"	Transfesa, Tilbury Riverside Terminal	Horwich 1961
D 3935–08767 x		North Norfolk Railway	Horwich 1961
D 3937–08769		Dean Forest Railway	Derby 1960
D 3940–08772 x		North Norfolk Railway	Derby 1960
D 3941–08773 x		UK Rail Shunter Hire, Manchester	Derby 1960
D 3942–08774 a	"ARTHUR VERNON DAWSON"	A.V. Dawson, Middlesbrough	Derby 1960
D 3948–08780 x		East Lancashire Railway	Derby 1960
D 3991–08823 a		Churnet Valley Railway	Derby 1960
D 3997–08829 x		West Coast Railway Company, Carnforth	Derby 1960
D 4014–08846 x	003	Bombardier Transportation, Derby Carriage Works	Horwich 1961
D 4018–08850 x		North Yorkshire Moors Railway	Horwich 1961
D 4038–08870 x		Lafarge Redland Aggregates, Barrow-upon-Soar	Darlington 1960
D 4115–08885 x		Nottingham Heritage Centre, Ruddington	Horwich 1962
D 4167–08937 x		Dartmoor Railways, Okehampton	Darlington 1962
D 4173–08943 x	PET II	Bombardier Transportation, Crewe Works	Darlington 1962
D 4174–08944 x		East Lancashire Railway	Darlington 1962

Note: D 3538 and D 4038 are on loan from RMS Locotec. D 3551 is on loan from RT Rail. D 3588 is being dismantled and used as a source of spares. D 3782 is on loan from Wabtec Rail.

CLASS 09   0-6-0

Built: 1959–62. Built at Darlington & Horwich. 26 built.
Engine: English Electric 6KT of 298 kW (400 h.p.) at 680 r.p.m.
Transmission: Electric: Two English Electric EE506 axle-hung traction motors.
Power at Rail: 201 kW (269 h.p.).
Max. T.E.: 111 kN (25000 lbf)   **Weight:** 50 tonnes.
Cont. T.E.: 39 kN (8800 lbf) at 11.6 m.p.h.   **Wheel Dia:** 1372 mm.
Max. Speed: 27 m.p.h.

D 3666–09002	South Devon Railway	Darlington 1959
D 3668–09004	Lavender Line, Isfield	Darlington 1959

CLASS 10   0-6-0

Built: 1955–62. Built at Darlington & Doncaster. 146 built.
Engine: Lister Blackstone ER6T of 261 kW (350 h.p.) at 750 r.p.m.
Transmission: Electric. Two GEC WT 821 axle-hung traction motors.
Power at Rail: 198 kW (265 h.p.).
Max. T.E.: 156 kN (35000 lbf).   **Weight:** 47 tonnes.
Cont. T.E.: 53.4 kN (12000 lbf) at 8.2 m.p.h.   **Wheel Dia:** 1372 mm.
Max. Speed: 20 m.p.h.

D 3452		Bodmin Steam Railway	Darlington 1957
D 3476		Colne Valley Railway	Darlington 1957
D 3489	"COLONEL TOMLINE"	Spa Valley Railway	Darlington 1958
D 4067	see below	Great Central Railway	Darlington 1961
D 4092	"CHRISTINE"	Barrow Hill Roundhouse	Darlington 1962

Notes: D 4067 is named "MARGARET ETHEL – THOMAS ALFRED NAYLOR".

CLASS 24   Bo-Bo

Built: 1958–61 at Derby, Crewe & Darlington. 151 built.
Engine: Sulzer 6LDA28A of 870 kW (1160 h.p.) at 750 r.p.m.
Transmission: Electric. Four BTH 137BY axle-hung traction motors.
Power at Rail: 629 kW (843 h.p.).
Max. T.E.: 178 kN (40000 lbf).   **Weight:** 78 (81*) tonnes.
Cont. T.E.: 95 kN (21300 lbf) at 4.38 m.p.h. **Wheel Dia:** 1143 mm.
Max. Speed: 75 m.p.h.   **Train Heating:** Steam.

D 5032–24032*	"HELEN TURNER"	North Yorkshire Moors Railway	Crewe 1959
D 5054–24054–ADB 968008		East Lancashire Railway	Crewe 1959
D 5061–24061–RDB 968007-97201		North Yorkshire Moors Railway	Crewe 1960
D 5081–24081		Gloucestershire-Warwickshire Railway	Crewe 1960

CLASS 25   Bo-Bo

Built: 1961–67. Built at Darlington, Derby & Beyer Peacock. 327 built.
Engine: Sulzer 6LDA28B of 930 kW (1250 h.p.) at 750 r.p.m.
Transmission: Electric. Four AEI 253AY axle-hung traction motors.
Power at Rail: 708 kW (949 h.p.).
Max. T.E.: 200 kN (45000 lbf).   **Weight:** 72–76 tonnes.
Cont. T.E.: 93 kN (20800 lbf) at 17.1 m.p.h. **Wheel Dia:** 1143 mm.
Max. Speed: 90 m.p.h.

Class 25/1. Dual braked except D 5217. Train heating: Steam.

D 5185–25035	"CASTELL DINAS BRAN"	Northampton & Lamport Railway	Darlington 1963
D 5207–25057		North Norfolk Railway	Derby 1963
D 5209–25059		Keighley and Worth Valley Railway	Derby 1963
D 5217–25067		Barrow Hill Roundhouse	Derby 1963
D 5222–25072		Dartmoor Railways, Okehampton	Derby 1963

Class 25/2. Dual braked (except D 5233). Train heating: Steam: D 5233, D 7585/94. None: D7523/35/41.

D 5233–25083		Caledonian Railway	Derby 1963
D 7523–25173	"John F. Kennedy"	West Somerset Railway	Derby 1965
D 7535–25185	"MERCURY"	Paignton & Dartmouth Railway	Derby 1965
D 7541–25191	"THE DIANA"	North Yorkshire Moors Railway	Derby 1965
D 7585–25235		Bo'ness & Kinneil Railway	Darlington 1964
D 7594–25244		Kent & East Sussex Railway	Darlington 1964

Class 25/3. Dual braked. Train heating: None.

D 7612–25262–25901		South Devon Railway	Derby 1966
D 7615–25265	"HARLECH CASTLE"	Great Central Railway	Derby 1966
D 7628–25278	"SYBILA"	North Yorkshire Moors Railway	BP 8038/1965
D 7629–25279		Nottingham Heritage Centre	BP 8039/1965
D 7633–25283–25904		Severn Valley Railway	BP 8043/1965
D 7659–25309–25909		The Railway Age, Crewe	BP 8069/1966
D 7663–25313	"CHIRK CASTLE/ CASTELL-Y-WAUN"	Llangollen Railway	Derby 1966
D 7671–25321		Midland Railway Centre	Derby 1967
D 7672–25322–25912	"TAMWORTH CASTLE"	Churnet Valley Railway	Derby 1967

CLASS 26 Bo-Bo

Built: 1958–59 by the Birmingham Railway Carriage & Wagon Company. 47 built.
Engine: Sulzer 6LDA28B of 870 kW (1160 h.p.) at 750 r.p.m.
Transmission: Electric. Four Crompton-Parkinson C171A1 (C171D3§) axle-hung traction motors.
Power at Rail: 671 kW (900 h.p.).
Max. T.E.: 187 kN (42000 lbf).   **Weight:** 72–75 tonnes.
Cont. T.E.: 133 kN (30000 lbf) at 14 m.p.h.   **Wheel Dia:** 1092 mm.
Max. Speed: 75 m.p.h.   Dual Braked.
Train Heating: Built with steam. Removed from D 5300/01/02/04 in 1967.
Class 26/0.

D 5300–26007	Barrow Hill Roundhouse	BRCW DEL/45/1958
D 5301–26001	Lakeside & Haverthwaite Railway	BRCW DEL/46/1958
D 5302–26002	Strathspey Railway	BRCW DEL/47/1958
D 5304–26004	Bo'ness & Kinneil Railway	BRCW DEL/49/1958
D 5310–26010	Northampton & Lamport Railway	BRCW DEL/55/1959
D 5311–26011	Barrow Hill Roundhouse	BRCW DEL/56/1959
D 5314–26014	Caledonian Railway	BRCW DEL/59/1959

Class 26/1.§

D 5324–26024	Bo'ness & Kinneil Railway	BRCW DEL/69/1959
D 5325–26025	Strathspey Railway	BRCW DEL/70/1959
D 5335–26035	Caledonian Railway	BRCW DEL/80/1959
D 5338–26038	Pullman TPL, Cardiff Cathays	BRCW DEL/83/1959
D 5340–26040	Kingdom of Fife Railway	BRCW DEL/85/1959
D 5343–26043	Gloucestershire-Warwickshire Railway	BRCW DEL/88/1959

CLASS 27 Bo-Bo

Built: 1961–62 by the Birmingham Railway Carriage & Wagon Company. 69 built.
Engine: Sulzer 6LDA28B of 930 kW (1250 h.p.) at 750 r.p.m.
Transmission: Electric. Four GEC WT459 axle-hung traction motors.
Power at Rail: 696 kW (933 h.p.).
Max. T.E.: 178 kN (40000 lbf).   **Weight:** 72–75 tonnes.
Cont. T.E.: 111 kN (25000 lbf) at 14 m.p.h.   **Wheel Dia:** 1092 mm.
Max. Speed: 90 m.p.h.
Train Heating: Built with steam (except D 5370 – no provision). Replaced with electric on D 5386 and D 5410 but subsequently removed.

Dual braked except D 5353.

D 5347–27001	Bo'ness & Kinneil Railway	BRCW DEL/190/1961
D 5351–27005	Bo'ness & Kinneil Railway	BRCW DEL/194/1961
D 5353–27007	Watercress Line	BRCW DEL/196/1961
D 5370–27024–ADB 968028	Caledonian Railway	BRCW DEL/213/1962
D 5386–27103–27212–27066	North Norfolk Railway	BRCW DEL/229/1962
D 5394–27106–27050	Bo'ness & Kinneil Railway	BRCW DEL/237/1962
D 5401–27112–27056	Northampton & Lamport Railway	BRCW DEL/244/1962
D 5410–27123–27205–27059	Severn Valley Railway	BRCW DEL/253/1962

Note: D 5394 is on loan from the Strathspey Railway.

CLASS 31 A1A-A1A

Built: 1957–62 by Brush Traction. 263 built.
Engine: Built with Mirrlees JVS12T of 930 kW (1250 h.p.). Re-engined 1964 - 9 with English Electric 12SVT of 1100 kW (1470 h.p.) at 850 r.p.m.
Transmission: Electric. Four Brush TM73-68 axle-hung traction motors.
Power at Rail: 872 kW (1170 h.p.).
Max. T.E.: 190 kN (42800 lbf).   **Weight:** 110 tonnes.
Cont. T.E.: 99 kN (22250 lbf) at 19.7 m.p.h.   **Wheel Dia:** 1092 mm.
Max. Speed: 90 (80§) m.p.h. D 5518, D 5522 and D 5526 were originally 80 m.p.h. but have been regeared for 90 m.p.h.
Train Heating: Built with steam heating. Electric heating fitted and steam heating removed on D 5522, D 5557, D 5600, D 5641, D 5823, D 5830 & D 5844.

Note: D 5500, D 5522, D 5526 and D 5562 were built without roof-mounted headcode boxes. They were subsequently fitted to D 5518.

Class 31/0. Electromagnetic Control.

D 5500–31018§	National Railway Museum	BE 71/1957

Class 31/1. Electro-pneumatic Control. Dual braked.

D 5518–31101 "Brush Veteran"	Battlefield Railway	BE 89/1958
D 5522–31418	Midland Railway Centre	BE 121/1959
D 5526–31108	Nene Valley Railway	BE 125/1959
D 5537–31119	UK Rail Shunter Hire, Manchester	BE 136/1959
D 5541–31123	Gloucestershire-Warwickshire Railway	BE 140/1959
D 5548–31130	Battlefield Railway	BE 147/1959
D 5557–31139–31438–31538	Mid-Norfolk Railway	BE 156/1959
D 5562–31144	UK Rail Shunter Hire, Manchester	BE 161/1959
D 5580–31162	North Norfolk Railway	BE 180/1960
D 5581–31163	Chinnor & Princes Risborough Railway	BE 181/1960
D 5584–31166	West Coast Railway Company, Carnforth	BE 184/1960
D 5600–31179–31435	East Lancashire Railway	BE 200/1960
D 5611–31188	West Coast Railway Company, Carnforth	BE 211/1960
D 5627–31203	Brush Traction, Loughborough	BE 227/1960
D 5630–31206	Brush Traction, Loughborough	BE 230/1960
D 5634–31210	Dean Forest Railway	BE 234/1960
D 5641–31216–31467	East Lancashire Railway	BE 241/1961
D 5662–31235	Mid-Norfolk Railway	BE 262/1960
D 5679–31251–31442	The Railway Age, Crewe	BE 279/1960
D 5683–31255	Colne Valley Railway	BE 284/1961
D 5800–31270	Colne Valley Railway	BE 301/1961
D 5801–31271	Midland Railway Centre	BE 302/1961
D 5821–31289	Northampton & Lamport Railway	BE 322/1961
D 5823–31291–31456–31556	East Lancashire Railway	BE 324/1961
D 5830–31297–31463–31563	Great Central Railway	BE 366/1962
D 5844–31310–31422–31522	Tyseley Locomotive Works, Birmingham	BE 380/1962
D 5862–31327 Phillips-Imperial	Bo'ness & Kinneil Railway	BE 398/1962

Note: D 5526 and D 5580 are on loan from the Midland Railway Centre.

CLASS 28   METROVICK   Co-Bo

Built: 1958–59 by Metropolitan Vickers. 20 built.
Engine: Crossley HSTVee 8 of 896 kW (1200 h.p.) at 625 r.p.m.
Transmission: Electric. Five MV 137BZ axle-hung traction motors.
Power at Rail: 671 kW (900 h.p.).
Max. T.E.: 223 kN (50000 lbf).   **Weight**: 99 tonnes.
Cont. T.E.: 111 kN (25000 lbf) at 13.5 m.p.h.   **Wheel Dia**: 1003 mm.
Max. Speed: 75 m.p.h.   **Train Heating**: Steam.

D 5705–S 15705–TDB 968006	East Lancashire Railway	MV 1958

CLASS 33   Bo-Bo

Built: 1961–62 by the Birmingham Railway Carriage & Wagon Company. 98 built.
Engine: Sulzer 8LDA28A of 1160 kW (1550 h.p.) at 750 r.p.m.
Transmission: Electric. Four Crompton-Parkinson C171C2 axle-hung traction motors.
Power at Rail: 906 kW (1215 h.p.).
Max. T.E.: 200 kN (45000 lbf).   **Weight**: 78 tonnes.
Cont. T.E.: 116 kN (26000 lbf) at 17.5 m.p.h.   **Wheel Dia**: 1092 mm.
Max. Speed: 85 m.p.h.   **Train Heating**: Electric.
Dual braked.

* built to former loading gauge of the Tonbridge–Battle line.
§ fitted for push-pull operation.

D 6513–33102§	Churnet Valley Railway	BRCW DEL/105/1960
D 6515–33012	Swanage Railway	BRCW DEL/107/1960
D 6525–33109§ Captain Bill Smith RNR	Watercress Line	BRCW DEL/117/1960

D 6527–33110§		Bodmin Steam Railway	BRCW DEL/119/1960
D 6528–33111§		Barrow Hill Roundhouse	BRCW DEL/120/1960
D 6530–33018		The Railway Age, Crewe	BRCW DEL/122/1960
D 6534–33019		Bo'ness & Kinneil Railway	BRCW DEL/126/1960
D 6535–33116§	Hertfordshire Railtours	National Railway Museum	BRCW DEL/127/1960
D 6536–33117§		East Lancashire Railway	BRCW DEL/128/1960
D 6552–33034		Swanage Railway	BRCW DEL/144/1961
D 6553–33035		Barrow Hill Roundhouse	BRCW DEL/145/1961
D 6566–33048		West Somerset Railway	BRCW DEL/170/1961
D 6570–33052	Ashford	Kent & East Sussex Railway	BRCW DEL/174/1961
D 6574–33056	The Burma Star	Churnet Valley Railway	BRCW DEL/178/1961
D 6583–33063		East Kent Light Railway	BRCW DEL/187/1962
D 6585–33065	Sealion	East Kent Light Railway	BRCW DEL/189/1962
D 6586–33201*		Midland Railway Centre	BRCW DEL/157/1962
D 6593–33208*		Watercress Line	BRCW DEL/164/1962

Note: D 6535 is currently stored at Old Oak Common Depot, London.

CLASS 37 Co-Co

Built: 1960–65 by English Electric Company at Vulcan Foundry, Newton le Willows or Robert Stephenson & Hawthorn, Darlington. 309 built.
Engine: English Electric 12CSVT of 1300 kW (1750 h.p.) at 850 r.p.m.
Transmission: Electric. Six English Electric 538/A.
Power at Rail: 932 kW (1250 h.p.).
Max. T.E.: 245 kN (55000 lbf). **Weight:** 103–108 tonnes.
Cont. T.E.: 156 kN (35000 lbf) at 13.6 m.p.h. **Wheel Dia:** 1092 mm.
Max. Speed: 80 m.p.h.
Train Heating: Steam (§ possibly built without heating, * built without heating, but later fitted to D 6961 & D 6964).
Dual braked.

D 6700–37119–37350		National Railway Museum	EE/VF 2863/D579/1960
D 6703–37003		East Anglian Railway Museum	EE/VF 2866/D582/1960
D 6725–37025		Bo'ness & Kinneil Railway	EE/VF 2888/D604/1961
D 6732–37032–37353		North Norfolk Railway	EE/VF 2895/D611/1961
D 6738–37038		East Lancashire Railway	EE/VF 2901/D621/1962
D 6775–37075		Nottingham Heritage Centre	EE/RSH 3067/8321/1962
D 6799–37099–37324	Clydebridge	Gloucestershire-Warwickshire Railway	EE VF 3228/D753/1962
D 6808–37108–37325	Lanarkshire Steel	West Coast Railway Company, Carnforth	EE/VF 3237/D762/1963
D 6858–37158§		West Coast Railway Company, Carnforth	EE/VF 3333/D832/1963
D 6890–37190–37314	Dalzell	Midland Railway Centre	EE/RSH 3368/8411/1964
D 6897–37197§		East Lancashire Railway	EE/RSH 3375/8418/1964
D 6907–37207§		Plym Valley Railway	EE VF 3385/D851/1963
D 6915–37215§		Gloucestershire-Warwickshire Railway	EE/VF 3393/D859/1964
D 6935–37235*		East Lancashire Railway	EE/VF 3421/D879/1964
D 6940–37240*		Llangollen Railway	EE/VF 3497/D928/1964
D 6961–37261*	Caithness	East Lancashire Railway	EE/VF 3521/D950/1965
D 6964–37264*		Tyseley Locomotive Works	EE/VF 3524/D953/1965

Notes: D 6703 was named First East Anglian Regiment for a short time in 1963. D 6935 is named The Coal Merchants' Association of Scotland.

CLASS 35 HYMEK B-B

Built: 1961–64. Beyer Peacock. 101 built.
Engine: Maybach MD 870 of 1269 kW (1700 h.p.) at 1500 r.p.m.
Transmission: Hydraulic. Mekydro K184U.
Max. T.E.: 207 kN (46600 lbf). **Weight:** 77 tonnes.
Cont. T.E.: 151 kN (33950 lbf) at 12.5 m.p.h. **Wheel Dia:** 1143 mm.
Max. Speed: 90 m.p.h. **Train Heating:** Steam.

D 7017	West Somerset Railway	BP 7911/1962
D 7018	West Somerset Railway	BP 7912/1962
D 7029	Old Oak Common Depot, London	BP 7923/1962
D 7076	East Lancashire Railway	BP 7980/1963

CLASS 20 Bo-Bo

Built: 1957–68 by English Electric. 228 built.
Engine: English Electric 8SVT of 746 kW (1000 h.p.) at 850 r.p.m.
Transmission: Electric. Four EE 526/5D axle-hung traction motors.
Power at Rail: 574 kW (770 h.p.).
Max. T.E.: 187 kN (42000 lbf). **Weight:** 74 tonnes.
Cont. T.E.: 111 kN (25000 lbf) at 11 m.p.h. **Wheel Dia:** 1092 mm.
Max. Speed: 75 m.p.h. **Train Heating:** None.

Dual braked except D 8000.

BR	Present			
D 8000–20050		National Railway Museum	EE/VF 2347/D375	1957
D 8001–20001		Victa Railfreight, Beechbrook Farm, Kent	EE/VF 2348/D376	1957
D 8007–20007		Churnet Valley Railway	EE/VF 2354/D382	1957
D 8020–20020		Strathspey Railway	EE/RSH 2742/8052	1959
D 8031–20031		Keighley & Worth Valley Railway	EE/RSH 2753/8063	1960
D 8035–20035	2001	CFD Industrie, France	EE/VF 2757/D482	1959
D 8048–20048		Victa Railfreight, Beechbrook Farm, Kent	EE/VF 2770/D495	1959
D 8056–20056		Barrow Hill Roundhouse	EE/RSH 2962/8214	1961
D 8059–20059		Somerset & Dorset Loco Co., Yeovil Jn.	EE/RSH 2965/8217	1961
D 8063–20063	2002	CFD Industrie, France	EE/RSH 2969/8221	1961
D 8069–20069		Mid Norfolk Railway	EE/RSH 2975/8227	1961
D 8087–20087		East Lancashire Railway	EE/RSH 2993/8245	1961
D 8096–20096		Barrow Hill Roundhouse	EE/RSH 3003/8255	1961
D 8098–20098		Great Central Railway	EE/RSH 3004/8256	1961
D 8107–20107	HL 010	Faber Prest Ports, Flixborough Wharf	EE/RSH 3013/8265	1961
D 8110–20110		South Devon Railway	EE/RSH 3016/8268	1962
D 8118–20118	Saltburn by the Sea	South Devon Railway	EE/RSH 3024/8276	1962
D 8128–20228	2004	CFD Industrie, France	EE/VF 3599/D998	1966
D 8137–20137	Murray B. Hofmeyr	Gloucestershire-Warwickshire Railway	EE/VF 3608/D1007	1966
D 8139–20139	2003	CFD Industrie, France	EE/VF 3610/D1009	1966
D 8142–20142		Victa Railfreight, Beechbrook Farm, Kent	EE/VF 3613/D1013	1966
D 8154–20154		Churnet Valley Railway	EE/VF 3625/D1024	1966
D 8166–20166		Bodmin Steam Railway	EE/VF 3637/D1036	1966
D 8168–20168		Barrow Hill Roundhouse	EE/VF 3639/D1038	1966
D 8169–20169		Stainmore Railway, Kirkby Stephen East	EE/VF 3640/D1039	1966
D 8177–20177		Somerset & Dorset Loco Co., Yeovil Jn.	EE/VF 3648/D1047	1966
D 8188–20188		Victa Railfreight, Beechbrook Farm, Kent	EE/VF 3669/D1064	1967
D 8189–20189		Victa Railfreight, Beechbrook Farm, Kent	EE/VF 3670/D1065	1967
D 8197–20197		Bodmin Steam Railway	EE/VF 3678/D1073	1967
D 8305–20205		Midland Railway Centre	EE/VF 3686/D1081	1967
D 8314–20214		Lakeside & Haverthwaite Railway	EE/VF 3695/D1090	1967
D 8327–20227		Victa Railfreight, Beechbrook Farm, Kent	EE/VF 3685/D1080	1968

Note: D 8001 and D 8327 are on loan from the Midland Railway Centre. D 8020 is on loan from the Bo'ness & Kinneil Railway. D 8107 is on loan from RMS Locotec, Dewsbury. D 8048 is on loan from Nottingham Heritage Centre. D 8142 is on loan from the Llangollen Railway. D 8188 is on loan from the Watercress Line. D 8189 is on loan from the Embsay & Bolton Abbey Railway. D 8327 is named 'Sir John Betjemen".

CLASS 15 Bo-Bo

Built: 1957–59 by BTH/Clayton Equipment Company. 44 built.
Engine: Paxman 16YHXL of 597 kW (800 h.p.) at 1250 r.p.m.
Transmission: Electric. Four BTH 137AZ axle-hung traction motors.
Power at Rail:
Max. T.E.: 178 kN (40000 lbf). **Weight:** 69 tonnes.
Cont. T.E.: 88 kN (19700 lbf) at 11.3 m.p.h. **Wheel Dia:** 1003 mm.
Max. Speed: 60 m.p.h. **Train Heating:** None.

D 8233–ADB968001	The Railway Age, Crewe	BTH 1131/1960

CLASS 17   Bo-Bo

Built: 1962–65. Clayton Equipment Company. 117 built.
Engine: Two Paxman 67HXL of 336 kW (450 h.p.) at 1500 r.p.m.
Transmission: Electric. Four GEC WT421 axle-hung traction motors.
Power at Rail: 461 kW (618 h.p.).
Max. T.E.: 178 kN (40000 lbf).   **Weight:** 69 tonnes.
Cont. T.E.: 80 kN (18000 lbf) at 12.8 m.p.h.   **Wheel Dia:** 1003 mm.
Max. Speed: 60 m.p.h.   **Train Heating:** None.

D 8568	Chinnor & Princes Risborough Railway	CE 4365U/69	1964

CLASS 55   DELTIC   Co-Co

Built: 1961–62. English Electric. 22 built.
Engine: Two Napier Deltic T18-25 of 1230 kW (1650 h.p.) at 1500 r.p.m.
Transmission: Electric. Six EE 538 axle-hung traction motors.
Power at Rail: 1969 kW (2640 h.p.).
Max. T.E.: 222 kN (50000 lbf).   **Weight:** 105 tonnes.
Cont. T.E.: 136 kN (30500 lbf) at 32.5 m.p.h.   **Wheel Dia:** 1092 mm.
Max. Speed: 100 m.p.h.
Train Heating: Built with Steam, electric subsequently fitted.
Dual braked.

D 9000–55022	ROYAL SCOTS GREY	Tyseley locomotive Works	EE/VF 2905/D557	1961
D 9002–55002	THE KINGS OWN YORKSHIRE			
	LIGHT INFANTRY	National Railway Museum	EE/VF 2907/D559	1961
D 9009–55009	ALYCIDON	Barrow Hill Roundhouse	EE/VF 2914/D566	1961
D 9015–55015	TULYAR	Midland Railway Centre	EE/VF 2920/D572	1961
D 9016–55016	GORDON HIGHLANDER	Tyseley locomotive Works	EE/VF 2921/D573	1961
D 9019–55019	ROYAL HIGHLAND FUSILIER	Barrow Hill Roundhouse	EE/VF 2924/D576	1961

Note: D 9002 is currently receiving attention at Wabtec Rail, Doncaster.

CLASS 14   0-6-0

Built: 1964–65 at Swindon. 56 built.
Engine: Paxman Ventura 6YJXL of 485 kW (650 h.p.) at 1500 r.p.m.
Transmission: Hydraulic. Voith L217u
Max. T.E.: 135 kN (30910 lbf).   **Weight:** 51 tonnes.
Cont. T.E.: 109 kN (26690 lbf) at 5.6 m.p.h.   **Wheel Dia:** 1219 mm.
Max. Speed: 40 m.p.h.   **Train Heating:** None.

Note: D 9524 has a Rolls Royce Type D 8 cyl of 336 kW (450 h.p.) engine which was fitted whilst in industrial use with BP. This engine was originally fitted to a Class 17.

a currently fitted with air brakes only.   x dual braked

BR	Present		
D 9500	9312/92	Barrow Hill Roundhouse	Swindon 1964
D 9502	9312/97	Peak Railway	Swindon 1964
D 9504		Victa Railfreight, Beechbrook Farm, Kent	Swindon 1964
D 9513	N.C.B. 38	Embsay & Bolton Abbey Railway	Swindon 1964
D 9515		Charmartin, Madrid, Spain	Swindon 1964
D 9516 x	56	Nene Valley Railway	Swindon 1964
D 9518	No. 7 9312/95	Rutland Railway Museum	Swindon 1964
D 9520	45	Nottingham Heritage Centre, Ruddington	Swindon 1964
D 9521		Swanage Railway	Swindon 1964
D 9523 x		Nene Valley Railway	Swindon 1964
D 9524 a	14901	Bo'ness & Kinneil Railway	Swindon 1964
D 9525		Battlefield Railway	Swindon 1965
D 9526		West Somerset Railway	Swindon 1965
D 9529	14029	Victa Railfreight, Beechbrook Farm, Kent	Swindon 1965
D 9531		East Lancashire Railway	Swindon 1965
D 9534		? Steelworks, Brescia, Italy	Swindon 1965
D 9537		Gloucestershire–Warwickshire Railway	Swindon 1965
D 9539		Gloucestershire–Warwickshire Railway	Swindon 1965

D 9548	937113106028	EC Nesso, Sagrera Yard, Barcelona, Spain	Swindon 1965
D 9549	?	Charmartin, Madrid, Spain	Swindon 1965
D 9551		Royal Deeside Railway	Swindon 1965
D 9553		Gloucestershire Warwickshire Railway	Swindon 1965
D 9555		Dean Forest Railway	Swindon 1965

Note: D 9504 and D 9529 are on loan from the Kent & East Sussex Railway. D 9555 is on loan from the Rutland Railway Museum.

CLASS 56   Co-Co

Built: 1976–84. by Electroputere, Craiova, Romania and BREL Doncaster & Crewe. 135 built.
Engine: Ruston-Paxman 16RK3CT of 2460 kW (3250 h.p.) at 900 r.p.m.
Transmission: Electric. Six Brush TM73-62 axle-hung traction motors.
Power at Rail: 1790 kW (2400 h.p.).
Max. T.E.: 275 kN (61800 lbf).   **Weight:** 125 tonnes.
Cont. T.E.: 240 kN (53950 lbf) at 32.5 m.p.h.   **Wheel Dia:** 1143 mm.
Max. Speed: 80 m.p.h.
Train Heating: None.
Air braked.

56009		Brush Traction, Loughborough	Electro 758/1976
56023		MoD Ashchurch, Gloucestershire	Electro 772/1977
56080	Selby Coalfield	MoD Ashchurch, Gloucestershire	Doncaster 1980
56097		Pullman TPL, Cardiff Cathays	Doncaster 1981

CLASS 98/1   0-6-0

Built: 1987 by Brecon Mountain Railway. 1 built for use on Aberystwyth–Devil's Bridge line.
Engine: Caterpillar 3304T of 105 kW (140 h.p.).
Transmission: Hydraulic. Twin Disc torque converter.
Gauge: 1' 11½"   **Weight:** 12.75 tonnes.
Max. Speed: 15 m.p.h.   **Wheel Dia:** 610 mm.

10	Vale of Rheidol Railway	BMR 1987

2.4. EXPERIMENTAL DIESEL LOCOMOTIVES

PROTOTYPE DELTIC   Co-Co

Built: 1955. English Electric. Used by BR 1959–1961.
Engine: Two Napier Deltic T18-25 of 1230 kW (1650 h.p.) at 1500 r.p.m.
Transmission: Electric. Six EE 526A axle-hung traction motors.
Power at Rail: 1976 kW (2650 h.p.).
Max. T.E.: 267 kN (60000 lbf).   **Weight:** 107.7 tonnes.
Cont. T.E.: 104 kN (23400 lbf) at 43.5 m.p.h.   **Wheel Dia:** 1092 mm.
Max. Speed: 105 m.p.h.   **Train Heating:** Steam.

DELTIC	National Railway Museum	EE 2003/1955

PROTOTYPE ENGLISH ELECTRIC SHUNTER   0-6-0

Built: 1957 by English Electric. Used by BR 1957–1960.
Engine: English Electric 6RKT of 373 kW (500 h.p.) at 750 r.p.m.
Transmission: Electric.
Power at Rail:
Max. T.E.: 147 kN (33000 lbf).   **Weight:** 48 tonnes.
Cont. T.E.: (lbf) at   m.p.h.   **Wheel Dia:** 1219 mm.
Max. Speed: 35 m.p.h.

D 226–D 0226	Keighley & Worth Valley Railway	EE/VF 2345/D226 1956

PROTOTYPE NORTH BRITISH SHUNTERS   0-4-0

Built: 1954. Used by BR Western Region (27414) and BR London Midland & Southern regions (27415). Subsequently sold for industrial use.
Engine: Paxman 6 VRPHXL of 160 kW (225 h.p.) at 1250 r.p.m.
Transmission: Hydraulic. Voith L24V.   **Weight:** tonnes.
Max. T.E.: 112 kN (22850 lbf).   **Max. Speed:** 12 m.p.h.
Wheel Dia: 1016 mm.   No train brakes.

BR	Present		
–	TOM	Telford Steam Railway	NBL 27414/1954
–	TIGER	Bo'ness & Kinneil Railway	NBL 27415/1954

PROTOTYPE NORTH BRITISH SHUNTER   0-4-0

Built: 1958. Used by BR Western Region at Old Oak Common in 1958. Subsequently sold for industrial use.
Engine: MAN W6V 17.5/22 OF 168 kW (225 h.p.).
Transmission: Hydraulic. Voith L24V.   **Weight:** tonnes.
Max. T.E.: 112 kN (22850 lbf).   **Max. Speed:** 12 m.p.h.
Wheel Dia: 940 mm.   No train brakes.

BR	Present		
–	D1	The Pallot Heritage Steam Museum, Jersey	NBL 27734/1958

2.5. DEPARTMENTAL DIESEL LOCOMOTIVES
CLASS 97/6 0-6-0

Built: 1952–59 by Ruston & Hornsby at Lincoln for BR Western Region Civil Engineers. 5 built.
Engine: Ruston 6VPH of 123 kW (165 h.p.).
Transmission: Electric. One British Thomson Houston RTA5041 traction motor.
Power at Rail:
Max. T.E.: 75 kN (17000 lbf).
Max. Speed: 20 m.p.h.
RA: 1.

Weight: 31 t.
Wheel Dia.: 978 mm.

PWM 650-97650	Lincolnshire Wolds Railway	RH 312990/1952
PWM 651-97651	Northampton & Lamport Railway	RH 431758/1959
PWM 653-97653	Long Marston Workshops	RH 431760/1959
PWM 654-97654	Jarvis Rail, Slateford, Edinburgh	RH 431761/1959

UNCLASSIFIED B

Built: 1975 by Matisa. Incorporated in ballast cleaner as power units. Rebuilt as locomotives by Kilmarnock Workshops 1986 (1988*).
Engine:
Transmission: Electric.
Max. T.E.:

Weight:
Wheel Dia:

97701	Wickham Rail Engineering, Thorrington	Matisa 2655/1975
97703*	Wickham Rail Engineering, Thorrington	Matisa 2654/1975

UNCLASSIFIED B

Built: 1958 for Beeston Sleeper Works. Ruston & Hornsby (36" gauge – being regauged to 1000 mm).
Engine: Ruston 4YC of 36 kW (48 h.p.) at 1375 r.p.m.
Transmission: Mechanical. Chain drive.
Max. T.E.: 18.7 kN (4200 lbf).
Wheel Dia: 762 mm.

Weight: 7.5 tonnes.
No train brakes.

ED 10	Irchester Narrow Gauge Railway	RH 411322/1958

UNCLASSIFIED B

Built: 1957 Ruston & Hornsby (18" gauge) for Horwich Works system. Now regauged to 600 mm.
Engine: Ruston 2VSH of 15 kW (20 h.p.) at 1200 r.p.m.
Transmission: Mechanical. Ruston 2 speed.
Max. T.E.: 8.4 kN (1890 lbf).
Wheel Dia: 420 mm.

Weight: 3.56 tonnes.
No train brakes.

ZM 32	Steeple Grange Light Railway	RH 416214/1957

UNCLASSIFIED B

Built: 1956–1957 Ruston & Hornsby (24" gauge) for Chesterton Junction Central Materials Depot, Cambridge.
Engine: Ruston 3VSH of 23.5 kW (31.5 h.p.)
Transmission: Mechanical. Chain drive.
No train brakes.

Weight: 4.5 tonnes.
Wheel Dia: 414 mm.

BR	Present		
85049	Unnumbered	Peak Railway	RH 393325/1956
85051		Cadeby Light Railway, Leicestershire	RH 404967/1957

UNCLASSIFIED A-1

Built: 1980. Noord Nederlandsche Machinefabriek B.V., Winschoten, Netherlands. Used on BREL Crewe works internal system.
Engine:
Transmission: Hydraulic.   **Weight:**
Max. T.E.:   **Wheel Dia:**

7158   Bombardier Transportation, Crewe Works NNM 77501/1980

UNCLASSIFIED D

Built: 1986 Allrad-Rangiertechnick GmbH., Düsseldorf, Germany. Used on BREL Crewe works internal system.
Transmission: Hydraulic.
Engine: **Weight:**
Max. T.E.:   **Wheel Dia:**

7207   Bombardier Transportation, Crewe Works Minilok 130/1986

UNCLASSIFIED A-1

Built: 1982 by Hugo Aeckerle & Company, Hamburg, Germany. Used on Glasgow Springburn Works internal system.
Engine:
Transmission: Mechanical.   **Weight:**
Max. T.E.:   **Wheel Dia:**

2777   Alstom, Springburn Works   Unilok 2091/1982

UNCLASSIFIED A-1

Built: 1978 by Simplex. Used on Wolverton Works internal system where it replaced 1311-G (see LMS petrol locomotive).
Engine: Petter PJ2 (20 h.p.)
Transmission: Mechanical – chain drive.   **Weight:** 3 tonnes.
Max. T.E.: 1500 lbf   **Wheel Dia:** 356 mm.

TITCHIE   Alstom, Wolverton Works   SMH 103GA078/1978

2.6. LONDON UNDERGROUND DIESEL LOCOMOTIVES

London Underground Ltd have only owned three diesel locomotives, two of which are now preserved with the third in industrial use.

UNCLASSIFIED ROLLS–ROYCE 0-6-0

Built: 1967–68. 3 built. Acquired 1971 from Thomas Hill, Kilnhurst.
Engine: Rolls–Royce C88FL of 242 kW (325 h.p.).
Transmission: Hydraulic.
Max. T.E.: 128 kN (28800 lbf).   **Weight:** 48 tonnes.
Wheel Dia: 1067 mm.

LUL	Present		
DL 81	00887131	Long Marston Workshops	RR 10278/1968 rebuilt YEC L152/1996
DL 82		Hardingham Station, Norfolk	RR 10272/1967
DL 83		Nene Valley Railway	RR 10271/1967

2.7. BRITISH MILITARY DIESEL LOCOMOTIVES

Many diesel shunting locomotives once used by the military are now either preserved or are in industrial use. Details of all those known to survive in Great Britain are given in this section. It should be noted that the Army Railway organisation of the Ministry of Defence still operates a sizeable fleet of diesel shunting locomotives.

2.7.1. WAR DEPARTMENT DIESEL LOCOMOTIVES

Locomotives in this section are listed in the order of their 1968 Army Department numbers. Many of the locomotives also carried earlier war department numbers and these are given in chronological order in the first column followed by the Army Department number in the second column. Locomotives not allocated numbers in the 1968 series are listed at the end of this section.

CLASS A2EQ   RUSTON & HORNSBY   B

Built: 1958. New to Weedon, Northamptonshire. To Bramshall, Staffordshire 1961. To Asfordby, Leicestershire 1964. To Shoeburyness, Essex 1968.
Engine: Ruston 4VRO of 36 kW (48 h.p.).
Transmission: Mechanical.   **Weight:** 6 tonnes.
Max. T.E.:   **Wheel Dia:** 762 mm.

WD	AD		
813	110	Museum of Army Transport, Beverley	RH 411319/1958

CLASS A4EQ   JOHN FOWLER   0-4-0

Built: 1938. Transferred to BAOR 1973 and displayed outside HQ 79 Railway Squadron RCT, Mönchengladbach. Returned to Marchwood for display 199x.
Engine: Fowler 6B of 45 kW (60 h.p.).
Transmission: Mechanical.   **Weight:** 15 tonnes.
Max. T.E.:   **Wheel Dia:** 914 mm.

WD	AD		
815	111	Marchwood Military Railway	JF 22503/1938

CLASS A5SA   RUSTON & HORNSBY   B

Built: 1952. New to Eskmeels, Cumbria. To Kirkintilloch, Strathclyde 1962. Sold for industrial use 1974.
Engine: ? of 66 kW (88 h.p.).
Transmission: Mechanical.   **Weight:** 17 tonnes.
Max. T.E.:   **Wheel Dia:** 914 mm.

WD	AD	Present		
8326	112	Unnumbered	Pleasurewood Hills Park, Lowestoft	RH 305315/1952

CLASS A7   BAGULEY/DREWRY   0-4-0

Built: 1941.
Engine: Gardner 6L3 of 114 kW (153 h.p.).
Transmission: Mechanical.
Max. T.E.:   **Weight:** 21 tonnes.
Wheel Dia: 990 mm.

WD	AD	Present		
70030–820	123	A7	Foxfield Railway	Bg/DC 2157/1941
70031–821	124	"Grumpy"	Avon Valley Railway	Bg/DC 2158/1941
70037		ED16	North Yorkshire Moors Railway	Bg/DC 2164/1941

CLASS A7   BARCLAY   0-4-0

Built: 1942. Sold for industrial use 1978.

Engine: Gardner 6L3 of 114 kW (153 h.p.).
Transmission: Mechanical.
Max. T.E.:
Weight: 21 tonnes.
Wheel Dia: 990 mm.

WD	AD	Present		
70048–828	127	Unnumbered	Rushden Station Museum	AB 363/1942

CLASS B1   BARCLAY   0–4–0

Built: 1942.
Engine: Gardner 6L3 of 114 kW (153 h.p.).
Transmission: Mechanical.
Max. T.E.: kN (lbf).
Weight: 21 tonnes.
Wheel Dia: 990 mm.

WD	AD	Present		
70042–823–869	202	OVERLORD	Royal Engineers Museum, Chatham	AB 357/1941
70043–824	200		Avon Valley Railway	AB 358/1941
70047–827	201		Stratford & Broadway Railway	AB 362/1942

Note: 70043 is currently receiving attention at Long Marston workshops.

CLASS B11   BARCLAY   0–4–0

Built: 1941, rebuilt from Class B3.
Engine: ? of 144 kW (193 h.p.).
Transmission: Mechanical.
Max. T.E.:
Weight: tonnes.
Wheel Dia: 990 mm.

WD	AD	Present		
70039–825	221	15	Lavender Line, Isfield	AB 354/1941
70044–823	220		Tarmac Precast Concrete, Hayes	AB 359/1941

CLASS B11   DREWRY/VULCAN FOUNDRY   0–4–0

Built: 1945, rebuilt from Class B3.
Engine: ? of 144 kW (193 h.p.).
Transmission: Mechanical.
Max. T.E.:
Weight: tonnes.
Wheel Dia: 990 mm.

WD	AD	Present		
72221–830	223	16	Lavender Line, Isfield	DC/VF 2176/5257/1945
72225–834	226		Wickham Rail Engineering, Thorrington	DC/VF 2180/5261/1945
72226–835	227		Direct Rail Services, Carlisle	DC/VF 2181/5262/1945

CLASS B11   BARCLAY   0–4–0

Built: 1945, rebuilt from Class B3.
Engine: ? of 144 kW (193 h.p.).
Transmission: Mechanical.
Max. T.E.:
Weight: tonnes.
Wheel Dia: 990 mm.

WD	AD		
72238–844	235	Isle of Wight Steam Railway	AB 371/1945

Note: For 240 see LMSR Diesel Locomotive section.

CLASS B7   JOHN FOWLER   0–4–0

Built: 1939.
Engine: McLaren of 112 kW (150 h.p.).
Transmission: Mechanical.
Max. T.E.:
Weight: 26 tonnes.
Wheel Dia: 914 mm.

WD	AD	Present		
70028–852	242	4	Watercress Line	JF 22889/1939

UNCLASSIFIED   BARCLAY (rebuild)   B

Built: 1966 by Rolls-Royce for Manchester Ship Canal Company. Acquires by AD in 1972. Rebuilt 1986 by Andrew Barclay, Kilmarnock.

Engine: Rolls-Royce C65FL of 190 kW (255 h.p.).
Transmission: Hydraulic.
Max. T.E.:
AD

242		Long Marston workshops		RR 10242/1966 rebuilt AB 1986

Weight: 32 tonnes.
Wheel Dia: 965 mm.

CLASS B8EQ THOMAS HILL (rebuild) 0–4–0

Built: 1942 by John Fowler, rebuilt 1963 by Thomas Hill.
Engine: Rolls Royce C6NFL of 112 kW (150 h.p.).
Transmission: Hydraulic. **Weight:** 27 tonnes.
Max. T.E.: **Wheel Dia:** 965 mm.

WD	AD	Present		
8311	244		J. Walker, Shawhill Station Yard	JF 22971/1942 rebuilt TH 130C/1963
8313	246	31469	Rutland Railway Museum	JF 22982/1942 rebuilt TH 132C/1963

UNCLASSIFIED RUSTON & HORNSBY 0–4–0

Built: 1956 for USAF. Transferred to AD in 1973 for use at Thatcham GSSD.
Engine: Ruston 6VPH of 123 kW (165 h.p.).
Transmission: Mechanical. **Weight:** 28 tonnes.
Max. T.E.: **Wheel Dia:** 914 mm.

AD	Present		
251	"FRANCIS BAILY OF THATCHAM"	GWR Preservation Group, Southall	RH 390772/1956

CLASS C1 NORTH BRITISH 0–4–0

Built: 1955–59.
Engine: National of 205 kW (275 h.p.).
Transmission: Hydraulic. **Weight:** 32 tonnes.
Max. T.E.: 96 kN (21 500 lbf). **Wheel Dia:** 1016 mm.

WD	AD	Present		
8200	400	"RIVER EDEN"	Kingdom of Fife Railway	NBL 27421/1955
8205	405	Unnumbered	Shropshire Locomotive Colection	NBL 27426/1955
8206	406		Mayer-Parry Recycling, Snailwell	NBL 27427/1955
8209	409	Unnumbered	Scottish Industrial Railway Centre	NBL 27644/1959
8210	410		Mayer-Parry Recycling, Snailwell	NBL 27645/1959
8213	413		Long Marston Workshops	NBL 27648/1959

CLASS C3SA RUSTON & HORNSBY 0–6–0

Built: 1961–63, some rebuilt after military use.
Engine: Paxman 6RPH of 214 kW (287 h.p.).
Transmission: Hydraulic. **Weight:** 42 tonnes.
Max. T.E.: **Wheel Dia:** 990 mm.

WD	AD	Present		
8214	420		Chinnor & Princes Risborough Railway	RH 459515/1961
8221	427		East Kent Light Railway	RH 466616/1961
8231	436	Unnumbered	AES Fiffonts Point Power Station	RH 468046/1963 rebuilt YEC L106/1992

Note: For 601 see LMSR Diesel Locomotives section.

CLASS D2 SENTINEL 0–8–0

Built: 1963.
Engine: Two Rolls Royce C8SFL of 239 kW (320 h.p.). New to Longmoor Military Railway. To Shoeburyness, Essex 1970.
Transmission: Hydraulic. **Weight:** 54 tonnes.
Max. T.E.: **Wheel Dia:** 1067 mm.

WD	AD	Present		
890	610	D2	Avon Valley Railway	S 10143/1963

UNCLASSIFIED   HUNSLET   0–4–0

Built: 1940. Sold for industrial use 1967.
Engine: Gardner 6L3 of 114 kW (153 h.p.).
Transmission: Mechanical.   **Weight:** tonnes.
Max. T.E.:   **Wheel Dia:** 1016 mm.

WD	AD	Present		
75519	849	ESSO	Buckinghamshire Railway Centre	HE 2067/1940

UNCLASSIFIED   RUSTON & HORNSBY   0–4–0

Built: 1945. Sold for industrial use 1974.
Engine: Ruston 4VRO of 36 kW (48 h.p.).
Transmission: Mechanical.   **Weight:** 6 tonnes.
Max. T.E.:   **Wheel Dia:** 762 mm.

WD	AD	Present		
72215	808	Unnumbered	Merseyside Development Corporation, Bootle	RH 224347/1945

UNCLASSIFIED   BARCLAY   0–6–0

Built: 1966 for use by BAOR. Returned to Great Britain in 1994.
Engine: Cummins NT400 of 230 kW (310 h.p.).
Transmission: Hydraulic.   **Weight:** tonnes.
Max. T.E.:   **Wheel Dia:** mm.

WD	Present		
870	"AWDAS"	ISTIL, Queenborough Wharf Scrapyard	AB 509/1966
871	"THOMPSON"	ISTIL, Queenborough Wharf Scrapyard	AB 510/1966
872	"CARR"	ISTIL, Queenborough Wharf Scrapyard	AB 511/1966
873	"BAGNALL"	ISTIL, Queenborough Wharf Scrapyard	AB 512/1966

UNCLASSIFIED   HUNSLET   0–4–0

Built: 1983–84 for use by BAOR. Returned to Great Britain in 199x.
Engine: Rolls-Royce C6TFL of 223 kW (300 h.p.) (*Caterpillar of 328 kW (440 h.p.).
Transmission: Mechanical.   **Weight:** 34.4 tonnes.
Max. T.E.:   **Wheel Dia:** 1143 mm.

875	Long Marston Workshops	HE 9222/1984
876	Long Marston Workshops	HE 9223/1984
877	Long Marston Workshops	HE 9224/1984
878*	Alstom, Asfordby Test Track	HE 9225/1984

2.7.1.1. ROYAL ORDNANCE FACTORY DIESEL LOCOMOTIVES

UNCLASSIFIED   BARCLAY   0–4–0

Built: 1972 for Royal Ordnance factory, Puriton, Bridgwater, Somerset.
Engine: Paxman 6RPHL Mk 7V6 of 225 kW (302 h.p.).
Transmission: Mechanical.   **Weight:**
Max. T.E.:   **Wheel Dia:**

6320–P5104	ROF BRIDGWATER No. 1	West Somerset Railway	AB 578/1972
6321	ROF BRIDGWATER No. 2	West Somerset Railway	AB 579/1972

UNCLASSIFIED   JOHN FOWLER   0–4–0

Built: 1962.
Engine:
Transmission: Hydraulic.   **Weight:**
Max. T.E.:   **Wheel Dia:**

18242	ROF CHORLEY No. 4	Stratford & Broadway Railway	JF422022/1962

2.7.2. AIR MINISTRY DIESEL LOCOMOTIVES
BARCLAY 0–4–0

Built: 1938. New to Hartlebury, Worcestershire.
Engine: Gleniffer 8-cyl of 119 kW (160 h.p.).
Transmission: Mechanical. **Weight:**
Max. T.E.: **Wheel Dia:**

AM	*Present*		
144	"JOHN PEEL"	East Anglian Railway Museum	AB 333/1938

ROBERT STEPHENSON & HAWTHORN 0–4–0

Built: 1940. New to Hartlebury, Worcestershire. Sold for industrial use 1952.
Engine: 112 kW (150 h.p.).
Transmission: Mechanical. **Weight:**
Max. T.E.: **Wheel Dia:**

AM	*Present*		
158	Unnumbered	Tanfield Railway	RSH 6980/1940

RUSTON & HORNSBY

Built: 1929. New to Dinton, Wiltshire. **Gauge:** 24"
Engine: Ruston 4VRO of 36 kW (48 h.p.).
Transmission: Mechanical. **Weight:** 7 tonnes
Max. T.E.: **Wheel Dia:** 457 mm.

AM			
165		Royal Air Force Museum, Hendon	RH 194784/1939

JOHN FOWLER 0–4–0

Built: 1939. New to Heywood, Lancashire. To Chilmark, Wiltshire 1956. To Burtonwood, Lancashire 1968. To St. Athan, Glamorgan 1959. Sold for industrial use 1973.
Engine: Fowler 4C of 112 kW (150 h.p.).
Transmission: Mechanical. **Weight:** 26 tonnes.
Max. T.E.: **Wheel Dia:** 990 mm.

AM	*Present*		
169	600	Erwood Station Craft Centre	JF 22878/1939

RUSTON & HORNSBY 0–4–0

Built: 1942. Sold for industrial use 1957.
Engine: 66 kW (88 h.p.).
Transmission: Mechanical. **Weight:** 17 tonnes.
Max. T.E.: **Wheel Dia:** 914 mm.

AM	*Present*		
238	Unnumbered	Somerset & Dorset Railway Trust	RH 210479/1942
239	Unnumbered	LCP Properties, Pensnett Trading Estate	RH 215755/1942

Note: 238 incorrectly carries worksplate RH 306089/19??

2.7.3. ADMIRALTY DIESEL LOCOMOTIVES
BARCLAY 0–6–0

Built: 1941. New to RN stores depot, Dalbeattie. To Kirkinton depot, Edinburgh 1948.
Engine:
Transmission: Mechanical. **Weight:**
Max. T.E.: **Wheel Dia:**

DS1		
	Bo'ness & Kinneil Railway	AB 343/1941

HUNSLET   0–4–0

Built: 1941. Used at Broughton Moor Armament Depot.
Engine:
Transmission: Mechanical.   **Weight:**
Max. T.E.:   **Wheel Dia:**

AM	*Present*		
S4	"Vortigern"ND6438	Bere Ferrers Station Museum	HE 2642/1941

HUNSLET   0–4–0

Built: 1968.
Engine:
Transmission: Hydraulic..   **Weight:**
Max. T.E.:   **Wheel Dia:**

12228	"ALLINGTON CASTLE"	Bressingham Steam Museum	HE 6975/1968

RUSTON & HORNSBY   0–4–0

Built: 1943.
Engine: Ruston 4VRO of 36 kW (48 h.p.).
Transmission: Mechanical.   **Weight:** 7.5 tonnes.
Max. T.E.: 20 kN (4200 lbf).   **Wheel Dia:** 762 mm.

YD43	Colne Valley Railway	RH 221639/1943

3. PETROL LOCOMOTIVES

L & YR   B

Built: 1919 by Motor Rail & Tram Car Company for departmental use.
Engine: Dorman 4JO of 30 kW (40 h.p.).
Transmission: Dixon Abbott two-speed gearbox with forward & reverse chain drive to axles.
Max. T.E.: 17 kN (3750 lbf).   **Weight:** 8 tonnes.
Max. Speed: 7 m.p.h.   **Wheel Dia:** 940 mm.

1	Chasewater Light Railway	MR 1947/1919

LMS   A–2

Built: 1927 by Mercury Truck and Tractor Company, Gloucester. Used at Wolverton works.
Engine:
Transmission: Chain drive.
Max. T.E.:   **Weight:**
Max. Speed: **Wheel Dia:**

1311-G	Midland Railway Centre	Mercury 5337/1927

LNER   B

Built: 1944. Used at Lowestoft Sleeper Depot.
Engine: Ruston 4VRO of 36 kW (48 h.p.).
Transmission: Chain drive.
Max. T.E.:   **Weight:** 5.5 tonnes.
Max. Speed: **Wheel Dia:** 457 mm.
Gauge: 3' 0"

BR	LNER	*Present*		
06/22/6/2	3	"MONTY"	A.J. Wilson, Leeds	RH 224337/1944

4. ELECTRIC LOCOMOTIVES

Electric railways have existed in Great Britain for over one hundred years. Prior to the second world war the majority of electrification was for the movement of passengers in and to metropolitan areas. The North Eastern Railway did however build a small fleet of electric locomotives for hauling heavy coal and steel trains in County Durham.

Notes

For notes on wheel arrangements, dimensions, tractive effort and brakes see 'Diesel Locomotives' section.

4.1. PRE-NATIONALISATION DESIGN ELECTRIC LOCOMOTIVES

LSWR   Bo

Built: 1898. Siemens design for operation on the Waterloo & City line.
System: 750 V d.c. third rail.   **Train Heating:** None
Traction Motors: Two Siemens 45 kW (60 h.p).
Wheel dia.: 3' 4".

BR	SR	LSWR		
DS75	75S	Unnumbered	National Railway Museum	SM 6/1898

NORTH EASTERN RAILWAY CLASS ES1   Bo-Bo

Built: 1905. 2 built. Used on Newcastle Riverside Branch.
System: 600 V d.c. overhead.   **Train Heating:** None
Traction Motors: 4 BTH design.
Weight: 46 tonnes.   **Wheel Dia:** 915 mm.

BR	LNER	NER		
26500	4075–6480	1	National Railway Museum	BE1905

LNER CLASS EM1 (BR CLASS 76)   Bo+Bo

Built: 1941–53 at Doncaster (26000) and Gorton (others) for Manchester–Sheffield/Wath system. 58 built.
System: 1500 V d.c. overhead.
Traction Motors: 4 MV 186 axle-hung.
Max Rail Power: 2460 kW (3300 h.p).
Continuous Rating: 970 kW (1300 h.p).
Max. T.E.: 200 kN (45000 lbf).   **Weight:** 88 tonnes.
Cont. T.E.: 39 kN (8800 lbf) at 56 m.p.h.   **Wheel Dia:** 1270 mm.
Max. Speed: 65 m.p.h.   **Train Heating:** Steam

26020–E26020–76020	National Railway Museum	Gorton 1027/1951

LNER CLASS EM2 (BR CLASS 77)   Co-Co

Built: 1953–55 at Gorton for BR to LNER design for Manchester–Sheffield route. 7 built. Sold to NS (Netherlands Railways) 1969.
System: 1500 V d.c. overhead.
Traction Motors: 6 MV 146 axle-hung.
Max Rail Power: 1716 kW (2300 hp).
Max. T.E.: 200 kN (45000 lbf).   **Weight:** 102 tonnes.
Cont. T.E.: 78 kN (15600 lbf) at 23 m.p.h.   **Wheel Dia:** 1092 mm.
Max. Speed: 90 m.p.h.
Train Heating: Steam whilst on BR, electric fitted by NS.
Air brakes.

NS	BR			
1502	27000–E 27000	ELECTRA	Midland Railway Centre	Gorton 1065/1953
1505	27001–E 27001	ARIADNE	Greater Manchester Museum of Science & Industry	Gorton 1066/1954
1501	27003–E 27003	(DIANA)	Leidschendamm, Den Haag (NS)	Gorton 1068/1954

4.2. BRITISH RAILWAYS ELECTRIC LOCOMOTIVES

Numbering System

Numbering of electric locomotives from 1957 was similar to that of diesel locomotives, except that the numbers were prefixed with an 'E' instead of a 'D'. Locomotives of pre-nationalisation design continued to be numbered in the 2xxxx series, although Classes EM1 and EM2 later acquired an 'E' prefix to their existing numbers. As with diesels, electric locomotives were later allocated a two-digit class number followed by a three-digit serial number.

CLASS 81   Bo-Bo

Built: 1959–64. Birmingham R.C.&W Company. 25 Built.
System: 25 kV a.c. overhead.
Max. T.E.: 222 kN (50000 lbf).
Cont. T.E.: 76 kN (17000 lbf) at 71 m.p.h.
Max. Speed: 100 m.p.h.
Dual braked.

Continuous Rating: 2390 kW (3200 h.p.).
Weight: 79 tonnes.
Wheel Dia: 1219 mm.
Train Heating: Electric

E3003–81002   Barrow Hill Roundhouse   BTH 1085/1960

CLASS 83   Bo-Bo

Built: 1960–62. Vulcan Foundry. 15 Built.
System: 25 kV a.c. overhead.
Max. T.E.: 169 kN (38000 lbf).
Cont. T.E.: 68 kN (15260 lbf) at 73 m.p.h.
Max. Speed: 100 m.p.h.
Dual braked.

Continuous Rating: 2200 kW (2950 h.p.).
Weight: 76 tonnes.
Wheel Dia: 1219 mm.
Train Heating: Electric

E3035–83012   Barrow Hill Roundhouse   EE 2941/VF E277/1961

CLASS 84   Bo-Bo

Built: 1960–61. North British Locomotive Company. 10 built.
System: 25 kV a.c. overhead.
Max. T.E.: 222 kN (50000 lbf).
Cont. T.E.: 78 kN (17600 lbf) at 66 m.p.h.
Max. Speed: 100 m.p.h.
Dual braked.

Continuous Rating: 2312 kW (3100 h.p.).
Weight: 76.6 tonnes.
Wheel Dia: 1219 mm.
Train Heating: Electric

E 3036–84001   Barrow Hill Roundhouse (N)   NBL 27793/1960

CLASS 82   Bo-Bo

Built: 1960–62. Beyer Peacock. 10 Built.
System: 25 kV a.c. overhead.
Max. T.E.: 222 kN (50000 lbf).
Cont. T.E.: 76 kN (17000 lbf) at 73 m.p.h.
Max. Speed: 100 m.p.h.
Dual braked.

Continuous Rating: 2460 kW (3300 h.p.).
Weight: 80 tonnes.
Wheel Dia: 1219 mm.
Train Heating: Electric

E3054–82008   Barrow Hill Roundhouse   BP 7893/1961

CLASS 85   Bo-Bo

Built: 1961–65. Doncaster. 40 Built.
System: 25 kV a.c. overhead.
Max. T.E.: 222 kN (50000 lbf).
Cont. T.E.: 76 kN (17000 lbf) at 71 m.p.h.
Max. Speed: 100 m.p.h.
Dual braked.

Continuous Rating: 2390 kW (3200 h.p.).
Weight: 82.5 tonnes.
Wheel Dia: 1219 mm.
Train Heating: Electric

E3061–85006–85101   Barrow Hill Roundhouse   Doncaster 1961

CLASS 71 Bo-Bo

Built: 1958–60. Doncaster. 24 built.
System: 660–750 V d.c. third rail or overhead.
Continuous Rating: 1715 kW (2300 h.p.).
Max. T.E.: 191 kN (43 000 lbf). **Weight:** 76.2 tonnes.
Cont. T.E.: 55 kN (12 400 lbf) at 69.6 m.p.h. **Wheel Dia:** 1219 mm.
Max. Speed: 90 m.p.h. **Train Heating:** Electric
Dual braked.

E 5001–71001 National Railway Museum Doncaster 1959

Note: In storage at Venice-Simplon Orient Express, Stewarts Lane, London.

CLASS 73/0 ELECTRO-DIESEL Bo-Bo

Built: 1962. Eastleigh. 6 built.
System: 660–750 V d.c. from third rail. **Continuous Rating:** Electric 1060 kW (1420 h.p.).
Continuous Tractive Effort: Diesel 72 kN (16100 lbf) at 10 m.p.h.
Maximum Tractive Effort: Electric 187 kN (42000 lbf). Diesel 152 kN (34100 lbf).
Weight: 76.3 tonnes. **Wheel Dia:** 1016 mm.
Max. Speed: 80 m.p.h.
Triple braked (vacuum, air and electro-pneumatic).
Train Heating: Electric

E 6001–73001–73901	Dean Forest Railway	Eastleigh 1962
E 6002–73002	Dean Forest Railway	Eastleigh 1962
E 6003–73003	Great Central Railway	Eastleigh 1962
E 6005–73005	Dean Forest Railway	Eastleigh 1962
E 6006–73006–73906	Dean Forest Railway	Eastleigh 1962

CLASS 73/1 ELECTRO-DIESEL Bo-Bo

Built: 1965–67. Vulcan Foundry. 43 built.
System: 660–750 V d.c. from third rail. **Continuous Rating:** Electric 1060 kW (1420 h.p.).
Continuous Tractive Effort: Diesel 60 kN (13600 lbf) at 11.5 m.p.h.
Maximum Tractive Effort: Electric 179 kN (40000 lbf). Diesel 152 kN (34100 lbf).
Weight: 76.8 tonnes. **Wheel Dia:** 1016 mm.
Max. Speed: 90 m.p.h.
Triple braked (vacuum, air and electro-pneumatic).
Train Heating: Electric

E 6033–73126	Fire Service College, Moreton-in-Marsh	EE/VF 3595/E365 1966
E 6047–73140	Lavender Line, Isfield	EE/VF 3719/E379 1966
E 6048–73141	Battlefield Railway	EE/VF 3720/E380 1967

4.3. LONDON UNDERGROUND ELECTRIC LOCOMOTIVES

CITY & SOUTH LONDON RAILWAY   B

Built: 1890 by Beyer-Peacock to Mather & Platt design. 14 built.
System: 500 V d.c. third rail system.   **Gauge:** 762 mm.
Max. T.E.:   **Weight:** 10.3 tonnes.
Cont. T.E.:.   **Wheel Dia:** 686 mm.
Max. Speed: **Continuous Rating:**

13	London Transport Depot Museum, Acton	BP 1890

METROPOLITAN RAILWAY   B–B

Built: 1922–23. 20 built.
System: 600 V d.c. 4-rail system.   **Continuous Rating:** 895 kW (1200 h.p.)
Max. T.E.: 100 kN (22600 lbf).   **Weight:** 62.5 tonnes
Cont. T.E.: 65 kN (14720 lbf).   **Wheel Dia:** 1105 mm
Max. Speed: 65 m.p.h.

5	JOHN HAMPDEN	London Transport Museum	VL 1922
12	SARAH SIDDONS	London Underground, West Ruislip Depot	VL 1922

4.4. BATTERY ELECTRIC LOCOMOTIVES

NORTH STAFFORDSHIRE RAILWAY   2–A

Built: 1917.
Battery: 108 cells giving an output of 61 kW (82 hp).
Transmission: Wilson four-speed gearbox driving a rear jackshaft.
Max. T.E.: 50 kN (15300 lbf).   **Wheel Dia:** 940 mm.

NSR	LMS		
2	BEL 2	Churnet Valley Railway (N)	Stoke 1917

LONDON PASSENGER TRANSPORT BOARD   1–A

Built: 1938. 9 built. Operates off either battery or rail supply.
Battery:
Traction Motors: 4 x 113 kW Metropolitan-Vickers MV145A2.
Weight: 54.6 tonnes.   **Max. T.E.:** 58 kN (17800 lbf).
Wheel Dia: 940 mm.
Max. Speed: 30 m.p.h. (rail supply), 15 m.p.h. (battery supply)

L 35	London Transport Depot Museum, Acton	GRCW 1938

5. GAS TURBINE VEHICLES
LOCOMOTIVE   AIA-AIA

Built: 1950. Brown Boveri
Power Unit: Brown Boveri gas turbine of 1828 kW (2450 h.p.).
Transmission: Electric. Four traction motors.
Max. T.E.: 140 kN (31500 lbf).
Cont. T.E.: 55 kN (12400 lbf) at 64 m.p.h.
Max. Speed: 90 m.p.h.
Weight: 117.1 tonnes.
Wheel Dias: 1232 mm.
Train Heating: Steam.

18000   The Railway Age, Crewe   BBC 4559/1950

EXPERIMENTAL ADVANCED PASSENGER TRAIN (APT-E)

Built: 1972 at Derby Litchurch Lane Works.
Power Units: Eight Leyland 350 automotive gas turbines of 222 kW (298 h.p.).
Traction Motors: Four GEC 253AY. Articulated unit.

PC1   National Railway Museum   Derby 1972
PC2   National Railway Museum   Derby 1972
TC1   National Railway Museum   Derby 1972
TC2   National Railway Museum   Derby 1972

6. DIESEL MULTIPLE UNIT VEHICLES
GENERAL

Prior to nationalisation, several schemes to transfer road bus technology to rail vehicles had taken place with little success, the exception being the GWR where the concept was developed resulting in a fleet of distinctive diesel railcars.

During the 1950s British Railways took the idea far more seriously as part of the modernisation plan and consequently numerous designs appeared. The preservation of these has expanded enormously in recent years.

Type Codes

The type codes used by the former BR operating departments to describe the various types of multiple unit vehicles are used, these being:

B   Brake, i.e. a vehicle with luggage space and a guard's/conductor's compartment.

BDM	Battery driving motor	L	Open or semi-open with lavatory
C	Composite	O	Open vehicle
Cso	Semi-open composite	PMV	Parcels & miscellaneous van
DT	Driving trailer	S	Second (now known as standard)
K	Side corridor with lavatory	T	Trailer
M	Motor	RB	Buffet car
BDT	battery driving trailer	Sso	Semi-open second
DM	Driving motor	T	Third (reclassified second in 1956)
F	First		

All diesel mechanical and diesel hydraulic vehicles are assumed to be open unless stated otherwise and do not carry an 'O' in the code. Certain DMU vehicles are nowadays used as hauled stock and these are denoted by a letter 'h' after the number.

Prefixes and Suffixes

Coaching stock vehicles used to carry regional prefix letters to denote the owning region. These were removed in the 1980s. These are not shown. Pre-nationalisation number series vehicles carried both prefix and suffix letters, the suffix denoting the pre-nationalisation number series. The prefixes and suffixes are shown for these vehicles.

Dimensions

Dimensions are shown as length (over buffers or couplers) x width (over bodysides including door handles)

Seating Capacities

These are shown as nF/nS relating to first and second class seats respectively, e.g. a car with 12 first class seats and 51 second class seats would be shown as 12/51. Prior to 3rd June 1956 second class was referred to as "third" class and is now referred to as "standard" class. Certain old vehicles are thus shown as third class.

Bogies

All vehicles are assumed to have two four-wheeled bogies unless otherwise stated.

6.1. GWR DIESEL RAILCARS

UNCLASSIFIED

PARK ROYAL

Built: 1934 by Park Royal. Single cars with two driving cabs.
Engines: Two AEC 90 kW (121 h.p.).
Body: 19.58 x 2.70 m.
Max. Speed: 75 m.p.h.
Transmission: Mechanical.
Weight: 26.6 tonnes.
Seats: –/44.

BR	GWR		
W 4 W	4	Steam – Museum of the Great Western Railway, Swindon (N)	PR 1934

UNCLASSIFIED

GWR

Built: 1940. Single cars with two driving cabs.
Engines: Two AEC 78 kW (105 h.p.).
Body: 20.21 x 2.70 m.
Max. Speed: 40 m.p.h.
Transmission: Mechanical.
Weight: 36.2 tonnes.
Seats: –/48.

BR	GWR		
W 20 W	20	Kent & East Sussex Railway	Swindon 1940
W 22 W	22	Didcot Railway Centre	Swindon 1941

6.2. BRITISH RAILWAYS DMUS

Numbering System

Early BR diesel multiple units were numbered in the 79XXX series, but when it was evident that this series did not contain enough numbers the 5XXXX series was allocated to this type of vehicle and the few locomotive-hauled non-corridor coaches which were in the 5XXXX series were renumbered into the 4XXXX series. Power cars in the 50XXX series and driving trailers in the 56XXX series were eventually renumbered into the 53XXX and 54XXX series respectively to avoid conflicting numbers with Class 50 and 56 diesel locomotives.

Diesel-electric multiple unit power cars were renumbered in the 60000–60499 series, trailers in the 60500–60799 series and driving trailers in the 60800–60999 series.

6.2.1. HIGH SPEED DIESEL TRAINS

The prototype high speed diesel train appeared in 1972. The two power cars (41001/2) were constructed to a locomotive lot (No. 1501) whilst the intermediate vehicles (10000, 10100, 11000–11002 & 12000–12002) were constructed to coaching stock lots. On 10th July 1974 the power cars were reclassified as coaching stock and issued with a coaching stock lot number. All prototype HSDT vehicles were thus categorised as multiple unit stock and renumbered into the 4XXXX series, Class No. 252 being allocated for the complete set.

CLASS 252

PROTOTYPE HST POWER CAR

Built: 1972. (2 built).
Engine: Paxman Valenta 12RP200L of 1680 kW (2250 h.p.) at 1500 r.p.m.
Traction Motors: Four Brush TMH 68-46.
Power at Rail: 1320 kW (1770 h.p.).
Max. T.E.: 80 kN (17 980 lbf.).
Cont. T.E.: 46 kN (10 340 lbf.) at 64.5 m.p.h.
Max. Speed: 125 m.p.h.
Weight: 67 tonnes
Wheel Dia: 1020 mm.
Air braked.

41001–43000–ADB 975812	National Railway Museum	Derby 1972

6.2.2. DIESEL MECHANICAL MULTIPLE UNITS
CLASS 100   GRCW TWIN UNITS

Built: 1957–58. Normal formation: DMBS–DTCL.
Engines: Two AEC 220 of 112 kW (150 h.p.).
Transmission: Mechanical.
Max. Speed: 70 m.p.h.

DMBS	18.49 x 2.82 m	30.5 tonnes	–/52
DTCL	18.49 x 2.82 m	25.5 tonnes	12/54

51118	DMBS	Midland Railway Centre	GRCW 1957
56097	DTCL	Midland Railway Centre	GRCW 1957
56301	DTCL	Mid-Norfolk Railway	GRCW 1957
56317	DTCL	Essex Traction Group, Boxted	GRCW 1958

CLASS 101   METRO-CAMMELL UNITS

Built: 1958–59. Various Formations.
Engines: Two AEC 220 of 112 kW (150 h.p.).
Transmission: Mechanical.
Max. Speed: 70 m.p.h.

DMBS	18.49 x 2.82 m	32.5 tonnes	–/52
DMCL	18.49 x 2.82 m	32.5 tonnes	12/46 (originally 12/53)
DTCL	18.49 x 2.82 m	25.5 tonnes	12/53
TCL	18.49 x 2.82 m	25.5 tonnes	12/53

51434	DMBS	Mid-Norfolk Railway	MC 1959
51503	DMCL	Mid-Norfolk Railway	MC 1959
56356–54356–6300h	DTCL	Gloucestershire–Warwickshire Railway	MC 1959
59117	TCL	Mid-Norfolk Railway	MC 1958

CLASS 103   PARK ROYAL TWIN UNITS

Built: 1958. Normal formation: DMBS–DTCL.
Engines: Two AEC 220 of 112 kW (150 h.p.).
Transmission: Mechanical.
Max. Speed: 70 m.p.h.

DMBS	18.49 x 2.82 m	34 tonnes	–/52
DTCL	18.49 x 2.82 m	27 tonnes	16/48

50397	DMBS	Coventry Railway Centre	PR 1958
50413	DMBS	West Somerset Railway	PR 1958
56160–DB 975228	DTCL	Denbigh & Mold Junction Railway, Sodom	PR 1958
56169	DTCL	West Somerset Railway	PR 1958

Note: 50397 was allocated number DB 975137 but this was never carried.

CLASS 104   BRCW UNITS

Built: 1957–58. Various formations.
Engines: Two BUT (Leyland) of 112 kW (150 h.p.).
Transmission: Mechanical.
Max. Speed: 70 m.p.h.

DMBS	18.49 x 2.82 m	31.5 tonnes	–/52
TCL	18.49 x 2.82 m	24.5 tonnes	12/54
TBSL	18.49 x 2.82 m	25.5 tonnes	–/51
DMCL	18.49 x 2.82 m	31.5 tonnes	12/54 (12/51*)
DTCL	18.49 x 2.82 m	24.5 tonnes	12/54

50437–53437	DMBS	Churnet Valley Railway	BRCW 1957
50447–53447	DMBS	Llangollen Railway	BRCW 1957
50454–53454	DMBS	Llangollen Railway	BRCW 1957
50455–53455	DMBS	Churnet Valley Railway	BRCW 1957

50479–53479	DMBS	Telford Steam Railway	BRCW 1958
50494–53494	DMCL	Churnet Valley Railway	BRCW 1957
50517–53517	DMCL	Churnet Valley Railway	BRCW 1957
50528–53528	DMCL	Llangollen Railway	BRCW 1958
50531–53531	DMCL	Telford Steam Railway	BRCW 1958
50556–53556*	DMCL	Telford Steam Railway	BRCW 1958
56182–54182–977554	DTCL	Churnet Valley Railway	BRCW 1958
59137	TCL	Churnet Valley Railway	BRCW 1957
59228	TBSL	Telford Steam Railway	BRCW 1958

CLASS 105   CRAVEN TWIN UNITS

Built: 1957–59. Normal formation: DMBS–DTCL or DMCL.
Engines: Two AEC 220 of 112 kW (150 h.p.).
Transmission: Mechanical.
Max. Speed: 70 m.p.h.

DMBS	18.49 x 2.82 m	29.5 tonnes	–/52
DTCL	18.49 x 2.82 m	23.5 tonnes	12/51

51485	DMBS	East Lancashire Railway	Cravens 1959
56121	DTCL	East Lancashire Railway	Cravens 1957
56456–54456	DTCL	Llangollen Railway	Cravens 1959

CLASS 107   DERBY HEAVYWEIGHT TRIPLE UNITS

Built: 1960–61. Normal formation: DMBS–TSL–DMCL.
Engines: Two BUT (Leyland) of 112 kW (150 h.p.).
Transmission: Mechanical.
Max. Speed: 70 m.p.h.

DMBS	18.49 x 2.82 m	35 tonnes	–/52
DMCL	18.49 x 2.82 m	35.5 tonnes	12/53
TSL	18.49 x 2.82 m	28.5 tonnes	–/71

51990–977830	DMBS	Strathspey Railway	Derby 1960
51993–977834	DMBS	Caledonian Railway	Derby 1961
52005–977832	DMBS	Embsay & Bolton Abbey Railway	Derby 1961
52006	DMBS	Embsay & Bolton Abbey Railway	Derby 1961
52008	DMBS	Strathspey Railway	Derby 1961
52012–977835	DMCL	Caledonian Railway	Derby 1960
52025–977833	DMCL	Bridgend Valleys Railway	Derby 1961
52029 h	DMCL	Pullman TPL, Cardiff Cathays	Derby 1961
52030–977831	DMBS	Strathspey Railway	Derby 1961
52031	DMCL	Embsay & Bolton Abbey Railway	Derby 1961
59791	TSL	Embsay & Bolton Abbey Railway	Derby 1961

CLASS 108   DERBY LIGHTWEIGHT UNITS

Built: 1958–1961. Various formations.
Engines: Two Leyland of 112 kW (150 h.p.).
Transmission: Mechanical.
Max. Speed: 70 m.p.h.

DMBS	18.49 x 2.79 m	29.5 tonnes	–/52
TBSL	18.49 x 2.79 m	21.5 tonnes	–/50
TSL	18.49 x 2.79 m	21.5 tonnes	–/68
DMCL	18.49 x 2.79 m	28.5 tonnes	12/53
DTCL	18.49 x 2.79 m	21.5 tonnes	12/53

50599–53599	DMBS	East Anglian Railway Museum	Derby 1958
50619–53619	DMBS	Dean Forest Railway	Derby 1958
50627–53627–977853	DMBS	Peak Railway	Derby 1958
50628–53628	DMBS	Keith & Dufftown Railway	Derby 1958

50632–53632	DMCL	Pontypool & Blaenavon Railway	Derby	1958
50645–53645	DMCL	Nottingham Heritage Centre, Ruddington	Derby	1958
50926–53926–977814	DMBS	Nottingham Heritage Centre, Ruddington	Derby	1959
50928–53928	DMBS	Keighley & Worth Valley Railway	Derby	1959
50933–53933	DMBS	Peak Railway	Derby	1960
50971–53971	DMBS	Kent & East Sussex Railway	Derby	1959
50980–53980	DMBS	Bodmin Steam Railway	Derby	1959
51562	DMCL	National Railway Museum	Derby	1959
51565	DMCL	Keighley & Worth Valley Railway	Derby	1959
51566	DMCL	Peak Railway	Derby	1959
51567-977854	DMCL	Peak Railway	Derby	1959
51568	DMCL	Keith & Dufftown Railway	Derby	1959
51571	DMCL	Kent & East Sussex Railway	Derby	1960
51572	DMCL	Mid-Norfolk Railway	Derby	1960
51907	DMBS	Llangollen Railway	Derby	1960
51909	DMBS	Avon Valley Railway	Derby	1960
51914	DMBS	Dean Forest Railway	Derby	1960
51919	DMBS	Swanage Railway	Derby	1960
51922	DMBS	National Railway Museum	Derby	1960
51933	DMBS	Swanage Railway	Derby	1960
51935	DMBS	Severn Valley Railway	Derby	1960
51937–977806	DMBS	Peak Railway	Derby	1960
51941	DMBS	Severn Valley Railway	Derby	1960
51942	DMBS	Pontypool & Blaenavon Railway	Derby	1961
51947	DMBS	Bodmin Steam Railway	Derby	1961
51950	DMBS	Gloucestershire-Warwickshire Railway	Derby	1961
52044	DMCL	Pontypool & Blaenavon Railway	Derby	1960
52048	DMCL	Swanage Railway	Derby	1960
52053–977807	DMCL	Keith & Dufftown Railway	Derby	1960
52054	DMCL	Bodmin Steam Railway	Derby	1960
52060–977813	DMCL	Nottingham Heritage Centre, Ruddington	Derby	1961
52062	DMCL	Gloucestershire-Warwickshire Railway	Derby	1961
52064	DMCL	Severn Valley Railway	Derby	1961
56207–54207 h	DTCL	Appleby-Frodingham RPS	Derby	1958
56208–54208	DTCL	Severn Valley Railway	Derby	1958
56223–54223	DTCL	Keith & Dufftown Railway	Derby	1959
56224–54224	DTCL	Mid-Norfolk Railway	Derby	1959
56270–54270	DTCL	Pontypool & Blaenavon Railway	Derby	1959
56271–54271	DTCL	Avon Valley Railway	Derby	1960
56274–54274 h	DTCL	Rutland Railway Museum	Derby	1960
56279–54279	DTCL	Vale of Glamorgan Railway	Derby	1960
56484–54484	DTCL	Peak Railway	Derby	1960
56490–54490	DTCL	Llangollen Railway	Derby	1960
56491–54491	DTCL	East Anglian Railway Museum	Derby	1960
56492–54492	DTCL	Dean Forest Railway	Derby	1960
56495–54495	DTCL	Dean Forest Railway	Derby	1960
56504–54504	DTCL	Swanage Railway	Derby	1960
59245 h	TBSL	Appleby-Frodingham RPS	Derby	1958
59250	TBSL	Severn Valley Railway	Derby	1958
59387	TSL	Peak Railway	Derby	1958

Note: 51909 and 56271 are currently under restoration at Long Marston Workshops.

CLASS 109   D. WICKHAM TWIN UNITS

Built: 1957. Normal formation: DMBS–DTCL.
Engines: Two BUT (Leyland) of 112 kW (150 h.p.).
Transmission: Mechanical.
Max. Speed: 70 m.p.h.

DMBS	17.53 x 2.82 m	27.5 tonnes	–/52	
DTCL	17.53 x 2.82 m	20.5 tonnes	16/50	

50416–DB 975005	DMBS	Midland Railway Centre	Wkm	1957
56171–DB 975006	DTCL	Midland Railway Centre	Wkm	1957

CLASS 110   BRCW CALDER VALLEY UNITS

Built: 1961–2. Normal formation: DMBC–TSL–DMCL.
Engines: Two Rolls-Royce C6NFLH38D of 134 kW (180 h.p.).
Transmission: Mechanical.
Max. Speed: 70 m.p.h.

DMBC	18.48 x 2.82 m	32.5 tonnes	12/33
DMCL	18.48 x 2.82 m	32.5 tonnes	12/54
TSL	18.48 x 2.82 m	24.5 tonnes	–/72

51813	DMBC	East Lancashire Railway	BRCW 1961
51842	DMCL	East Lancashire Railway	BRCW 1961
52071	DMBC	Lakeside & Haverthwaite Railway	BRCW 1962
52077	DMCL	Lakeside & Haverthwaite Railway	BRCW 1961
59701	TSL	East Lancashire Railway	BRCW 1961

CLASS 111   METRO-CAMMELL TRAILER BUFFET

Built: 1960. Used to augment other units as required.
Max. Speed: 70 m.p.h.

TSLRB	18.49 x 2.82 m	25.5 tonnes	–/53

59575	TSLRB	Mid-Norfolk Railway	MC 1960

CLASS 114   DERBY HEAVYWEIGHT TWIN UNITS

Built: 1956–57. Normal formation: DMBS–DTCL.
Engines: Two Leyland Albion of 149 kW (200 h.p.).
Transmission: Mechanical.
Max. Speed: 70 m.p.h.

DMBS	20.45 x 2.82 m	38 tonnes	–/62
DTCL	20.45 x 2.82 m	30 tonnes	12/62

50019–53019	DMBS	Midland Railway Centre	Derby 1957
56006–54006	DTCL	Midland Railway Centre	Derby 1956
56047–54047	DTCL	Strathspey Railway	Derby 1957

CLASS 115   DERBY SUBURBAN QUAD UNITS

Built: 1960. Non-gangwayed when built, but gangways subsequently fitted. Normal formation: DMBS–TSso–TCL–DMBS.
Engines: Two Leyland Albion of 149 kW (200 h.p.).
Transmission: Mechanical.
Max. Speed: 70 m.p.h.

DMBS	20.45 x 2.82 m	38.5 tonnes	–/74 (originally –/78)
TCL	20.45 x 2.82 m	30.5 tonnes	28/38 (originally 30/40)
TSso	20.45 x 2.82 m	29.5 tonnes	–/98 (originally –/106)

BR	Present			
51655		DMBS	Epping & Ongar Railway	Derby 1960
51663		DMBS	West Somerset Railway	Derby 1960
51669		DMBS	Spa Valley Railway	Derby 1960
51677		DMBS	Epping & Ongar Railway	Derby 1960
51849		DMBS	Spa Valley Railway	Derby 1960
51852		DMBS	West Somerset Railway	Derby 1960
51859		DMBS	West Somerset Railway	Derby 1960
51880		DMBS	West Somerset Railway	Derby 1960
51886		DMBS	Buckinghamshire Railway Centre	Derby 1960
51887		DMBS	West Somerset Railway	Derby 1960
51899		DMBS	Buckinghamshire Railway Centre	Derby 1960
59659 h	"9659"	TSso	South Devon Railway	Derby 1960
59664 h		TCL	Mangapps Farm Railway Museum	Derby 1960
59678		TCL	West Somerset Railway	Derby 1960
59719		TCL	South Devon Railway	Derby 1960

| 59740 h | "9740" | TSso | South Devon Railway | Derby 1960 |
| 59761 | | TCL | Buckinghamshire Railway Centre | Derby 1960 |

CLASS 116   DERBY SUBURBAN TRIPLE UNITS

Built: 1957–58. Non-gangwayed when built, but gangways subsequently fitted. Normal formation: DMBS–TS or TC–DMS.
Engines: Two Leyland of 112 kW (150 h.p.).
Transmission: Mechanical.
Max. Speed: 70 m.p.h.

DMBS	20.45 x 2.82 m	36.5 tonnes	–/65
DMS	20.45 x 2.82 m	36.5 tonnes	–/89 (originally –/95)
TS§	20.45 x 2.82 m	29 tonnes	–/98 (originally –/102)
TC	20.45 x 2.82 m	29 tonnes	20/68 (originally 28/74)

§-converted from TC.

51131		DMBS	Battlefield Railway	Derby 1958
51134		DMBS	Swansea Vale Railway	Derby 1958
51135		DMBS	Swansea Vale Railway	Derby 1958
51138–977921		DMBS	Nottingham Heritage Centre, Ruddington	Derby 1958
51147		DMS	Swansea Vale Railway	Derby 1958
51148		DMS	Swansea Vale Railway	Derby 1958
51151		DMS	Nottingham Heritage Centre, Ruddington	Derby 1958
59003 h		TS	Paignton & Dartmouth Railway	Derby 1957
59004 h	"Emma"	TS	Paignton & Dartmouth Railway	Derby 1957
59444 h		TC	Chasewater Light Railway	Derby 1958
59445		TC	Swansea Vale Railway	Derby 1958

CLASS 117   PRESSED STEEL SUBURBAN TRIPLE UNITS

Built: 1960. Non-gangwayed when built, but gangways subsequently fitted. Normal formation: DMBS–TCL–DMS.
Engines: Two Leyland of 112 kW (150 h.p.).
Transmission: Mechanical.
Max. Speed: 70 m.p.h.

DMBS	20.45 x 2.82 m	36.5 tonnes	–/65
TCL	20.45 x 2.82 m	30.5 tonnes	22/48 (originally 24/50)
DMS	20.45 x 2.82 m	36.5 tonnes	–/89 (originally –/91)

51342	DMBS	Epping & Ongar Railway	PS 1960
51346	DMBS	North Norfolk Railway	PS 1960
51347	DMBS	Nene Valley Railway	PS 1960
51351	DMBS	Pontypool & Blaenavon Railway	PS 1960
51352	DMBS	West Somerset Railway	PS 1960
51354	DMBS	Pullman TPL, Cardiff Cathays	PS 1960
51359	DMBS	Northampton & Lamport Railway	PS 1960
51360	DMBS	Mid-Norfolk Railway	PS 1960
51363	DMBS	Watercress Line	PS 1960
51365	DMBS	Plym Valley Railway	PS 1960
51367	DMBS	Northampton & Lamport Railway	PS 1960
51370	DMBS	Chasewater Light Railway	PS 1960
51372	DMBS	Chasewater Light Railway	PS 1960
51375	DMS	Tyseley Locomotive Works, Birmingham	PS 1960
51376	DMS	West Somerset Railway	PS 1960
51384	DMS	Epping & Ongar Railway	PS 1960
51386	DMS	Mid-Norfolk Railway	PS 1960
51388	DMS	North Norfolk Railway	PS 1960
51396	DMS	Pullman TPL, Cardiff Cathays	PS 1960
51397	DMS	Pontypool & Blaenavon Railway	PS 1960
51400	DMS	Northampton & Lamport Railway	PS 1960
51401	DMS	Nene Valley Railway	PS 1960
51402	DMS	Northampton & Lamport Railway	PS 1960
51405	DMS	Watercress Line	PS 1960
51407	DMS	Plym Valley Railway	PS 1960
51412	DMS	Chasewater Light Railway	PS 1960

▲ Standard Class 4MT 4-6-0 No. 75027 is seen climbing Freshfield Bank on the Bluebell Railway with the 14.05 Sheffield Park–Kingscote on 10 November 2001. **Alan Barnes**

▼ Standard Class 4MT 2-6-0 No. 76079 is seen here passing Langstone Rock, Dawlish with a "Dawlish Donkey" shuttle from Paignton to Exeter. 19 August 2002. **Chris Booth**

▲ Standard Class 4MT 2-6-4T No. 80135 leaves Goathland, North Yorkshire Moors Railway with a Grosmont–Pickering train on 17 August 2002. **George Allsop**

◄ Standard Class 9F 2-10-0 No. 92212 is seen at Rabbit Bridge on the Great Central Railway with a demonstration freight train for Rothley on 20 April 2000. **Brian Dobbs**

▲ WD 2-10-0 No. 90775 passes Kinchley Lane with a mineral train from Loughborough Central to Leicester North on 28 July 2002.

▼ USATC Class S160 2-8-0 No. 5197 visited various preserved lines in 2002. Here it is seen passing Kinchley Lane on the GCR with the 16.30 Loughborough–Leicester on 28 July 2002. **Hugh Ballantyne (2)**

▲ Class 45 No. D123 is seen during a special night photo-shoot on the Great Central Railway on 19 October 2001. **Paul Chancellor**

▼ 50035 "Ark Royal" is seen at Kidderminster, Severn Valley Railway with the 18.05 to Bridgnorth on 28 April 2001. **Hugh Ballantyne**

▲ "Warship" No. D821 "GREYHOUND" leaves Kidderminster with the 11.15 to Bridgnorth on 28 April 2001. **Hugh Ballantyne**

▼ "Western" No. D1013 "WESTERN RANGER" crosses Oldbury Viaduct with the 15.35 Bridgnorth–Kidderminster on 10 August 2002. **Keith Satterly**

▲ BR Green liveried Class 47 No. D1566 (47449), complete with Union Jack flag for HM the Queen's Golden Jubilee celebrations, is seen at Carrog with the 14.00 to Llangollen on 1 June 2002.
Doug Birmingham

▼ Rarely photographed 03399 resides at the Mangapps Farm museum, Burnham-on-Crouch, Essex. Here it is seen shunting a brake van on 15 July 2002.
Iain Scotchman

▲ Class 01 No. D2953 stands at Rowsley, Peak Rail on 5 May 2002. This loco had moved here from the South Yorkshire Railway at Meadowhall. **Chris Booth**

▼ Class 08 No. D3014 "SAMSON" is seen shunting at the Paignton terminus of the Paignton and Dartmouth Railway on 21 September 2002. **Robert Pritchard**

▲ BR Blue liveried 24081 is seen leaving Greet Tunnel at the head of the 14.45 Toddington–Gotherington service at the Gloucestershire Warwickshire Railway on 21 July 2000.   **John Chalcraft**

▼ BR Blue liveried 25059 is a regular and reliable performer at the Keighley and Worth Valley Railway. Here the "rat" leaves Keighley with an Oxenhope train on 30 March 2002.   **Les Nixon**

▲ Trainload coal-liveried 26004 and BR Blue 26024 make for a fine sight as they leave Bo'ness with the 13.10 Bo'ness–Birkhill service on 5 May 2002. **Paul Robertson**

▼ Trainload Freight liveried 31108, on hire to the ELR from the Midland Railway Centre, is seen working the 13.00 Rawtenstall–Bury on 4 August 2001. **George Allsop**

▲ The Midland Railway Centre's 33201 pilots DRS's 33025 (not a preserved loco) on a Keighley–Oxenhope service during the Keighley and Worth Valley Railways diesel weekend on 3 August 2002. **Dick Crane**

▼ Superbly restored 37215 is resident at the 'diesel-friendly' Gloucestershire and Warwickshire Railway. Here it awaits departure from Toddington with a Gotherington service. **John Chalcraft**

Class 20 D8087 (20087) is seen in as-built condition with the 14.30 Ramsbottom–Bury at Touch Hill, Burrs on 25 June 2002.
Brian Dobbs

▲ Porterbrook Purple liveried "DELTIC" No. 9016 "GORDON HIGHLANDER" passes Colton, on its former ECML stomping ground, with the 17.00 Scarborough–Crewe railtour of 6 April 2002.
Chris Booth

▼ Class 14 No. D9539 approaches Winchcombe with the 14.15 Gotherington–Toddington on 6 April 2002. **Alan Barnes**

▲ The only preserved Class 82 No. 82008 is seen at its home, the Barrow Hill Roundhouse in the company of Class 81 No. E3003 (81002). **Phil Quine**

▼ Class 108 2-car DMU set No. L0262 (56490/54490) is seen at Llangollen with a Carrog service on 5 May 2002. **Doug Birmingham**

▲ Class 114 Derby Heavyweight DMU vehicles 50019 and 56006 are seen at Swanwick Shed, Midland Railway Centre on 16 May 2002. **John Eggleshaw**

▼ Class 116 DMU Nos. 51136 and 51151 with Class 117 centre car 59501 lead Class 108 Nos. 50645 and 50926 at Hotchley Hill at the Nottingham Heritage Centre. 21 July 2002. **Paul Robertson**

▲ Class 122 "Bubble car" No. 55003 is seen arriving at Ropley with an Alresford–Alton service on the Watercress line. 21 April 2002. **Darren Ford**

▼ Class 311 No. 311 103 (ex-Railtrack sandite unit No. 936 103) was donated to Summerlee Heritage Centre, Coatbridge in 2002. The type used to work regularly in the Glasgow area. It is seen shortly after arrival on 4 July 2002 alongside former Brussels tram No. 9062. **Douglas Third**

▲ Ex-SJ 4-6-0 No. 1697 (restored as SWJB 101) is currently resident at the Nene Valley Railway. Here it is seen at Orton Mere with the 12.30 Wansford–Peterborough on 4 May 2002.

Horace Gamble

▼ Polish-built USA-style 0-6-0T No. 3135 "SPARTAN" is seen at Groombridge on the Spa Valley Railway with the 12.30 Groombridge–Tunbridge Wells West. 1 September 2001. **P.G. Barnes**

59488 h	TCL	Paignton & Dartmouth Railway	PS 1960
59490	TCL	Swansea Vale Railway	PS 1960
59493 h	TCL	West Somerset Railway	PS 1960
59494 h	TCL	Paignton & Dartmouth Railway	PS 1960
59496 h	TCL	Battlefield Railway	PS 1960
59501	TCL	Nottingham Heritage Centre, Ruddington	PS 1960
59503 h	TCL	Paignton & Dartmouth Railway	PS 1960
59505	TCL	West Somerset Railway	PS 1960
59506 h	TCL	West Somerset Railway	PS 1960
59507 h	TCL	Paignton & Dartmouth Railway	PS 1960
59508	TCL	Nene Valley Railway	PS 1960
59510 h	TCL	West Somerset Railway	PS 1960
59511 h	TCL	Lavender Line, Isfield	PS 1960
59513 h	TCL	Paignton & Dartmouth Railway	PS 1960
59514	TCL	West Somerset Railway	PS 1960
59515 h	TCL	West Somerset Railway	PS 1960
59516	TCL	North Norfolk Railway	PS 1960
59517 h	TCL	Paignton & Dartmouth Railway	PS 1960
59520	TCL	Pontypool & Blaenavon Railway	PS 1960
59522 h	TCL	Battlefield Railway	PS 1960

CLASS 118   BRCW SUBURBAN TRIPLE UNITS

Built: 1960. Non-gangwayed when built, but gangways subsequently fitted.Normal formation: DMBS–TCL–DMS.
Engines: Two Leyland of 112 kW (150 h.p.).
Transmission: Mechanical.
Max. Speed: 70 m.p.h.

DMS	20.45 x 2.82 m	36.5 tonnes	–/89 (originally –/91)	
51321–977753	DMS	Battlefield Railway		BRCW 1960

CLASS 119   GRCW CROSS-COUNTRY UNITS

Built: 1959. Normal formation: DMBC–TSLRB–DMSL.
Engines: Two Leyland of 112 kW (150 h.p.).
Transmission: Mechanical.
Max. Speed: 70 m.p.h.

DMBC	20.45 x 2.82 m	37.5 tonnes	18/16	
DMSL	20.45 x 2.82 m	38.5 tonnes	–/68	
51073	DMBC	Mid-Norfolk Railway		GRCW 1959
51074	DMBC	Swindon & Cricklade Railway		GRCW 1959
51104	DMSL	Swindon & Cricklade Railway		GRCW 1959

CLASS 120   SWINDON CROSS-COUNTRY UNITS

Built: 1958. Normal formation: DMBC–TSLRB–DMSL.
Max. Speed: 70 m.p.h.

TSLRB	20.45 x 2.82 m	31.5 tonnes	–/60	
59276	TSLRB	Great Central Railway		Swindon 1958

CLASS 121   PRESSED STEEL SINGLE UNITS & DRIVING TRAILERS

Built: 1960–61. Non-gangwayed single cars with two driving cabs plus driving trailers used for augmentation. The driving trailers were latterly fitted with gangways for coupling to power cars of other classes.
Engines: Two Leyland of 112 kW (150 h.p.).
Transmission: Mechanical.
Max. Speed: 70 m.p.h.

DMBS	20.45 x 2.82 m	38 tonnes	–/65
DTS	20.45 x 2.82 m	30 tonnes	–/89 (originally –/91)

55023	DMBS	Chinnor & Princes Risborough Railway	PS 1960
55026–977824	DMBS	Swansea Vale Railway	PS 1960
55032–977842	DMBS	The Railway Age, Crewe	PS 1960
55033–977826	DMBS	Colne Valley Railway	PS 1960
55034–977828	DMBS	Tyseley Locomotive Works, Birmingham	PS 1961
56285–54285–977486 h	DTS	Northamptonshire Ironstone Railway	PS 1961
56287–54287 h	DTS	Mangapps Farm Railway Museum	PS 1961
56289–54289 h	DTS	Battlefield Railway	PS 1961

CLASS 122   GRCW SINGLE UNITS

Built: 1958. Non-gangwayed single cars with two driving cabs.
Engines: Two AEC 220 of 112 kW (150 h.p.).
Transmission: Mechanical.
Max. Speed: 70 m.p.h.

DMBS	20.45 x 2.82 m	36.5 tonnes	–/65

55000	DMBS	South Devon Railway	GRCW 1958
55001-DB975023	DMBS	Northampton & Lamport Railway	GRCW 1958
55003	DMBS	Watercress Line	GRCW 1958
55005	DMBS	Battlefield Railway	GRCW 1958
55006	DMBS	Mid-Norfolk Railway	GRCW 1958
55009	DMBS	Mid-Norfolk Railway	GRCW 1958

CLASS 126   SWINDON INTER-CITY UNITS

Built: 1956–59. Various formations.
Engines: Two AEC 220 of 112 kW (150 h.p.).
Transmission: Mechanical.
Max. Speed: 70 m.p.h.

DMBSL	19.66 x 2.82 m	38.5 tonnes	–/52
TSK	19.66 x 2.82 m	32.3 tonnes	–/56 (originally TCK 18/32)
TFKRB	19.66 x 2.82 m	34 tonnes	18/12
DMSL	19.66 x 2.82 m	38.5 tonnes	–/64

BR	*Present*			
51017		DMSL	Bo'ness & Kinneil Railway	Swindon 1959
51043		DMBSL	Bo'ness & Kinneil Railway	Swindon 1959
59404		TSK	Bo'ness & Kinneil Railway	Swindon 1959
79091	91	DMBSL	Lamco, Nimba, Liberia	Swindon 1957
79093	93	DMBSL	Lamco, Nimba, Liberia	Swindon 1957
79094	94	DMBSL	Lamco, Nimba, Liberia	Swindon 1957
79096 h	96	DMBSL	Lamco, Nimba, Liberia	Swindon 1956
79097	97	DMBSL	Lamco, Nimba, Liberia	Swindon 1956
79443		TFKRB	Bo'ness & Kinneil Railway	Swindon 1957

Note: 51017 and 51043 are currently under restoration at the Lancastrian Carriage & Wagon Company, Heysham

CLASS 127   DERBY SUBURBAN QUAD UNITS

Built: 1959. Non-gangwayed. Normal formation: DMBS–TSL–TS–DMBS. Some DMBS rebuilt as DMPMV Normal formation: DMPMV(A)-DMPMV(B).

Engines: Two Rolls-Royce C8 of 177 kW (238 h.p.).

Transmission: Hydraulic.
Max. Speed: 70 m.p.h.

DMBS	20.45 x 2.82 m	40.6 tonnes	–/76
DMPMV (A)	20.45 x 2.82 m	40 tonnes	
DMPMV (B)	20.45 x 2.82 m	40 tonnes	
TSL	20.45 x 2.82 m	30.5 tonnes	–/86

51592	DMBS	South Devon Railway	Derby 1959
51604	DMBS	South Devon Railway	Derby 1959

51616	DMBS	Great Central Railway	Derby 1959
51618	DMBS	Llangollen Railway	Derby 1959
51622	DMBS	Great Central Railway	Derby 1959
51591–55966	DMPMV(A)	Midland Railway Centre	Derby 1959
51610–55967	DMPMV(B)	Rogart Station	Derby 1959
51625–55976	DMPMV(A)	Midland Railway Centre	Derby 1959
59603	TSL	Chasewater Light Railway	Derby 1959
59609	TSL	Midland Railway Centre	Derby 1959

UNCLASSIFIED   DERBY LIGHTWEIGHT TWIN UNIT

Built: 1955. Normal formation. DMBS–DTCL.
Engines: Two BUT (AEC) of 112 kW (150 h.p.).
Transmission: Mechanical.
Max. Speed: 70 m.p.h.

| DMBS | 17.53 x 2.82 m | 27.4 tonnes | –/61 |
| DTCL | 17.53 x 2.82 m | 21.3 tonnes | 9/53 |

| 79018–DB 975007 | DMBS | Midland Railway Centre | Derby 1955 |
| 79612–DB 975008 | DTCL | Midland Railway Centre | Derby 1955 |

UNCLASSIFIED   DERBY LIGHTWEIGHT SINGLE UNITS

Built: 1956. Non-gangwayed single cars with two driving cabs.
Engines: Two AEC of 112 kW (150 h.p.).
Transmission: Mechanical.
Max. Speed: 70 m.p.h.

| DMBS | 17.53 x 2.82 m | 27 tonnes | –/52 |

| 79900–DB975010 | DMBS | Midland Railway Centre | Derby 1956 |

6.2.3. DIESEL RAILBUSES

Note: All vehicles in this section are four-wheeled.

UNCLASSIFIED   WAGGON UND MASCHINENBAU

Built: 1958. 5 built.
Engine: Buessing of 112 kW (150 h.p.) at 1900 rpm. (§ AEC 220 of 112 kW (150h.p.))
Transmission: Mechanical.
Max. Speed: 70 m.p.h.

| DMS | 13.95 x 2.67 m | 15 tonnes | –/56 |

79960		North Norfolk Railway	WMD 1265/1958
79962		Keighley & Worth Valley Railway	WMD 1267/1958
79963		North Norfolk Railway	WMD 1268/1958
79964§		Keighley & Worth Valley Railway	WMD 1298/1958

UNCLASSIFIED   AC CARS

Built: 1958. 5 built.
Engine: AEC 220 of 112 kW (150 h.p.). (§ engine removed)
Transmission: Mechanical.
Max. Speed: 70 m.p.h.

| DMS | 11.33 x 2.82 m | 11 tonnes | –/46 |

| 79976§ | | Colne Valley Railway | AC 1958 |
| 79978 | | Colne Valley Railway | AC 1958 |

UNCLASSIFIED   BR DERBY/LEYLAND

Built: 1977.
Engine: Leyland 510 of 149 kW (200 h.p.). (Fitted 1979).
Transmission: Mechanical. Self Changing Gears.

Max. Speed: 75 m.p.h.		Air braked.	
DMS	12.32 x 2.50 m	16.67 tonnes	–/40
R1-RDB 975874		National Railway Museum	RTC Derby 1977

UNCLASSIFIED   BREL DERBY/LEYLAND/WICKHAM

Built: 1980.
Engine: Leyland 690 of 149 kW (200 h.p.).
Transmission: Mechanical. Self changing gears.
Max. Speed: 75 m.p.h.   Air braked.

DMS	15.30 x 2.50 m	19.8 tonnes	–/56
R3.01		Connecticut Trolley Museum, East Windsor, CT, USA	Wkm 1980

UNCLASSIFIED   BREL DERBY/LEYLAND

Built: 1981.
Engine: Leyland 690 of 149 kW (200 h.p.).
Transmission: Mechanical. Self Changing Gears SE4 epicyclic gearbox and cardan shafts to SCG RF28 final drive.
Max. Speed: 75 m.p.h.   Air braked.
Gauge: Built as 1435 mm but converted to 1600 mm when sold to Northern Ireland Railways.

DMS	15.30 x 2.50 m		19.96 tonnes	–/56
R3.03–RDB 977020	RB3	Downpatrick Steam Railway, NI		RTC Derby 1981

UNCLASSIFIED   BRE-LEYLAND

Built: 1984.
Engine: Leyland TL11 of 152 kW (205 h.p.)   **Transmission:** Mechanical.
Max. Speed: 75 m.p.h.   Air braked.

DMS	x 2.50 m	37.5 tonnes	–/64 (–/40§)
RE 002	'DENMARK'	Riverstown Mill Railway, Dundalk, Ireland	BRE-Leyland 1984
RE 004§	'USA'	Embsay & Bolton Abbey Railway	BRE-Leyland 1984

CLASS 140   DERBY/LEYLAND BUS PROTOTYPE TWIN RAILBUS

Built: 1981.
Engine: Leyland TL11 of 152 kW (205 h.p.).
Transmission: Mechanical. Self-Changing Gears 4-speed gearbox.
Max. Speed: 75 m.p.h.   Air braked.

DMSL	16.20 x 2.50 m	23.2 tonnes	–/50
DMS	16.20 x 2.50 m	23.0 tonnes	–/52
55500	DMS	Keith & Dufftown Railway	Derby 1981
55501	DMSL	Keith & Dufftown Railway	Derby 1981

CLASS 141   BREL/LEYLAND BUS TWIN RAILBUS

Built: 1983–84. Modified by Barclay 1988–89.
Engine: Leyland TL11 of 152 kW (205 h.p.)
Transmission: Hydraulic. Voith T211r.
Max. Speed: 75 m.p.h.   Air braked.

DMS	15.45 x 2.50 m	26.0 tonnes	–/50
DMSL	15.45 x 2.50 m	26.5 tonnes	–/44
55502	DMS	Iranian Islamic Republic Railways	BRE-Leyland 1983
55503	DMS	Weardale Railway	BRE-Leyland 1984
55507	DMS	Iranian Islamic Republic Railways	BRE-Leyland 1984
55508	DMS	Mid-Norfolk Railway	BRE-Leyland 1984
55509	DMS	Iranian Islamic Republic Railways	BRE-Leyland 1984
55510	DMS	Weardale Railway	BRE-Leyland 1984
55511	DMS	Iranian Islamic Republic Railways	BRE-Leyland 1984
55513	DMS	Midland Railway Centre	BRE-Leyland 1984

55514	DMS	Iranian Islamic Republic Railways	BRE-Leyland 1984
55515	DMS	Iranian Islamic Republic Railways	BRE-Leyland 1984
55516	DMS	Fire Service College, Moreton-in-Marsh	BRE-Leyland 1984
55517	DMS	Iranian Islamic Republic Railways	BRE-Leyland 1984
55519	DMS	Iranian Islamic Republic Railways	BRE-Leyland 1984
55520	DMS	Iranian Islamic Republic Railways	BRE-Leyland 1984
55522	DMSL	Iranian Islamic Republic Railways	BRE-Leyland 1983
55523	DMSL	Weardale Railway	BRE-Leyland 1984
55527	DMSL	Iranian Islamic Republic Railways	BRE-Leyland 1984
55528	DMSL	Mid-Norfolk Railway	BRE-Leyland 1984
55529	DMSL	Iranian Islamic Republic Railways	BRE-Leyland 1984
55530	DMSL	Weardale Railway	BRE-Leyland 1984
55531	DMSL	Iranian Islamic Republic Railways	BRE-Leyland 1984
55533	DMS	Midland Railway Centre	BRE-Leyland 1984
55534	DMSL	Iranian Islamic Republic Railways	BRE-Leyland 1984
55535	DMSL	Iranian Islamic Republic Railways	BRE-Leyland 1984
55536	DMSL	Fire Service College, Moreton-in-Marsh	BRE-Leyland 1984
55537	DMSL	Iranian Islamic Republic Railways	BRE-Leyland 1984
55539	DMSL	Iranian Islamic Republic Railways	BRE-Leyland 1984
55540	DMSL	Iranian Islamic Republic Railways	BRE-Leyland 1984

UNCLASSIFIED　　WICKHAM TRACK RECORDING CAR

Built: 1958 for BR Research. Later known as the Wickham Self-propelled Laboratory.
Engine:
Transmission: Mechanical.
Max. Speed:

999507-RDB 999507	East Lancashire Railway	Wkm 1958

6.2.4. DIESEL ELECTRIC MULTIPLE UNITS
CLASS 201　　HASTINGS LINE 6-CAR DIESEL-ELECTRIC UNIT

Built: 1957 by BR Eastleigh Works on frames constructed at Ashford. Special
narrow-bodied units built to the former loading gauge of the Tonbridge–Battle line.
Normal formation: DMBSO–TSOL–TSOL–TFK–TSOL–DMBSO.
Engines: English Electric 4SRKT of 370 kW (500 h.p.).
Transmission: Two EE 507 traction motors on the inner power car bogie.
Max. Speed: 75 m.p.h.

DMBSO	18.35 x 2.50 m	54 tonnes	–/22
TSOL	18.35 x 2.50 m	29 tonnes	–/52
TFK	18.36 x 2.50 m	30 tonnes	42/–

60000	"Hastings"	DMBSO	St. Leonards Railway Engineering	Eastleigh 1957
60001		DMBSO	St. Leonards Railway Engineering	Eastleigh 1957
60500		TSOL	St. Leonards Railway Engineering	Eastleigh 1957
60501		TSOL	St. Leonards Railway Engineering	Eastleigh 1957
60502		TSOL	St. Leonards Railway Engineering	Eastleigh 1957
60700		TFK	St. Leonards Railway Engineering	Eastleigh 1957

CLASS 202　　HASTINGS LINE 6-CAR DIESEL-ELECTRIC UNITS

Built: 1957–58 by BR Eastleigh Works on frames constructed at Ashford. Special
narrow-bodied units built to the former loading gauge of the Tonbridge–Battle line.
Normal formation: DMBSO–TSOL–TSOL (or TRB)–TFK–TSOL–DMBSO.
Engines: English Electric 4SRKT of 370 kW (500 h.p.).
Transmission: Two EE 507 traction motors on the inner power car bogie.
Max. Speed: 75 m.p.h.

DMBSO	20.34 x 2.50 m	55 tonnes	–/30
TSOL	20.34 x 2.50 m	29 tonnes	–/60
TFK	20.34 x 2.50 m	31 tonnes	48/–
TRB	20.34 x 2.50 m	34 tonnes	–/21

Note: 60755 was converted to the Southern Region General Manager's saloon in 1970.

60016	"Mountfield"	DMBSO	St. Leonards Railway Engineering	Eastleigh	1957
60018	"60118"	DMBSO	St. Leonards Railway Engineering	Eastleigh	1957
60019		DMBSO	St. Leonards Railway Engineering	Eastleigh	1957
60527		TSOL	St. Leonards Railway Engineering	Eastleigh	1957
60528		TSOL	St. Leonards Railway Engineering	Eastleigh	1957
60529		TSOL	St. Leonards Railway Engineering	Eastleigh	1957
60708		TFK	St. Leonards Railway Engineering	Eastleigh	1957
60709		TFK	St. Leonards Railway Engineering	Eastleigh	1957
60750–RDB 975386		TRB	St. Leonards Railway Engineering	Eastleigh	1958
60755–RDB 975025		TRB	Venice-Simplon-Orient Express	Eastleigh	1958

CLASS 205   "HAMPSHIRE" 3-CAR DIESEL-ELECTRIC UNITS

Built: 1958–59 by BR Eastleigh Works on frames constructed at Ashford. Non-gangwayed.
Normal formation: DMBSO–TSO–DTCsoL.
Engines: English Electric 4SRKT of 370 kW (500 h.p.).
Transmission: Two EE 507 traction motors on the inner power car bogie.
Max. Speed: 75 m.p.h.

DMBSO	20.34 x 2.82 m	56 tonnes	–/52
TSO	20.28 x 2.82 m	30 tonnes	–/104
DTCsoL	20.34 x 2.82 m	32 tonnes	19/50

60122	DMBSO	St. Leonards Railway Engineering	Eastleigh	1959
60661	TSO	Hampshire & Sussex UPS, Selhurst	Eastleigh	1959
60668	TSO	St. Leonards Railway Engineering	Eastleigh	1959
60669	TSO	Hampshire & Sussex UPS, Selhurst	Eastleigh	1959
60820	DTCsoL	St. Leonards Railway Engineering	Eastleigh	1958
60822	DTCsoL	Hampshire & Sussex UPS, Selhurst	Eastleigh	1959

CLASS 207   "OXTED" 3-CAR DIESEL-ELECTRIC UNITS

Built: 1962 by BR Eastleigh Works on frames constructed at Ashford. Reduced body width
to allow operation through Somerhill Tunnel. Non-gangwayed.
Normal formation: DMBSO–TCsoL–DTSO.
Engines: English Electric 4SRKT of 370 kW (500 h.p.).
Transmission: Two EE 507 traction motors on the inner power car bogie.
Max. Speed: 75 m.p.h.

DMBSO	20.34 x 2.74 m	56 tonnes	–/42
TCsoL	20.34 x 2.74 m	31 tonnes	24/42

60138–977907	DMBSO	St. Leonards Railway Engineering	Eastleigh	1962
60616	TCsoL	Hampshire & Sussex UPS, Selhurst	Eastleigh	1962

CLASS 210
DERBY PROTOTYPE 3-CAR (4-CAR*) DIESEL-ELECTRIC UNITS

Built: 1981 by BR Derby Works.
Normal formation: DMSO–TSO–DTSO (*DMBSO–TSO–TSOL–DTSO).
Engines: Ruston-Paxman 6RP200 of 840 kW (*MTU 12V396TC11 of 850 kW).
Transmission:
Max. Speed: 75 m.p.h.

DMSO	20.52 x 2.82 m	62 tonnes	–/45
DMBSO	20.52 x 2.82 m	62 tonnes	–/28
DTSO	20.52 x 2.82 m	29 tonnes	–/74

53000–60200–977649	DMSO	Coventry Railway Centre	Derby	1981
53001–60201–977650*	DMBSO	Coventry Railway Centre	Derby	1981
54000–60300–67300*	DTSO	Coventry Railway Centre	Derby	1981
54001–60301–67301	DTSO	Coventry Railway Centre	Derby	1981

Note: 53000 and 53001 are stored at Alstom, Eastleigh Works.

6.3. TROLLEYS

Note: These are small four-wheeled vehicles normally used for the transportation of railway personnel or track inspection.

6.3.1. BRITISH RAILWAYS TROLLEYS

INSPECTION TROLLEY BAGULEY-DREWRY

Built: 1950. Two built for Manchester–Sheffield/Wath line. Later transferred to the Great Eastern section of the Eastern Region.
Engine: **Transmission:** Mechanical **Weight:**

998901	Middleton Railway	BD 2268/1950

PERSONNEL CARRIER PERMAQUIP

Built: 1985–86. 11 built. DX 68800–04 used on London Midland Region, DX 68805–08 used on Southern Region. Two remain in use with railway maintenance contractors (not listed here).
Engine: **Transmission:** Mechanical.
Weight: **Gauge:** Standard (1'11½"*).

DX 68800	Wooler Railway Collection	Permaquip 001/1985
DX 68801	Telford Steam Railway	Permaquip 002/1985
DX 68802–RTU 8802	Wooler Railway Collection	Permaquip 003/1985
DX 68803–RTU 8803	Wooler Railway Collection	Permaquip 004/1985
DX 68804*	Vale of Rheidol Railway	Permaquip 005/1985
DX 68805	Wyvern Rail, Wirksworth	Permaquip 006/1986
DX 68806	Wyvern Rail, Wirksworth	Permaquip 007/1986
DX 68807	Nottingham Heritage Centre	Permaquip 008/1986
DX 68808	Wyvern Rail, Wirksworth	Permaquip 009/1986

PERSONNEL CARRIER (TYPE 18) WICKHAM

Built: 1947–75. 16 built for BR. Used on Southern and Scottish Regions. Eight have now been preserved whist five others are in use with railway maintenance contractors (not listed here).
Engine: Perkins (Ford*). **Transmission:** Mechanical **Weight:**

DS 3057–PWM 5643*	Dean Forest Railway	Wkm 4254/1947
970213	Bo'ness & Kinneil Railway	Wkm 6049/1952
DB 965330–RMT 68/1–DX 68002	Scottish Industrial Railway Centre	Wkm 10180/1968
DB 965331–RMT 68/2–DX 68003	Scottish Industrial Railway Centre	Wkm 10179/1968
DB 965990–DX 68073	Bluebell Railway	Wkm 10705/1974
DB 965991–DX 68075	Watercress Line	Wkm 10707/1974
DB 965992–DX 68078	Bluebell Railway	Wkm 10708/1974
DB 966031–DX 68082	Watercress Line	Wkm 10839/1974

PERSONNEL CARRIER (TYPE 27) WICKHAM

Built: 1949–72. 73 built for BR. Used on Eastern, London Midland, Southern & Western regions.
Engine: Ford. **Transmission:** Mechanical **Weight:**

PWM2830–B193W	East Anglian Railway Museum	Wkm 5008/1949
PWM2831–B194W–DX 68004	Exeter & Teign Valley Railway	Wkm 5009/1949
PWM3763–B2W–DS3319–PWM5647	Watercress Line	Wkm 6642/1953
PWM3764–B3W–TR38–DX 68065	Oswestry Cycle & Railway Museum	Wkm 6643/1953
PWM3766–B5W–DS3320	Isle of Wight Steam Railway	Wkm 6645/1953
PWM3767–B6W–DS3321–PWM5648	South Devon Railway	Wkm 6646/1953
PWM3769–B8W	Avon Valley Railway	Wkm 6648/1953
PWM3773–B12W	South Devon Railway	Wkm 6652/1953
PWM3776–B15W–DS3324	Alderney Railway	Wkm 6655/1953
PWM3951–B25W–TR16–DX 68054	Lavender Line, Isfield	Wkm 6936/1955
PWM3954–B28W	Alderney Railway	Wkm 6939/1955
PWM3956–B30W	Rowden Mill Station, Herefordshire	Wkm 6941/1955
PWM3957–B31W	Epping Forest Railway	Wkm 6942/1955
PWM3959–B33W–DS3327	Bluebell Railway	Wkm 6944/1955

PWM3962–B36W		Pontypool & Blaenavon Railway	Wkm 6947/1955
PWM4301–B40W–TR18–DX 68055		Battlefield Railway	Wkm 7504/1956
PWM4302–B41W–TR19–DX 68056		Battlefield Railway	Wkm 7505/1956
PWM4303–B42W–DX 68007		Didcot Railway Centre	Wkm 7506/1956
PWM4305–B44W–DX 68009		Didcot Railway Centre	Wkm 7508/1956
PWM4306–B45W–TR39–DX 68066		Bluebell Railway	Wkm 7509/1956
PWM4311–B50W–TR21–DX 68058		Rippingale Station, Lincolnshire	Wkm 7514/1956
PWM4312–B51W–TR22–DX 68059		Watercress Line	Wkm 7515/1956
PWM4313–B52W–TR23–DX 68060		Gloucestershire-Warwickshire Railway	Wkm 7516/1956
PWM4314–B53W–TR40–DX 68067		Fencote Station, Herefordshire	Wkm 7517/1956
PWM4316–B55W		Cholsey & Wallingford Railway	Wkm 7519/1956
TS52P–TR34–DX 68062		Midland Railway Centre	Wkm 8272/1959
DB 965949–68/005–DX 68005		Elsecar Heritage Centre	Wkm 10645/1972

Note: PWM 3764, PWM 3954, PWM 3957, PWM 4301 and PWM 4302 are currently off-site receiving attention.

6.3.2. MILITARY TROLLEYS
PERSONNEL CARRIER (TYPE 27)   WICKHAM

Built: 1954–60. 22 built for military use. 13 have now been preserved whilst three others are in use with railway maintenance contractors (not listed here)

Engine: Ford.   **Transmission:** Mechanical   **Weight:**

9020			Wkm 8084/1958
9021	"6"	Severn Valley Railway	Wkm 8085/1958
9022	"7"	Alderney Railway	Wkm 8086/1958
9024	"7090"	Chinnor & Princes Risborough Railway	Wkm 7090/1955
9025	"1 GEORGE"	Alderney Railway	Wkm 7091/1955
9029	"8 SHIRLEY"	Alderney Railway	Wkm 7095/1955
9031		Swindon & Cricklade Railway	Wkm 8089/1958
9035		Museum of Army Transport, Beverley	Wkm 8195/1958
9037		Buckinghamshire Railway Centre	Wkm 8197/1958
9038		South Devon Railway	Wkm 8198/1958
9043		Kent & East Sussex Railway	Wkm 6965/1958
9044		Kent & East Sussex Railway	Wkm 7438/1958
9045	"WILLY SKUNK"	Cholsey & Wallingford Railway	Wkm 8774/1958

INSPECTION TROLLEY (TYPE 40)   WICKHAM

Built: 1955–57. Four were built for military use. One has been preserved whilst one remains in military service.

Engine: Ford.   **Transmission:** Mechanical   **Weight:**

9040	Buckinghamshire Railway Centre	Wkm 6963/1955

PERSONNEL CARRIER   BAGULEY

Built: 1959. Two personnel carriers were built for the War Department in 1959. Both were converted to fire-fighting trailers in 1981 (1979*) at Bromley. 9112 was subsequently used as a mobile bird-watching platform. It has been restored as a powered personnel carrier.
* Rebuilt to 2' gauge and no longer powered.

Engine: Perkins of 26 kW (35 h.p.).   **Transmission:** Mechanical   **Weight:**

9112	Fawley Hill Railway	Bg 3538/1959
9113*	Leighton Buzzard Narrow Gauge Railway	Bg 3539/1959

PERSONNEL CARRIER   BAGULEY-DREWRY

Built: 1975–76. 14 of these were built for the Army Department of the Ministry of Defence. Five have now been preserved whist several others remain in military service.

Engine: Perkins of 50 kW (68 h.p.).   **Transmission:** Mechanical   **Weight:** 6.25 tonnes.

9117	East Anglian Railway Museum	BD 3706/1975
9118	Midland Railway Centre	BD 3707/1975
9119	Gloucestershire-Warwickshire Railway	BD 3708/1975
9124	Beacon Farm, Maxstoke	BD 3713/1975
9127	Gloucestershire-Warwickshire Railway	BD 3743/1975

7. ELECTRIC MULTIPLE UNITS
Type Codes
For type codes see the DMU section (section 6).

7.1. SOUTHERN RAILWAY EMU STOCK
CLASS 487   WATERLOO & CITY LINE UNITS
Built: 1940. No permanent formations.
System: 630 V d.c. third rail.
Traction Motors: Two EE 500 of 140 kW (185 h.p.).   **Max. Speed:** 35 m.p.h.

DMBTO   14.33 x 2.64 m   29 tons   –/40

BR	SR				
S 61 S	61	DMBTO		National Railway Museum	EE 1940

1285 CLASS (later 3 Sub)   SUBURBAN UNITS
Built: 1925. Normal formation. DMBT–TT–DMBT.
System: 630 V d.c. third rail.
Traction Motors: Two MV 167 kW (225 h.p.).   **Max. Speed:** 75 m.p.h.

DMBT   18.90 x 2.44 m   39 tons   –/70

BR	SR				
S 8143 S	8143	DMBT	(Ex. unit 1293 later 4308)	National Railway Museum	MC 1925

4 Cor   "NELSONS"   PORTSMOUTH EXPRESS STOCK
Built: 1937–38. Normal formation. DMBTO–TTK–TCK–DMBTO.
System: 630 V d.c. third rail.
Traction Motors: Two MV 167 kW (225 h.p.) per power car. **Max. Speed:** 75 m.p.h.

DMBTO   19.54 x 2.88 m   46.5 tons   –/52
TTK   19.54 x 2.85 m   32.65 tons   –/68
TCK   19.54 x 2.85 m   32.6 tons   30/24

BR	SR				
S 10096 S	10096	TTK	(Ex. unit 3142)	St. Leonards Railway Engineering	Eastleigh 1937
S 11161 S	11161	DMBTO	(Ex. unit 3142)	St. Leonards Railway Engineering	Eastleigh 1937
S 11179 S	11179	DMBTO	(Ex. unit 3131)	National Railway Museum	Eastleigh 1937
S 11187 S	11187	DMBTO	(Ex. unit 3135)	St. Leonards Railway Engineering	Eastleigh 1937
S 11201 S	11201	DMBTO	(Ex. unit 3142)	St. Leonards Railway Engineering	Eastleigh 1937
S 11825 S	11825	TCK	(Ex. unit 3142)	St. Leonards Railway Engineering	Eastleigh 1937

Notes: S 11161 S was originally in unit 3065 and S11825S in unit 3135.

4 Sub (later Class 405)   SUBURBAN UNITS
Built: 1941–51. Normal formation DMBTO–TT–TTO–DMBTO.
System: 630 V d.c. third rail.
Traction Motors: Two EE507 of 185 kW (250 h.p.).   **Max. Speed:** 75 m.p.h.

DMBTO   19.05 x 2.82 m   42 tons   –/82
TT   18.90 x 2.82 m   27 tons   –/120
TTO   18.90 x 2.82 m   26 tons   –/102

BR	SR				
S 10239 S	10239	TT	(Ex. unit 4732)	Coventry Railway Centre	Eastleigh 1947
S 12354 S		TTO	(Ex. unit 4732)	Coventry Railway Centre	Eastleigh 1948
S 12795 S		DMBTO	(Ex. unit 4732)	Coventry Railway Centre	Eastleigh 1951
S 12796 S		DMBTO	(Ex. unit 4732)	Coventry Railway Centre	Eastleigh 1951

Note: S 10239 S was originally in unit 4413 and S 12354 S in unit 4381.

2 Bil　　　　　　　　　　　　SEMI-FAST UNITS

Built: 1937. Normal formation DMBTK–DTCK.
System: 630 V d.c. third rail.
Traction Motors: Two EE of 205 kW (275 h.p.).　　**Max. Speed:** 75 m.p.h.

DMBTK	19.24 x 2.85 m	43.5 tons	–/52
DTCK	19.24 x 2.85 m	31.25 tons	24/30

BR	SR					
S 10656 S	10656	DMBTK	(Ex. unit 1890–2090)	St. Leonards Railway Engineering (N)	Eastleigh 1937
S 12123 S	12123	DTCK	(Ex. unit 1890–2090)	St. Leonards Railway Engineering (N)	Eastleigh 1937

4 Buf　　　PORTSMOUTH EXPRESS STOCK

Built: 1937. Normal formation. DMBTO–TCK–TRBT–DMBTO.
System: 630 V d.c. third rail.　　**Max. Speed:** 75 m.p.h.

TRBT	19.60 x 2.84 m	37 tons	–/26

BR	SR				
S 12529 S	12529	TRBT	(Ex. unit 3084)	Nene Valley Railway (N)	Eastleigh 1938

4 DD　　　DOUBLE-DECK SUBURBAN UNITS

Built: 1949. Normal formation DMBT–TT–TT–DMBT.
System: 630 V d.c. third rail.
Traction Motors: Two EE of 185 kW (250 h.p.).　　**Max. Speed:** 75 m.p.h.

DMBT	19.24 x 2.85 m	39 tons	–/121

S 13003 S	DMBT	(Ex unit 4002 –4902)	Hope Farm, Sellindge	Lancing 1949
S 13004 S	DMBT	(Ex unit 4002 –4902)	Northamptonshire Ironstone Railway	Lancing 1949

4 EPB (later Class 415)　　SUBURBAN UNITS

Built: 1951–57. Normal formation DMBTO–TT–TTO–DMBTO.
System: 630 V d.c. third rail.
Traction Motors: Two EE507 of 185 kW (250 h.p.).　　**Max. Speed:** 75 m.p.h.

DMBTO	19.05 x 2.82 m	42 tons	–/82
TTO	18.90 x 2.82 m	26 tons	–/102

S 14351 S	DMBTO	(Ex unit 5176)	Northamptonshire Ironstone Railway	Eastleigh 1955
S 15354 S	TTO	(Ex unit 5176)	Coventry Railway Centre	Eastleigh 1955
S 15396 S	TTO	(Ex unit 5176)	Northamptonshire Ironstone Railway	Eastleigh 1956
S 14352 S	DMBTO	(Ex unit 5176)	Northamptonshire Ironstone Railway	Eastleigh 1955

Note: 15396 was originally in unit 5208.

2 EPB (later Class 416)　　SUBURBAN UNITS

Built: 1959. Normal formation DMBSO–DTSO.
System: 630 V d.c. third rail.
Traction Motors: Two EE of 185 kW (250 h.p.).　　**Max. Speed:** 75 m.p.h.

DMBSO	19.05 x 2.82 m	40 tons	–/82
DTSO	18.90 x 2.82 m	30 tons	–/92

S 14573 S	DMBSO	(Ex unit 5667–6307)	Coventry Railway Centre	Eastleigh 1959
S 16117 S	DTSO	(Ex unit 5667–6307)	Coventry Railway Centre	Eastleigh 1959

Note: In addition, the underframes of six other Southern railway EMU cars converted to crane match wagons (welded rail wagon*) have also been preserved.

BR Departmental	BR	SR		
DS 70277	S 12275 S	12275	(ex 6 Pan TSK ex unit 3036)	Spa Valley Railway
DS 70278	S 10027 S	10027	(ex 6 Pan TSK ex unit 3024)	Chasewater Light Railway
DS 70279	S 12270 S	12270	(ex 6 Pan TFK ex unit 3031)	Keighley & Worth Valley Railway
DS 70280	S 11861 S	11861	(ex 4 Cor TCK ex unit 3158)	Midland Railway Centre
DS 70281	S 12235 S	12235	(ex 4 Cor TFK ex unit 3065)	Eden Valley Railway
DB 975514-083656*	S 10050 S	10050	(ex 6 Pan TTK ex unit 3047)	Swanage Railway

Note: S 10050 S was originally in unit 3035 and S 12235 S in unit 3062.

7.2. PULLMAN CAR COMPANY EMU STOCK
GENERAL

Pullman cars owned by the Pullman Car Company operated as parts of EMU formations on the Southern Railway (later BR Southern Region). In addition the three Brighton Belle EMU sets were composed entirely of Pullman vehicles.

All vehicles are used as hauled stock except * – static exhibits.

6 Pul

Built: 1932. Six car sets incorporating one Pullman kitchen composite.
Normal formation: DMBTO–TTK–TCK–TPCK–TCK–DMBTO.

TPCK   20.40 x 2.77 m   43 tons   12/16

RUTH	S 264 S	TPCK	(Ex. unit 2017–3042)	Venice–Simplon Orient Express	MC 1932
BERTHA	S 278 S	TPCK	(Ex. unit 2012–3001)	Swanage Railway	MC 1932

5 Bel   BRIGHTON BELLE UNITS

Built: 1932. Five car all pullman sets.
System: 630 V d.c. Third rail.
Formation: DMPBT–TPT–TPKF–TPKF–DMPBT.
Traction Motors: Four BTH of 167 kW (225 hp).

TPKF	20.40 x 2.77 m	42 tons	20/–
TPT	20.40 x 2.77 m	41 tons	–/56
DMPBT	20.62 x 2.77 m	62 tons	–/48

HAZEL *	S279S	TPKF	(Ex. unit 2051–3051)	Black Bull, Moulton, N. Yorks	MC 1932
AUDREY	S280S	TPKF	(Ex. unit 2052–3052)	Venice–Simplon Orient Express	MC 1932
GWEN	S281S	TPKF	(Ex. unit 2053–3053)	Venice–Simplon Orient Express	MC 1932
DORIS *	S282S	TPKF	(Ex. unit 2051–3051)	CIL Storefitters, Finsbury Park	MC 1932
MONA	S283S	TPKF	(Ex. unit 2053–3053)	Venice–Simplon Orient Express	MC 1932
VERA	S284S	TPKF	(Ex. unit 2052–3052)	Venice–Simplon Orient Express	MC 1932
CAR No. 85	S285S	TPT	(Ex. unit 2053–3053)	Venice–Simplon Orient Express	MC 1932
CAR No. 86	S286S	TPT	(Ex. unit 2051–3051)	Venice–Simplon Orient Express	MC 1932
CAR No. 87	S287S	TPT	(Ex. unit 2052–3052)	Keith & Dufftown Railway	MC 1932
CAR No. 88	S288S	DMPBT	(Ex. unit 2051–3051)	Venice–Simplon Orient Express	MC 1932
CAR No. 89*	S289S	DMPBT	(Ex. unit 2051–3051)	Little Mill Inn, Rowarth, Derbys.	MC 1932
CAR No. 91	S291S	DMPBT	(Ex. unit 2052–3052)	Keith & Dufftown Railway	MC 1932
CAR No. 92	S292S	DMPBT	(Ex. unit 2053–3053)	Venice–Simplon Orient Express	MC 1932
CAR No. 93	S293S	DMPBT	(Ex. unit 2053–3053)	Venice–Simplon Orient Express	MC 1932

Note: CAR No. 89 is now named DERBYSHIRE BELLE.

7.3. LMS & CONSTITUENTS EMU STOCK

LNWR — EUSTON–WATFORD STOCK

Built: 1915. Oerlikon design. Normal formation: DMBTO–TTO–DTTO.
System: 630 V d.c. third rail. Used on Euston–Watford line.
Traction Motors: Four Oerlikon 179 kW (240 h.p.).
Max. Speed:

DMBTO   17.60 x 2.73 m   54.75 tonnes.   –/48

BR	LMS			
M 28249 M	28249	DMBTO	National Railway Museum	MC 1915

CLASS 502 — LIVERPOOL–SOUTHPORT STOCK

Built: 1939. Normal formation: DMBTO–TTO–DTTO (originally DTCO).
System: 630 V d.c. third rail.
Traction Motors: Four EE 175 kW.   **Max. Speed:** 65 m.p.h.

DMBTO   20.26 x 2.90 m   42.5 tonnes.   –/88
DTTO   20.26 x 2.90 m   25.5 tonnes.   –/79 (built as DTCO 53/25)

BR	LMS			
M 28361 M	28361	DMBTO	MoD BAD Kineton (N)	Derby 1939
M 29896 M	29896	DTTO	MoD BAD Kineton (N)	Derby 1939

CLASS 503 — MERSEY–WIRRAL STOCK

Built: 1938. Normal formation: DMBTO–TTO (originally TCO)–DTTO.
System: 630 V d.c. third rail.
Traction Motors: 4 BTH 100 kW.   **Max. Speed:** 65 m.p.h.

DMBTO   17.68 x 2.77 m   36.5 tonnes.   –/56
TTO   17.07 x 2.77 m   20.5 tonnes.   –/58 (built as TCO 40/19)
DTTO   17.68 x 2.77 m   21.5 tonnes.   –/66

BR	LMS			
M 28690 M	28690	DMBTO	Coventry Railway Centre	Derby 1938
M 29720 M	29720	TTO	Coventry Railway Centre	Derby 1938
M 29289 M	29289	DTTO	Woodside Museum, Birkenhead	Derby 1938

MSJ&A STOCK

Built: 1931. Normal formation: DMBT–TC–DTT.
System: 1500 V d.c. overhead. Used on Manchester South Junction and Altrincham line until it was converted to 25 kV a.c. This line is now part of the Manchester Metrolink system.
Traction Motors: **Max. Speed:** 65 m.p.h.

TC   17.60 x 2.85 m   31 tonnes.   24/72

BR	LMS	MSJ&A			
M 29663 M	29663	114	TC	Midland Railway Centre	MC 1931
M 29666 M	29666	117	TC	Midland Railway Centre	MC 1931
M 29670 M	29670	121	TC	Midland Railway Centre	MC 1931

7.4. LNER & CONSTITUENTS EMU STOCK

NORTH EASTERN RAILWAY   DMLV

Built: 1904. Driving motor luggage van for North Tyneside line. After withdrawal from capital stock, this vehicle was used as a rail de-icing car.
System: 675 V d.c. third rail.
Traction Motors: **Max. Speed:**

DMLV   17.40 x 2.77 m   46.5 tonnes

BR	LNER	NER			
DE 900730	23267	3267	DMLV	Stephenson Railway Museum (N)	MC 1904

GRIMSBY & IMMINGHAM LIGHT RAILWAY   A1-1A

Built: 1915 by GCR Dukinfield.
Type: Single deck tram.
Seats: 64 + 8 tip-up.
Bogies: Brush.
Motors: 2 x 25 hp Dick Kerr DK9 of 18 kW.

14	Crich Tramway Village	GCR Dukinfield 1914

7.5. BR EMU STOCK

BR EMU power cars were numbered in the 6XXXX series starting with 61000 whilst trailer cars were numbered in the 7XXXX series. This does not apply to the APT-P or the battery EMU.

CLASS 307   BR EASTLEIGH

Built: 1954–56 for Liverpool Street–Southend Victoria Services.
System: 1500 V d.c. overhead. Converted 1960–61 to 25 kV a.c. overhead.
Formation: DTBSO (originally DTS)–MSO–(originally MBS)–TSOL(originally TCOL)–DTCOL(originally DTSsoL).
Traction Motors: Four GEC WT344 of 130 kW.
Max. Speed: 75 m.p.h.

DTBSO	19.50 x 2.83 m	43 tonnes	–/66 (originally –/108)

75018–977018	DTBSO (Ex unit 118))	Barrow Hill Roundhouse	Eastleigh 1956

CLASS 310   BR DERBY

Built: 1965–67 for West Coast Main Line outer suburban services. Later used for LTS services.
System: 25 kV a.c. overhead.
Formation: DTSO–MBSO–TSO–DTCO.
Traction Motors: Four AEI of 165 kW.
Max. Speed: 75 m.p.h.

DTSO	19.86 x 2.82 m	37.3 tonnes	–/80
DTCO	19.86 x 2.82 m	34.4 tonnes	25/43

76161	DTSO	(Ex unit 077)	MoD RAF Caerwent, Monmouthshire	Derby 1966
76211	DTCO	(Ex unit 077)	MoD RAF Caerwent, Monmouthshire	Derby 1966

CLASS 311   CRAVENS

Built: 1967 for Glasgow "South Side electrification" extension to Gourock and Wemyss Bay.
System: 25 kV a.c. overhead.
Formation: DTSO(A)–MBSO–DTSO(B).
Traction Motors: Four AEI of 165 kW.
Max. Speed: 75 m.p.h.

MBSO	19.36 x 2.83 m	56.4 tonnes	–/70
DTSO(A)	19.50 x 2.83 m	34.4 tonnes	–/83
DTSO(B)	19.50 x 2.83 m	38.4 tonnes	–/83

62174–977845	MBSO	(Ex unit 103)	Summerlee Heritage Park, Coatbridge	Cravens 1967
76414–977844	DTSO(A)	(Ex unit 103)	Summerlee Heritage Park, Coatbridge	Cravens 1967
76433–977846	DTSO(B)	(Ex unit 103)	Summerlee Heritage Park, Coatbridge	Cravens 1967

CLASS 370
PROTOTYPE ADVANCED PASSENGER TRAIN (APT-P)

Built: 1978–80. Designed to run as pairs of six-car articulated units with two power cars in the middle, these electric trains featured active hydraulic tilt and proved to be a maintenance nightmare. The power cars were reasonably successful, and are partly the basis of the class 91 electric locomotive.
System: 25 kV a.c. overhead.
Normal Formation of Trailer Rake: DTSOL–TSOL–TSRB–TUOL–TFOL–TBFOL.
Formation of preserved set: DTSOL–TBFOL–M–TRSB–TBFOL–DTSOL.
Traction Motors: Four ASEA LJMA 410F body mounted.
Wheel Dia: 853 mm.
Max. Speed: 125 m.p.h.

DTSOL	21.44 x 2.72 m	33.7 tonnes	–/52
TBFOL	21.20 x 2.72 m	31.9 tonnes	25/–

TRSBL	21.20 x 2.72 m	26.75 tonnes	−/28
M	20.40 x 2.72 m	67.5 tonnes	

48103	DTSOL	The Railway Age, Crewe (N)	Derby 1978
48106	DTSOL	The Railway Age, Crewe (N)	Derby 1979
48602	TBFOL	The Railway Age, Crewe (N)	Derby 1978
48603	TBFOL	The Railway Age, Crewe (N)	Derby 1978
48404	TSRBL	The Railway Age, Crewe (N)	Derby 1979
49002	M	The Railway Age, Crewe (N)	Derby 1979
49006	M	MoD BAD Kineton (N)	Derby 1980

CLASS 411 (4 Cep)   BR EASTLEIGH

Built: 1956–63 for Kent Coast electrification.
System: 750 V d.c. third rail.
Original Formation: DMBSO–TSK–TCK–DMBSO.
Rebuilt Formation: DMSO–TSOL–TBCK–DMSO.
Traction Motors: Two EE507 of 185 kW.
Max. Speed: 90 m.p.h.

DMSO	20.34 x 2.82 m	49 tonnes	−/56 (built as DMBSO −/64)
TSOL	20.18 x 2.82 m	36 tonnes	−/64 (built as TSK −/64)
TBCK	20.18 x 2.82 m	34 tonnes	24/8 (built as TCK 24/24)

61383	DMSO	(Ex units 7150–1523)	Coventry Railway Centre	Eastleigh 1958
61390	DMSO	(Ex units 7003–1532)	Coventry Railway Centre	Eastleigh 1958
61742	DMSO	(Ex units 7178–1589)	Dartmoor Railways, Okehampton	Eastleigh 1960
61743	DMSO	(Ex units 7178–1589)	Dartmoor Railways, Okehampton	Eastleigh 1960
70035	TSOL	(Ex units 7103–1505)		Eastleigh 1956
70262	TSOL	(Ex units 7113–1524)	St. Leonards Railway Engineering	Eastleigh 1958
70284	TSOL	(Ex units 7135–1520)	Northamptonshire Ironstone Railway	Eastleigh 1959
70296	TSOL	(Ex units 7147–1559)	Northamptonshire Ironstone Railway	Eastleigh 1959
70302	TSOL	(Ex units 7153–1560)	Coventry Railway Centre	Eastleigh 1959
70345	TBCK	(Ex units 7153–1500)	Coventry Railway Centre	Eastleigh 1959
70346	TBCK	(Ex units 7003–1532)	Elletson Arms PH, Stake Pool, Lancs.	Eastleigh 1959
70510	TSOL	(Ex units 7161–1597)	Northamptonshire Ironstone Railway	Eastleigh 1960
70576	TBCK	(Ex units 7178–1589)	Snibston Discovery Park	Eastleigh 1960

Note: 70346 is now named "STAKE POOL BELLE".

CLASS 414 (2 Hap)   BR EASTLEIGH

Built: 1959 for the South-Eastern Division of the former BR Southern Region.
System: 750 V d.c. third rail.
Formation: DMBSO–DTCsoL.
Traction Motors: Two EE507 of 185 kW.
Max. Speed: 90 m.p.h.

DMBSO	20.44 x 2.82 m	42 tonnes	−/84
DTCsoL	20.44 x 2.82 m	32.5 tonnes	19/60

61287	DMBSO	(Ex units 6089-4311)	Coventry Railway Centre	Eastleigh 1959
75407	DTCsoL	(Ex units 6089-4311)	Coventry Railway Centre	Eastleigh 1959

CLASS 416 (2 EPB)   BR EASTLEIGH

Built: 1955–56. 65373 & 77558 were built for the South Eastern Division of BR Southern Region. 65321 & 77112 were originally used between Newcastle and South Shields but were transferred to join the rest of the class on the Southern Region when the South Tyneside line was de-electrified in 1963.
System: 750 V d.c. third rail.
Formation: DMBSO–DTSso.
Traction Motors: Two EE507 of 185 kW.
Max. Speed: 75 m.p.h.

DMBSO	20.44 x 2.82 m	42 tonnes	−/82
DTSso	20.44 x 2.82 m	30.5 tonnes	−/102

65321–977505	DMBSO	(Ex unit 5791–6291)	Coventry Railway Centre	Eastleigh	1955
65373	DMBSO	(Ex unit 5759–6259)	East Kent Light Railway	Eastleigh	1956
77112–977508	DTSso	(Ex unit 5793–6293)	Coventry Railway Centre	Eastleigh	1955
77558	DTSso	(Ex unit 5759–6259)	East Kent Light Railway	Eastleigh	1956

CLASS 419 (MLV)   BR EASTLEIGH

Built: 1959–61. Motor luggage vans for Kent Coast electrification. Fitted with batteries to allow operation on non-electrified lines.
System: 750 V d.c. third rail.
Traction Motors: Two EE507 of 185 kW.
Max. Speed: 90 m.p.h.
Also fitted with vacuum brakes for hauling parcels trains.

DMLV   20.45 x 2.82 m   45.5 tonnes

68001	East Kent Light Railway	Eastleigh 1959
68003	Eden Valley Railway	Eastleigh 1961
68004	Mid-Norfolk Railway	Eastleigh 1961
68005	Eden Valley Railway	Eastleigh 1961
68007	Coventry Railway Centre	Eastleigh 1961
68008	Coventry Railway Centre	Eastleigh 1961
68009	Colne Valley Railway	Eastleigh 1961
68010	Colne Valley Railway	Eastleigh 1961

CLASS 422 (4 Big)   BR YORK

Built: 1963–69 for the Central Division of BR Southern Region.
System: 750 V d.c. third rail.
Formation: DTCsoL–MBSO–TSRB–DTCsoL.
Traction Motors: Two EE507 of 185 kW.
Max. Speed: 90 m.p.h.

TSRB   20.18 x 2.82 m   35 tonnes   –/40

69302	TSRB	(Ex units 7032–1276–2251)	Abbey View Disabled Day Centre, Neath	York 1963
69304	TSRB	(Ex units 7034–1299–2260)	Northamptonshire Ironstone Railway	York 1963
69306	TSRB	(Ex units 7036–1282–2254)	Spa Valley Railway	York 1963
69307	TSRB	(Ex units 7037–1297–2256)	Widnes International Rail Depot	York 1963
69310	TSRB	(Ex units 7040–1290–2255)	Dartmoor Railways, Okehampton	York 1963
69313	TSRB	(Ex units 7043–1284–2253)	East Somerset Railway	York 1963
69316	TSRB	(Ex units 7046–1296–2258)	Waverley Route Heritage Association, Whitrope	York 1963
69318	TSRB	(Ex units 7048–1298–2259)	Colne Valley Railway	York 1963
69332	TSRB	(Ex units 7051–2203)	Dartmoor Railways, Okehampton	York 1969
69333	TSRB	(Ex units 7055–1802–2260)	Lavender Line, Isfield	York 1969
69334	TSRB	(Ex units 7056–2208)	East Somerset Railway	York 1969
69335	TSRB	(Ex units 7057–2209)	Wensleydale Railway, Leeming Bar	York 1969
69337	TSRB	(Ex units 7058–2210)	St. Leonards Railway Engineering	York 1969
69338	TSRB	(Ex units 7054–2206)	Station Restaurant, Gulf Corporation, Bahrain	York 1969
69339	TSRB	(Ex units 7053–2205)	Coventry Railway Centre	York 1969

CLASS 491 (4 TC)   BR YORK

Built: 1967. Unpowered units designed to work push-pull with Class 430 (4 Rep) tractor units and Class 33/1, 73 and 74 locomotives. Converted from locomotive hauled coaching stock built 1952–57 (original number in brackets).
System: 750 V d.c. third rail.
Formation: DTSO–TFK–TBSK–DTSO.
Max. Speed: 90 m.p.h.

DTSO	20.18 x 2.82 m	32 tonnes	–/64
TFK	20.18 x 2.82 m	33.5 tonnes	42/–
TBSK	20.18 x 2.82 m	35.5 tonnes	–/32

70812 (34987)	TBSK	(Ex unit 401)	Dartmoor Railways, Okehampton	MC 1957
70823 (34970)	TBSK	(Ex unit 412)	London Underground, West Ruislip Depot	MC 1957
70824 (34984)	TBSK	(Ex unit 413)	London Underground, West Ruislip Depot	MC 1957

70826	(34980)	TBSK	(Ex unit 415)	Dartmoor Railways, Okehampton	MC	1957
70855	(13018)	TFK	(Ex unit 412)	London Underground, West Ruislip Depot	Swindon	1952
70859	(13040)	TFK	(Ex unit 412)	Stravithie Station, Fife	Swindon	1952
70860	(13019)	TFK	(Ex unit 417)	Dartmoor Railways, Okehampton	Swindon	1952
71163	(13097)	TFK	(Ex unit 430)	London Underground, West Ruislip Depot	Swindon	1954
76297	(3938)	DTSO	(Ex unit 415)	London Underground, West Ruislip Depot	Eastleigh	1955
76298	(4004)	DTSO	(Ex unit 415)	London Underground, West Ruislip Depot	Eastleigh	1957
76301	(4375)	DTSO	(Ex unit 417)	Dartmoor Railways, Okehampton	Swindon	1957
76302	(4382)	DTSO	(Ex unit 417)	Dartmoor Railways, Okehampton	Swindon	1957
76322	(3936)	DTSO	(Ex unit 427)	London Underground, West Ruislip Depot	Eastleigh	1955
76324	(4009)	DTSO	(Ex unit 428)	London Underground, West Ruislip Depot	Eastleigh	1957

CLASS 501   BR EASTLEIGH

Built: 1957 for Euston–Watford and North London lines. Now used as hauled stock.
Normal Formation: DMBSO–TSO–DTBSO.
System: 630 V d.c. third rail.
Max. Speed: 60 m.p.h.

TSO	19.96 x 2.82 m	29.5 tonnes	–/92	
DTBSO	20.06 x 2.82 m	30.5 tonnes	–/74	

BR	AD			
70170	WGP 8808	TSO	Marchwood Military Railway	Eastleigh 1957
75186	WGP 8809	DTBSO	Marchwood Military Railway	Eastleigh 1957

CLASS 504   BR WOLVERTON

Built: 1959 for Manchester–Bury line.
Normal Formation: DMBSO–DTSO.
System: 1200 V d.c. protected side-contact third rail.
Max. Speed: 65 m.p.h.
Traction Motors: Four EE of 90 kW.

DMBSO	20.12 x 2.82 m	50 tonnes	–/84
DTSO	20.12 x 2.82 m	33 tonnes	–/94

65451	DMBSO	East Lancashire Railway	Wolverton 1959
77172	DTSO	East Lancashire Railway	Wolverton 1959

TRAMS   GRIMSBY & IMMINGHAM LIGHT RAILWAY

Built: 1925.(1927*). Single-deck trams built for Gateshead & District Tramways Company.
Sold to British Railways in 1951 for use on Grimsby & Immingham Light Railway.
Motors: 2 x Dick Kerr 31A (25A*) of 18 kW (25 h.p.).
Bogies: Brill 39E.
Seats: 48 (reduced to 44 on BR*).

BR	Gateshead		
20 *	5	Crich Tramway Village	Gateshead & District Tramways Co. 1927
26	10	North of England Open Air Museum	Gateshead & District Tramways Co. 1925

BATTERY EMU   BR DERBY/COWLAIRS TWIN UNIT

Built: 1958. Normal formation. BDMBSO–BDTCOL.
Power: 216 lead-acid cells of 1070 Ah.
Traction Motors: Two 100 kW Siemens nose-suspended motors.
Max. Speed: 70 m.p.h.
Braking: Vacuum

BDMBSO	17.52 x 2.79 m	37.5 tonnes	–/52
BDTCOL	17.52 x 2.79 m	32.5 tonnes	12/53

79998–DB 975003	BDMBS	Royal Deeside Railway	Derby/Cowlairs 1958
79999–DB 975004	BDTCL	Royal Deeside Railway	Derby/Cowlairs 1958

7.6. LONDON UNDERGROUND EMU STOCK

System: 630 V d.c. third rail.
Traction Motors:.

"TUNNEL" STOCK   CENTRAL LONDON RAILWAY

Built: 1903. In 1939 the two cars below were converted to a sleet locomotive numbered ESL 107.

CLR	LPTB	LTE		
208	3944-ESL 107	ESL 107	London Transport Depot Museum, Acton	MC 1903
252	3981-ESL 107	ESL 107	London Transport Depot Museum, Acton	BRCW 1903

G CLASS   DISTRICT RAILWAY

Built: 1923 for District Railway.
Traction Motors: Two BTH GE69 of 200 h.p.

DM   15.77 x 2.62 m   29.5 tonnes   –/44

DR	LER	LPTB	LTE			
644	238	4148	4248	DM	London Transport Museum	GRCW 1923
662	274	4184		DM	London Transport Depot Museum, Acton	GRCW 1923

T STOCK   METROPOLITAN RAILWAY

Built: 1932 for Metropolitan Railway. Converted 1961 for use as a sleet locomotive numbered ESL118.
Traction Motors: Two GEC WT54 of 210 h.p.

DM   16.00 x 2.79 m   tonnes   –/50

MR	LER	LPTB	LTE			
249	2749	2749	ESL 118B	DM	Spa Valley Railway	BRCW 1932
258	2758	2758	ESL 118A	DM	Spa Valley Railway	BRCW 1932

STANDARD STOCK   LONDON ELECTRIC RAILWAYS

Built: 1923–35 for London Electric Railways. Those shown * converted 1967 for BR Isle of Wight Line.
Traction Motors: Two ? of 240 h.p.

DM   16.70 x 2.60 m   29.5 tonnes   –/30
DT   15.70 x 2.60 m   19 tonnes   –/44
T   15.17 x 2.60 m   17 tonnes   –/48

LER	LPTB	LTE	BR			
3080	3080	L11		DM	London Underground, Acton Works	MC 1931
3109	3109	L11		DM	London Underground, Acton Works	MC 1932
3209	3209*		7	DM	London Underground, Acton Works	MC 1932
297–3327	3327			DM	London Transport Depot Museum, Acton	MC 1927
320–3370	3370	L134		DM	London Transport Depot Museum, Acton	MC 1927
3690	3690	L130		DM	London Underground, Acton Works	MC 1934
3693	3693	L131		DM	London Transport Depot Museum, Acton	MC 1934
3701	3701	L135		DM	London Underground, Acton Works	MC 1934
3706	3706*		2	DM	London Underground, Acton Works	MC 1935
1789–5279	5279*		27	DT	London Transport Depot Museum, Acton	MC 1925
7061	7061	PC850		T	London Underground, Acton Works	BRCW 1932
7063	7063	PC851		T	London Underground, Acton Works	BRCW 1932
7071	7071	PC855		T	London Underground, Acton Works	BRCW 1932
831–7281	7281*		44	T	London Underground, Acton Works	CL 1923
846–7296	7296*		49	T	London Transport Depot Museum, Acton	CL 1923

N CLASS   LONDON PASSENGER TRANSPORT BOARD

Built: 1936 for use on the Metropolitan line Hammersmith–Barking section.

T   15.58 x 2.72 m   tonnes   –/44

LPTB	LTE			
8063	08063	T	London Transport Depot Museum, Acton	MC1936

CO/CP STOCK   LONDON PASSENGER TRANSPORT BOARD

Built: 1938–39.   **Traction Motors:** Two MV145AZ of 152 b.h.p.

| DM | | 15.58 x 2.72 m | | tonnes | –/40 |
| T | | 15.58 x 2.72 m | | tonnes | –/44 |

LPTB	LTE					
13028	53028	"CO"	DM	Buckinghamshire Railway Centre	BRCW	1938
13063	013063	"CO"	T	Buckinghamshire Railway Centre	GRCW	1938
14233	54233	"CP"	DM	Buckinghamshire Railway Centre	GRCW	1939
14256	54256	"CP"	DM	Friends of the Pump House, Walthamstow	BRCW	1939

Q38 STOCK   LONDON PASSENGER TRANSPORT BOARD

Built: 1939 for Metropolitan Line.   **Traction Motors:** Two GEC WT45B of 152 b.h.p.

| DM | | 15.58 x 2.72 m | | tonnes | –/40 |

LPTB	LTE				
4416	L126	DM	London Transport Museum	GRCW	1939
4417	L127	DM	London Transport Depot Museum, Acton	GRCW	1939

Note: 4416 is currently being restored at London Underground, Acton Works.

1938 STOCK   LONDON PASSENGER TRANSPORT BOARD

Built: 1938–40.   **Traction Motors:**

DM	15.93 x 2.69 m	27.4 tonnes	–/42
M	15.60 x 2.60 m	25.9 tonnes	–/40
T	15.60 x 2.60 m	20.7 tonnes	–/40

Note: Although maintained and operated by London Transport, 012331 was designated LNER stock until passing into LT ownership in 1948.

LPTB	LTE				
10012	10012	DM	London Transport Depot Museum, Acton	MC	1938
11012	11012	DM	London Transport Depot Museum, Acton	MC	1938
11182	11182	DM	London Transport Museum	MC	1939
92048	92048–12048	M	London Transport Depot Museum, Acton	MC	1939
012229	012229-4927	T	Epping Forest Railway	BRCW	1939
012256	012256	T	London Transport Depot Museum, Acton	BRCW	1939
012331	012331-TRC912	T	London Underground, Acton Works	BRCW	1940

Notes: 012229 is stored at West Ruislip Depot. A number of cars are in use with Island Line on the Isle of Wight, details of these are given in other Platform 5 titles.

R38 STOCK   LONDON TRANSPORT EXECUTIVE

Built: 1938 as Q38 stock. Rebuilt 1950 as R38 stock for District Line.   **Traction Motors:**

| DM | | x   m | | tonnes | –/ |

| 22624 | | DM | Mangapps Farm, Burnham-on-Crouch | GRCW | 1938 |

R49 SURFACE STOCK   LONDON TRANSPORT EXECUTIVE

Built: 1952–53 for District Line.   **Traction Motors:** Two LT 111 of 110 h.p.

| DM | | 15.58 x 2.72 m | | tonnes | –/40 |

LTE				
21147		DM	Friends of the Pump House, Walthamstow	MC	1953
22679		DM	London Transport Depot Museum, Acton	MC	1952

1959 TUBE STOCK   LONDON TRANSPORT EXECUTIVE

Built: 1959 for Piccadilly Line   **Traction Motors:**

| DM | | 15.98 x 2.60 m | | 26.62 tonnes | –/42 |

| 1018 | | DM | London Transport Museum | MC | 1959 |
| 1030 | | DM | Mangapps Farm, Burnham-on-Crouch | MC | 1959 |

1044	DM	Alderney Railway Mannez Quarry	MC 1959
1045	DM	Alderney Railway Mannez Quarry	MC 1959
1085–1031	DM	Bombardier Transportation, Morden Metrocare Depot	MC 1959
1304	DM	The Stable Block, Broad Oak, Herefordshire	MC 1959
1305	DM	Sutton Hall, Rochford, Essex	MC 1959
1306	DM	Police Training Centre, Denton, Gravesend, Kent	MC 1959
2044	T	Mangapps Farm, Burnham-on-Crouch	MC 1959

Note: 1018 is stored at MoD Pig's Bay, Essex.

1960 TUBE STOCK   LONDON TRANSPORT EXECUTIVE

Built: 1960 for Central Line.   **Traction Motors:**

DM	15.86 x 2.60 m	29.89 tonnes	–/40

3906	DM	Epping Forest Railway	Cravens 1960
3907	DM	Epping Forest Railway	Cravens 1960

Note: 3906 and 3907 are stored at West Ruislip Depot.

1962 TUBE STOCK   LONDON TRANSPORT EXECUTIVE

Built: 1962 for Central Line.   **Traction Motors:** Two LT 112 of ? h.p.

DM	15.90 x 2.60 m	26.62 t	–/42
M	15.60 x 2.60 m	24.28 t	–/40

1506	DM	Epping Forest Railway	BRCW 1962
1507	DM	Epping Forest Railway	BRCW 1962
1676	DM	Metropolitan Police, Hounslow Heath Training Area	BRCW 1962
1744	DM	Epping & Ongar Railway	BRCW 1962
1745	DM	Epping & Ongar Railway	BRCW 1962
2506	T	Epping Forest Railway	BRCW 1962
2744	T	Epping & Ongar Railway	BRCW 1962
9507	M	Epping Forest Railway	BRCW 1962
9745	M	Epping & Ongar Railway	BRCW 1962
9749	M	British Airports Authority, Heathrow Airport	BRCW 1962

Note: 1506, 1507, 2506 and 9507 are stored at Hainault Depot.

1967 TUBE STOCK   LONDON TRANSPORT EXECUTIVE

Built: 1968 for Victoria Line..   **Traction Motors:** .

DM	16.09 x 2.64 m	28.50 t	–/40

3016	DM	Friends of the Pump House, Walthamstow	MC 1968

1972 TUBE STOCK   LONDON TRANSPORT EXECUTIVE

Built: 1972 for Northern Line.   **Traction Motors:** .

DM	16.09 x 2.64 m	28.20 t	–/40

3530	DM	London Transport Depot Museum, Acton	MC 1972

1983 TUBE STOCK   LONDON TRANSPORT EXECUTIVE

Built: 1983–86 for Jubilee Line.   **Traction Motors:** .

DM	17.23 x 2.60 m	26.34 tons	–/48

3721	DM	Tyne and Wear Fire Service Training Centre, Washington	MC 1984
3734	DM	London Transport Depot Museum, Acton	MC 1984

1986 PROTOTYPE TUBE STOCK   LONDON TRANSPORT EXECUTIVE

Built: 1986–87 for Central Line.   **Traction Motors:** .

DM

16	DM	London Transport Depot Museum, Acton	MC 1986

8. OVERSEAS STEAM LOCOMOTIVES PRESERVED IN GREAT BRITAIN

Note: All locomotives are standard gauge unless shown otherwise. Only locomotives of minimum 750 mm gauge are listed.

8.1. ANTIGUA

Gauge: 760 mm (2'6").

Rly.	No.	Builder	Works No.	Built	Wheels	Name/Present	Location
ANT	?	KS	4404	1927	0-6-2T	JOAN "No. 12"	Welshpool & Llanfair Railway

8.2. AUSTRIA

Gauge: 760 mm (2'6").

Rly.	No.	Builder	Works No.	Built	Wheels	Name	Location
StLB	699.01	FB	2855	1944	0-8-0T	"SIR DREFALDWYN No. 10"	Welshpool & Llanfair Railway

8.3. CHINA

Rly.	No.	Type	Builder	Works Number	Built	Wheels	Name	Location
CNR	607	KF7	VF	4674	1935	4-8-4		National Railway Museum

8.4. DENMARK

Rly.	No.	Type	Builder	Works Number	Built	Wheels	Name	Location
DSB	385	WS	Hartmann	2110	1895	0-4-0T		Middleton Railway
DSB	656	F	Frichs	360	1949	0-6-0T		Nene Valley Railway
DSB	996	E	Frichs	415	1950	4-6-2		Railworld, Peterborough

8.5. FINLAND

Gauge: 1524 mm (5'0").

Rly.	No.	Type	Builder	Works Number	Built	Wheels	Name	Location
VR	794	Vr1	TK	350	1925	0-6-0T		Epping & Ongar Railway
VR	799	Vr1	TK	355	1925	0-6-0T		Hope Farm, Sellindge
VR	792	Vr1	TK	373	1927	0-6-0T	"HEN"	Enfield Timber Company
VR	1103	Tk3	LO	141	1945	2-8-0		Spirit of the West American Theme Park
VR	1134	Tk3	TK	531	1946	2-8-0		Epping & Ongar Railway
VR	1008	Hr1	LO	157	1948	4-6-2		Epping & Ongar Railway
VR	1016	H1	TK	946	1948	4-6-2		Long & Somerville, Southbury, London
VR	1144	Tk3	TK	571	1948	2-8-0		Steam Traction, Acton, Suffolk
VR	1157	Tk3	Frichs	403	1949	2-8-0		HLPG, Binbrook Trading Estate
VR	1077	Tr1	Jung	11787	1953	2-8-2		Steam Traction, Acton, Suffolk
VR	1060	Tr1	LO	172	1954	2-8-2		Epping & Ongar Railway

Gauge: 760 mm (2'6").

Rly.	No.	Builder	Works No.	Built	Wheels	Name	Location
JR	?	Niv	2369	1948	2-6-2T	"ORION No. 5"	Welshpool & Llanfair Railway

8.6. FRANCE

Rly.	No.	Builder	Works Number	Built	Wheels	Location
SNCF	230.D.116	Hen	10745	1911	4-6-0	Nene Valley Railway
(EX NORD RAILWAYS 3628)						

Gauge: 1000 mm (3'3³/₈").

Rly.	No.	Builder	Works No.	Built	Wheels	Name	Location
CFCA	1	Corpet	493	1888	0-6-0T	CAMBRAI	Irchester Narrow Gauge Railway

8.7. GERMANY

Rly.	No.	Type	Builder	Works Number	Built	Wheels	Location
DB	64.305	64	Krupp	1308	1934	2-6-2T	Nene Valley Railway

8.8. NORWAY

Rly.	No.	Type	Builder	Works Number	Built	Wheels	Name	Location
NSB	376	21	NOHAB	1163	1919	2-6-0		Kent & East Sussex Railway
NSB	377	21	NOHAB	1164	1919	2-6-0	KING HAAKON VII	Bressingham Steam Museum
NSB	5865	63a	Schichau	Unknown	1944	2-10-0	PEER GYNT	Bressingham Steam Museum

8.9. PAKISTAN

Gauge: 1676 mm (5'6").

Railway	No.	Builder	Works Number	Built	Wheels	Location
PWR	3157	VF	3064	1911	4-4-0	Greater Manchester Museum of Science & Industry

8.10. POLAND

Rly. No.	Builder	Works No.	Built	Wheels	Name	Location
Ind Ty2.7173	Florids	16626	1943	2-10-0		Nene Valley Railway
Ind TKh.2871	Chr	2871	1951	0-6-0T		Bridgend Valleys Railway
Ind TKh.2944	Chr	2944	1952	0-6-0T	"HOTSPUR"	Spa Valley Railway
Ind TKh.3135	Chr	3135	1953	0-6-0T	"SPARTAN"	Spa Valley Railway
Ind TKh.3138	Chr	3138	1954	0-6-0T	"HUTNIK"	Appleby-Frodingham RPS
Ind TKh.4015	Chr	4015	1954	0-6-0T	"KAROL"	North Norfolk Railway
Ind TKh.5374	Chr	5374	1959	0-6-0T	"VANGUARD"	Northampton & Lamport Railway
Ind TKh.5380	Chr	5380	1960	0-6-0T		
Ind TKh.5697	Chr	5697	1959	0-6-0T		
Ind Tkh.17646	Chr	3112	1952	0-6-0T	"Northamptonshire"	Northampton & Lamport Railway
Ind TKp.5485	Chr	5485	1961	0-8-0T		Nene Valley Railway
Ind TKp.3399	Chr	3399	19xx	0-8-0T		Pontypool & Blaenavon Railway

Notes: The type of loco is the same as the first three characters of the number, e.g. Tkh.2871 is a class Tkh. Tkh 5374 is at present receiving attention at Heritage Engineering (Swindon).

Gauge: 750 mm (2'5½").

Rly.	No.	Builder	Works No.	Built	Wheels	Location
LAS		Chr	2959	1951	0-6-0WT	Midland Railway Centre
LAS		Chr	3326	1954	0-6-0WT	Midland Railway Centre

8.11. ROMANIA

Gauge: 760 mm (2'6").

Rly.	No.	Builder	Works No.	Built	Wheels	Present	Location
CFI	764.423	Resita	1679	1954	0-8-0T	INV 60006	Apedale Light Railway

8.12. SIERRA LEONE

Gauge: 760 mm (2'6").

Rly.	No.	Builder	Works No.	Built	Wheels	Present	Location
SLR	85	HE	3815	1954	2-6-2T	"No. 14"	Welshpool & Llanfair Railway

8.13. SOUTH AFRICA

Gauge: 914 mm (3'6").

Rly.	No.	Builder	Works Number	Built	Wheels	Name	Location
SAR	2352	BP	6639	1930	4-8-2+2-8-4		Greater Manchester Museum of Science & Industry
SAR	4112	NBL	27770	1957	4-8-2+2-8-4	SPRINGBOK	Summerlee Heritage Park, Coatbridge
SAR	3405	NBL	27291	1958	4-8-4	CITY OF BLOEMFONTEIN	Buckinghamshire Railway Centre
SAR	390	SS	4150	1896	4-8-0		British Empire & Commonwealth Museum

Note: SAR 390 was latterly used by the Zambesi Sawmills Railway.

8.14. SWEDEN

Rly.	No.	Type	Builder	Works Number	Built	Wheels	Name	Location
SJ	1178	S	Motala	516	1904	2-6-2T		Nene Valley Railway
SJ	1313	B	Motala	586	1917	4-6-0		Stephenson Railway Museum
SJ	1697	B	NOHAB	2082	1944	4-6-0	"SWJB 101"	Nene Valley Railway
SJ	1928	Si	NOHAB	2229	1953	2-6-4T	"ALLEN GLADDEN"	Hope Farm, Sellindge

8.15. TASMANIA

Gauge: 914 mm (3'6").

Railway	No.	Builder	Works Number	Built	Wheels	Location
TGR	M2	RSHN	7430	1951	4-6-2	Tanfield Railway

8.16. THAILAND

Gauge: 760 mm (2'6").

Rly.	No.	Builder	Works No.	Built	Wheels	Name	Location
CHON	105	Hen	29582	1956	0-6-0T	SIAM	Bredgar & Wormshill Light Railway

8.17. TRINIDAD

Rly.	No.	Builder	Works No.	Built	Wheels	Name	Location
USM		HE	1450	1927	2-6-2T	PICTON	Middleton Railway

8.18. YUGOSLAVIA

Railway	No.	Builder	Works Number	Built	Wheels	Name/Present	Location
Ind	62-669	Brod	669	1960	0-6-0T	"30075"	East Somerset Railway

RAILWAY ABBREVIATIONS

ANT	Antigua Sugar Factory Railway	PKP	Polskie Koleje Panstwowe
CFCA	Chemins de Fer du Cambresia	SAR	South African Railways
CHON	Chonburn Sugar Mill Railway	SJ	Statens Järnväger
CNR	Canadian National Railway	SLR	Sierra Leone Railway
DB	Deutsche Bundesbahn	SNCF	Société Nationale des Chemins de Fer Francais
DSB	Danske Statsbaner	StLB	Steirmarkische Landesbahnen
JR	Jokioisten Railway	ITGR	Tasmanian Government Railways
Ind	Industrial Railway	USM	Usine Sainte Madeleine Sugar Mill Railway
LAS	? (Poland)	VR	Valtion Rautatiet
NSB	Norges Statsbaner		

9. LIST OF LOCATIONS

The following is a list of locations in Great Britain where locomotives and multiple units included in this book can be found, together with Ordnance Survey grid references where these are known. Please note that industrial sites where preserved locomotives are kept are classed as preservation sites. Industrial locations are those where the locomotives are in industrial use. At certain locations locomotives may be dispersed at several sites. In such cases the principle site where locomotives can normally be found is the one given. Enquiries at this location will normally reveal the whereabouts of other locomotives, but this is not guaranteed.

9.1. PRESERVATION SITES & OPERATING RAILWAYS

§ denotes not normally open to the public.

	OS GRID REF.
Abbey View Disabled Day Centre, Neath Abbey, Neath, Port Talbot.	SS 734973
A.J. Wilson, 35 Holt Park Road, Cookridge, Leeds, West Yorkshire.§	SE 261403
Apedale Light Railway, Apedale Heritage Centre, Chesterton, Staffordshire.	ST 823483
Appleby-Frodingham RPS, Corus, Appleby-Frodingham Works, Scunthorpe, Lincs.	SE 913109
Avon Valley Railway, Bitton Station, Bitton, Gloucestershire.	ST 670705
Barrow Hill Roundhouse, Campbell Drive, Barrow Hill, Staveley, Chesterfield, Derbyshire.	SK 414755
Battlefield Railway, Shackerstone Station, Shackerstone, Leicestershire.	SK 379066
Beacon Farm, Bentleys Lane, Maxstoke, Warwickshire.	SP 244874
Bere Ferrers Station Museum, Bere Ferrers, Devon.	SX 452635
Bicton Woodland Railway, Bicton Gardens, East Budleigh, near Sidmouth, Devon.	SY 074862
Birmingham Museum of Science & Industry, Discovery Centre, Millennium Point, Birmingham.	SP 079873
Bluebell Railway, Sheffield Park, Uckfield, East Sussex.	TQ 403238
Bodmin Steam Railway, Bodmin General Station, Bodmin, Cornwall.	SX 073664
Bombardier Transportation, Morden Metrocare Depot, Morden, London.§	TQ 256682
Bo'ness & Kinneil Railway, Bo'ness Station, Union Street, Bo'ness, Falkirk.	NT 003817
Bredgar & Wormshill Light Railway, The Warren, Swanton Street, Bredgar, near Sittingbourne.	TQ 873575
Bressingham Steam Museum, Bressingham Hall, Diss, Norfolk.	TM 080806
Bridgend Valleys Railway, Pontycymer, Cwm Garw, Bridgend.	SS 903913
Brighton Railway Museum, Preston Park, Brighton, West Sussex.§	TQ 302061
British Empire & Commonwealth Museum, Temple Meads, Bristol.	ST 596724
Bryn Engineering, Locomotive Restoration Centre, Pemberton, Wigan, Greater Manchester.§	
Buckinghamshire Railway Centre, Quainton Road Station, Aylesbury, Bucks.	SP 736189
Cadeby Light Railway, The Old Rectory, Cadeby, Market Bosworth, Leicestershire.	SK 426024
Caledonian Railway, Brechin Station, Brechin, Montrose, Angus.	NO 603603
Canterbury Heritage Centre, Stour Street, Canterbury, Kent.	TQ 146577
Cefn Coed Colliery Museum, Old Blaenant Colliery, Cryant, Neath Port Talbot.	SN 786034
Chasewater Light Railway, Chasewater Pleasure Park, Brownhills, Staffordshire.	SK 034070
Chatham Dockyard Historic Trust, Chatham Dockyard, Chatham, Kent.	TQ 758689
Chinnor & Princes Risborough Railway, Chinnor Cement Works, Chinnor, Oxon.	SP 756002
Cholsey & Wallingford Railway, St. John's Road, Wallingford, Oxfordshire.	SU 600891
Churnet Valley Railway, Cheddleton Station, Cheddleton, Leek, Staffordshire.	SJ 983519
CIL Storefitters, Finsbury Park, London.	TQ 313867
Colne Valley Railway, Castle Hedingham Station, Halstead, Essex.	TL 774362
Coventry Railway Centre, Rowley Road, Baginton, Coventry, Warwickshire.	SP 354751
Crich Tramway Village, Crich, nr Matlock, Derbyshire.	SK 345549
Darlington North Road Goods Shed, Station Road, Hopetown, Darlington, Co. Durham.	NZ 290156
Darlington North Road Museum, Station Road, Hopetown, Darlington, Co. Durham.	NZ 289157
Dartmoor Railways, Meldon Quarry, Okehampton, Devon.	SX 568927
Dean Forest Railway, Norchard, Lydney, Gloucestershire.	SO 629044
Denbigh & Mold Junction Railway, Sodom, near Bodfari, Denbighshire, Wales.	
Derwent Valley Light Railway, Yorkshire Museum of Farming, Murton, York, North Yorks.	SE 650524
Designer Outlet Village, Kemble Drive, Swindon, Wiltshire.	SU 142849
Didcot Railway Centre (Great Western Society), Didcot, Oxfordshire.	SU 524906
East Anglian Railway Museum, Chappel & Wakes Colne Station, Essex.	TL 898289
East Kent Light Railway, Shepherdswell, Kent.	TR 258483
East Lancashire Railway, Bolton Street Station, Bury, Greater Manchester.	SD 803109

East Somerset Railway, West Cranmore Station, Shepton Mallet, Somerset. ST 664429
Eden Valley Railway, Warcop Station, Warcop, Cumbria. NY 758152
Elham Valley Museum, Peene Yard, Peene, Folkestone, Kent. TR 185378
Elsecar Heritage Centre, Wath Road, Elsecar, Barnsley, South Yorkshire. SX 386998
Embsay & Bolton Abbey Railway, Embsay Station, Embsay, Skipton, North Yorks. SE 007533
Enfield Timber Company, The Ridge, Hertford Road, Enfield, Middlesex § TQ 352965
Epping & Ongar Railway, Ongar Station, Station Road, Chipping Ongar, Essex. TL 552035
Epping Forest Railway, The Bushes, Magdalen Laver, near Harlow, Essex.§ TL 526078
ERPS, Alstom, Eastleigh Works, Eastleigh, Hampshire.§ SU 457185
Erwood Station Craft Centre, Erwood Station, Erwood, Powys. SO 089439
Essex Traction Group, Boxted, near Colchester, Essex (exact location unknown).
Exeter & Teign Valley Railway, Christow (GWR) station, Doddiscombeleigh, Devon. SX 839868
F & W Saunders & Son, Huntingdon, Cambridgeshire. (exact location unknown).§
Fawley Hill Railway, Fawley Green, near Henley-on-Thames, Buckinghamshire.§ SU 755861
Foxcote Station, Hatfield, near Leominster, Herefordshire. SO 601589
Foxfield Railway, Blythe Bridge, Stoke-on-Trent, Staffordshire. SJ 976446
Friends of the Pump House, The Pump House, Lowe Hall Lane, Walthamstow, London TQ 362882
FSR, Southall Depot, Southall, Greater London.§ TQ 133798
Glasgow Museum of Transport, Kelvin Hall, Burnhouse Road, Coplawhill, Glasgow. NS 565663
Gloucestershire-Warwickshire Railway, Toddington Station, Gloucestershire. SP 049321
Great Central Railway, Loughborough Central Station, Loughborough, Leicestershire. SK 543194
Greater Manchester Museum of Science & Industry, Liverpool Road, Manchester. SJ 831978
Gwili Railway, Bronwydd Arms Station, Carmarthen, Carmarthenshire. SN 417236
GWR Preservation Group, Field Sidings, Southall, Greater London.§ TQ 131798
Hampshire & Sussex UPS, Selhurst Depot, Selhurst, London.§ TQ 333675
Hardingham Station, Low Street, Hardingham, Norfolk.§ TM 050055
Helical Technologies, Dock Road, Lytham St. Annes, Lancashire.§ SD 381276
Heritage Engineering (Swindon), Old No.20 Shop, Swindon Works, Swindon, Wiltshire.§ SU 143849
HLPG, Binbrook Trading Estate, Binbrook, Lincolnshire.§ TF 201958
Hope Farm (Southern Locomotives), Sellindge, near Ashford, Kent §. TR 119388
Ian Storey Engineering, Station Yard, Hepscott, Morpeth, Northumberland.§ NZ 223844
Irchester Narrow Gauge Railway, Irchester Country Park, Irchester, Northamptonshire. SP 906660
Isle of Wight Steam Railway, Haven Street Station, Isle of Wight. SZ 556898
Keighley & Worth Valley Railway, Haworth, Keighley, West Yorkshire. SE 034371
Keith & Dufftown Railway, Dufftown, Moray. NJ 323414
Kent & East Sussex Railway, Tenterden Town Station, Tenterden, Kent. TQ 882336
Kingdom of Fife Railway, Methill Power Station, Methill, Fife.§ NO 382001
Lakeside & Haverthwaite Railway, Haverthwaite, Cumbria. SD 349843
Lancastrian Carriage & Wagon, Bay Close, Port of Heysham Industrial Park, Heysham, Lancs.§SD 408604
Lavender Line, Isfield Station, Station Road, Isfield, East Sussex. TQ 452171
Leeds Industrial Museum, Armley Mills, Canal Road, Leeds, West Yorkshire. SE 275342
Leighton Buzzard Narrow Gauge Railway, Pages Park, Leighton Buzzard, Bedfordshire. SP 929242
Lincolnshire Wolds Railway, Ludborough Station, Ludborough, Lincolnshire. TF 309960
Llangollen Railway, Llangollen Station, Llangollen, Denbighshire. SJ 211423
London Transport Depot Museum, Gunnersby Lane, Acton, Greater London. TQ 194799
London Transport Museum, Covent Garden, London. TQ 303809
London Underground, Acton Works, Bollo Lane, London.§ TQ 196791
London Underground, Hainault Depot, Hainault, London.§ TQ 450918
London Underground, West Ruislip Depot, Ruislip, London.§ TQ 094862
Long & Somerville, Southbury Road, Potters End, Enfield, London.§ TQ 348962
Long Coppice, Moreton-on-Lugg, near Hereford, Herefordshire§. SO 503467
Long Marston Workshops, Long Marston, Warwickshire §. SP 152469
Madame Tussauds, Royalty & Empire Exhibition, Windsor & Eton Central Station. SU 966769
Mangapps Farm, Southminster Road, Burnham-on-Crouch, Essex. TQ 944980
Merseyside Development Corporation, Jn of Derby Road and Banksfield Street, Bootle, Merseyside. SJ 339937
Middleton Railway, Tunstall Road, Hunslet, Leeds, West Yorkshire. SE 305310
Midland Railway Centre, Butterley Station, Ripley, Derbyshire. SK 403520
Mid-Norfolk Railway, Dereham Station, Dereham, Norfolk. TG 003102
Milton Keynes Central Station, Milton Keynes, Buckinghamshire.
MNLPS, Stewarts Lane, Battersea, London.§ TQ 257798
MoD Ashchurch, Gloucestershire§. SO 932338
MoD BAD Kineton Military Railway,Temple Herdewyke, Southam, Warwickshire §.SP 373523
MoD Pig's Bay, Shoeburyness, Essex. TM 946856
Museum of Army Transport, Flemingate, Beverley, East Riding of Yorkshire. TA 041392

Museum of Liverpool Life, Mann Island, Liverpool Pier Head, Liverpool, Merseyside. SJ 339900
National Railway Museum, Leeman Road, York, North Yorkshire. SE 594519
NELPG, Former Carriage Works, Hopetown, Darlington, County Durham NZ 288157
Nene Valley Railway, Wansford Station, Peterborough, Cambridgeshire. TL 093979
Northampton & Lamport Railway, Pitsford, Northamptonshire. SP 736666
Northamptonshire Ironstone Railway, Hunsbury Hill, Northampton, Northamptonshire.SP 735584
North Norfolk Railway, Sheringham Station, Norfolk. TG 156430
North of England Open Air Museum, Beamish Hall, Beamish, County Durham. NZ 217547
North Woolwich Station Museum, Pier Road, North Woolwich, London. TQ 433798
North Yorkshire Moors Railway, Grosmont Station, North Yorkshire. NZ 828049
Nottingham Heritage Centre, Mereway, Ruddington, Nottinghamshire SK 575322
Old Oak Common Depot, Acton, Greater London.§ TQ 218823
Oswestry Cycle & Railway Museum, Oswestry Station Yard, Oswestry, Shropshire. SJ 294297
Paignton & Dartmouth Railway, Queen's Park Station, Paignton, Devon. SX 889606
Peak Railway, Darley Dale Station, Darley Dale, Matlock, Derbyshire. SK 273626
Pleasurewood Hills Park, Lowestoft, Suffolk. TM 545965
Plym Valley Railway, Marsh Mills, Plymouth, Devon. SX 520571
Pontypool & Blaenavon Railway, Furnoe Sidings, Big Pit, Blaenavon, Torfaen. SO 237093
Railworld (Museum of World Railways), Woodston, Peterborough, Cambs. TL 188982
Ribble Steam Railway, off Chain Caulway, Riversway, Preston, Lancashire SD 504295
Rippingale Station, Fen Road, Rippingale, Lincolnshire.§ TF 115283
Rogart Station, Rogart, Highland. NC 724020
Rowden Mill Station, Rowden Mill, near Bromyard, Herefordshire.§. SO 627565
Royal Air Force Museum, Graham Park Way, Hendon, Greater London. TQ 221904
Royal Deeside Railway, Milton, Crathes, Banchory, Aberdeen. NO 743962
Royal Engineers Museum, Prince Arthur Road, Chatham, Kent.
Rushden Station Museum, Rectory Road, Rushden, Northamptonshire. SP 957672
Rutland Railway Museum, Ashwell Road, Cottesmore, Oakham, Rutland. SK 887137
Science Museum, Imperial Institute Road, South Kensington, London. TQ 268793
Scolton Manor Museum, Scolton Manor, Haverfordwest, Pembrokeshire. SM 991222
Scottish Industrial Railway Centre, Minnivey Colliery, Dalmellington, East Ayrshire.NS 475073
Severn Valley Railway, Bridgnorth Station, Shropshire. SO 715926
Shropshire Locomotive Collection, Coton's Farm, Cross Houses, Atcham, Shrewsbury, Shropshire.§ SJ 558069
Snibston Discovery Park, Snibston Mine, Ashby Road, Coalville, Leicestershire. SK 420144
Somerset & Dorset Locomotive Company, Yeovil Junction, near Yeovil, Somerset ST 571141
Somerset & Dorset Railway Trust, Washford Station, Washford, Somerset. ST 044412
South Devon Railway, Buckfastleigh, Devon. SX 747663
Spa Valley Railway, Tunbridge Wells West Station, Tunbridge Wells, Kent. TQ 542346
Spirit of The West American Theme Park, Retallack, St Columb Major, Cornwall. SW 936658
St. Leonards Railway Engineering, West Marina Depot, Bridge Way, St Leonards, East Sussex.§ TQ 778086
Stainmore Railway, Kirkby Stephen East Station, Kirkby Stephen, Cumbria. NY 769075
Steam-Museum of the Great Western Railway, Old No. 20 Shop, Old Swindon Works,
    Kemble Drive, Swindon, Wiltshire. SU 143849
Steam Traction, Acton Place Industrial Estate, Acton, Sudbury, Suffolk.§ TL 883455
Steeple Grange Light Railway, Steeplehouse Junction, Wirksworth, Derbyshire SK 288554
Stephenson Railway Museum, Middle Engine Lane, West Chirton, Tyne & Wear. NZ 323693
Stratford & Broadway Railway, Long Marston, Warwickshire. SP 153473
Strathspey Railway, Aviemore, Highland Region. NH 898131
Stravithie Station, Stravithie, near St. Andrews, Fife. NO 533134
Summerlee Heritage Park, West Canal Street, Coatbridge, North Lanarkshire. NS 728655
Sutton Hall, Rochford, Essex. TQ 888892
Swanage Railway, Swanage Station, Swanage, Dorset. SZ 028789
Swansea Vale Railway, Llansamlet, Swansea. SS 660928
Swindon & Cricklade Railway, Blunsden Road Station, Swindon, Wiltshire. SU 110897
Swindon Railway Workshop, Flour Mill Engine House, Bream, Forest of Dean, Glos.§ SO 604067
Talyllyn Railway, Tywyn Pendre Depot, Tywyn, Gwynedd. SH 590008
Tanfield Railway, Marley Hill Engine Shed, Sunniside, Tyne & Wear. NZ 207573
Telford Steam Railway, Bridge Road, Horsehay, Telford, Shropshire. SJ 675073
The Railway Age, Crewe, Cheshire SJ 708552
The Rosemary Vineyard, Smallbrook Lane, Ryde, Isle of Wight§ SU 591901
The Stable Block, Broad Oak, near Hereford, Herefordshire § SO 480213
Timothy Hackworth Museum, Soho Works, Shildon, County Durham. NZ 233257
Tiverton Museum, St. Andrew's Street, Tiverton, Devon. SS 955124
Tyseley Locomotive Works, Warwick Road, Tyseley, Birmingham. SP 105841

Vale of Glamorgan Railway, Barry Island, Vale of Glamorgan.   ST 118667
Vale of Rheidol Railway, Aberystwyth, Ceredigian   SN 587812
Venice-Simplon Orient Express, Stewarts Lane , Battersea, London §.   TQ 288766
Watercress Line, Alresford Station, New Alresford, Hampshire.   SU 588325
Waverley Route Heritage Association, Whitrope, near Hawick, Scottish Borders.   NT 527005
Weardale Railway (Weardale Steel), Wolsingham, County Durham.   NZ 081370
Welshpool & Llanfair Railway, Llanfair Caereinon, Powys.   SJ 107069
Wensleydale Railway, Leeming Bar Station, Leeming Bar, North Yorkshire.   SE 286900
West Coast Railway Company, Warton Road, Carnforth, Lancashire.§   SD 496708
West Somerset Railway, Minehead Station, Minehead, Somerset.   SS 975463
Woodside Museum, Shore Road, Birkenhead, Merseyside.
Wooler Railway Collection, Unit A, Berwick Road, Wooler, Northumberland§.   NU 994287
Wyvern Rail, Wirksworth station, Wirksworth, Derbyshire.   SK 289542

9.2. INDUSTRIAL LOCATIONS

AES Fiffonts Point Power Station, Uskmouth, Newport   ST 325835
Alstom, Asfordby Test Track, Asfordby, Leicestershire
Alstom, Eastleigh Works, Campbell Road, Eastleigh, Hampshire.   SU 457185
Alstom, Springburn Works, Springburn Road, Glasgow.   NS 605665
Alstom, Wolverton Works, Stratford Road, Wolverton, Milton Keynes, Bucks.   SP 812413
A.V. Dawson, Ayrton Store & Railhead, Forty Foot Road, Middlesbrough, North Yorks.   NZ 493215
Bombardier Transportation, Crewe Works, Crewe, Cheshire.   SJ 691561
Bombardier Transportation, Derby Carriage Works, Litchurch Lane, Derby, Derbyshire.   SK 364345
Bombardier Transportation, Doncaster Works, Doncaster, South Yorkshire.   SE 565029
British Airports Authority, Heathrow Airport, London.
Brush Traction, Loughborough, Leicestershire.   SK 543207
Crouch Mining, Widdrington Disposal Point, Widdrington, Northumberland.   NZ 237957
Deanside Transit, Deanside Road, Hillington, Glasgow.   NS 526652
Direct Rail Services, Kingmoor Depot, Etterby, Carlisle, Cumbria.   NY 386575
ETOL, Wilton Works, Middlesbrough, North Yorkshire.   NZ 564218
European Metal Recycling, Trinity Road, Kingsbury, Warwickshire.   SP 219969
Faber Prest Ports, Flixborough Wharf, Flixborough, Scunthorpe, Lincolnshire.   SE 859197
Fire Service College, Moreton-in-Marsh, Gloucestershire.   SP 216329
Foster Yeoman, Isle of Grain, Rochester, Kent.   TQ 875473
Foster Yeoman, Merehead Stone Terminal, Shepton Mallet, Somerset.   ST 693426
Fragonset Railways, rtc Business Park, London Road, Derby, Derbyshire.   SK 365350
Petroplus International, Waterston, Milford Haven, Pembrokeshire.   SM 935055
Hanson Aggregates, Machen Quarry, near Newport.   ST 221886
Hanson Aggregates, Whatley Quarry, near Frome, Somerset.   ST 733479
Hayes Chemicals, Elworth Works, Sandbach, Cheshire   SJ 729633
Imerys, Blackpool Dries, Methrose, Burngullow, Cornwall.   SW 985526
Imerys, Rocks Dries, Bugle, Cornwall.   SX 025586
ISTIL, Queenborough Wharf Scrapyard, Isle of Sheppey, Kent.   TQ 911716
J. Walker, Shawhill Station Yard, Annan, Dumfries & Galloway.   NY 201664
Jarvis Rail, Slateford Plant Depot, Slateford, Edinburgh.   NT 228714
Lafarge Redland Aggregates, Barrow-upon-Soar rail-loading terminal, Leicestershire   SK 587168
LCP Properties, Pensnett Trading Estate, Shut End, West Midlands.   SO 901897
Marchwood Military Railway, Marchwood, Hampshire.   SU 395103
Mayer-Parry Recycling, Snailwell, Newmarket, Cambridgeshire.   TL 638678
Metropolitan Police, Hounslow Heath Training Area, Hounslow Heath, London.
MoD DSDA Bicester Military Railway, Bicester, Oxfordshire.   SP 581203
MoD RAF Caerwent, Monmouthshire   ST 48x90x
Police Training Centre, Denton, Gravesend, Kent
Port of Boston Authority, Boston Docks, Boston, Lincolnshire.   TF 329431
Pullman TPL, Cardiff Cathays, Cardiff.   ST 177779
RMS Locotec, Vanguard Works, Bretton Street, Dewsbury, West Yorkshire.   SE 249200
Tarmac Precast Concrete, Hayes, Middlesex.   TQ 105795
The Potter Group, Knowsley, Merseyside.
The Potter Group, Rail Distribution Centre, Selby, North Yorkshire   SE 629322
Tilcon, Swinden Quarry, Grassington, North Yorkshire.   SE 605539
Transfesa, Tilbury Riverside Terminal, Tilbury, Essex.   TQ 645754
Tyne & Wear Fire Service Training Centre, Nissan Way, Barmston Mier, Washington, Tyne & Wear.   NZ 329572
UK Rail Shunter Hire, Reliance Industrial Estate, Newton Heath, Manchester.

Wabtec Rail, Doncaster Wagon Works, Doncaster, South Yorkshire.   SK 569031
Wickham Rail Engineering, Cross Engineering Works, Thorrington, Essex.   TQ 087203
Widnes International Rail Depot, Widnes, Merseyside.   SJ 504844
Victa Railfreight, Beechbrook Farm, Kent

9.3. PUBLIC HOUSES & HOTELS

Black Bull, Moulton, North Yorkshire.   NZ 237037
Elletson Arms, Stake Pool, Pilling, Lancashire   SD 412479
Little Mill Inn, Rowarth, Mellor, Derbyshire.   SK 011890

10. ABBREVIATIONS USED

ABB	ASEA Brown Boveri.
AD	Army Department of the Ministry of Defence
BAD	Base Armament Depot
BAOR	British Army of the Rhine
BR	British Railways.
BREL	British Rail Engineering Ltd. (later BREL, then ABB, now Bombardier Transportation).
BRML	British Rail Maintenance Ltd.
BTH	British Thomson Houston.
C&W	Carriage & Wagon.
DE	Diesel electric.
DH	Diesel hydraulic.
DM	Diesel mechanical.
DMU	Diesel Multiple Unit
DSDA	Defence Distribution & Agency.
FS	Ferrovie dello Stato
FSR	Flying Scotsman Railways.
GEC	General Electric Company (UK).
GSSD	General Stores Sub Depot
GWR	Great Western Railway
HLPG	Humberside Locomotive Preservation Society.
ICI	Imperial Chemical Industries.
IRR	Iran Islamic Republic Railways
LC&W	Locomotive, Carriage & Wagon.
LER	London Electric Railways
LMS	London Midland & Scottish Railway.
LMS	London Midland & Scottish Railway.
LNER	London & North Eastern Railway.
LPTB	London Passenger Transport Board
LSWR	London & South Western Railway.
L&YR	Lancashire & Yorkshire Railway.
LTE	London Transport Executive
LTS	London Tilbury & Southend Railway
MNLPS	Merchant Navy Locomotive Preservation Society.
MoD	Ministry of Defence.
NS	Nederlandse Spoorwegen.
NSR	North Staffordshire Railway
RAF	Royal Air Force
RC&W	Railway Carriage & Wagon
Rly.	Railway
RPS	Railway Preservation Society.
SR	Southern Railway.
TCDD	Türkiye Cumhuryeti devlet Demiryollan.
UPS	Unit Preservation Society.
USAF	United States Air Force
USATC	United States of America Transportation Corps.
WD	War Department
WR	British Railways Western Region
a.c.	alternating current.
d.c.	direct current.
(s)	Stored

11. PRIVATE MANUFACTURER CODES

The following codes are used to denote private locomotive manufacturers. These are followed by the works number and build year, e.g.,AW 1360/1937 – built by Armstrong-Whitworth and Company, works number 1360, year 1937. Unless otherwise shown, locations are in England.

AB	Andrew Barclay, Sons & Company, Caledonia Works, Kilmarnock, Scotland.
AC	AC Cars, Thames Ditton, Surrey.
AE	Avonside Engine Company, Bristol, Avon.
AEC	Associated Equipment Company, Southall, Berkshire.
AL	American Locomotive Company, USA/Canada.
AP	Aveling & Porter, Invicta Works, Canterbury, Kent.
AW	Armstrong-Whitworth & Company, Newcastle, Tyne and Wear.
BBC	Brown-Boveri et Cie., Switzerland.
BCK	Bury, Curtis & Kennedy, Liverpool, Merseyside.
BD	Baguley-Drewry, Burton-on-Trent, Staffordshire.
BE	Brush Electrical Engineering Company, Loughborough, Leicestershire.
Bg	E.E. Baguley, Burton-on-Trent, Staffordshire.
BLW	Baldwin Locomotive Works, Philidelphia, Pennsylvania, USA.
BMR	Brecon Mountain Railway Company, Pant, Merthyr Tydfil, Wales.
BP	Beyer Peacock and Company, Gorton, Manchester.
BRCW	Birmingham Railway Carriage & Wagon Company, Smethwick, Birmingham.
Brod	PRVA Jugoslovenska Tvornica Vagona, Slavonski Brod, Yugoslavia
BTH	British Thomson-Houston Company, Rugby, Warwickshire.
Carn	Steamtown Railway Museum, Warton Road, Carnforth, Lancashire.
CE	Clayton Equipment Company, Hatton, Derbyshire.
Chr	Fabryka Locomotyw Im F. Dzierzynskiego, Chrzanow, Poland
CL	Cammell Laird & Company
Corpet	Corpet, Louvet & Compagnie, Seine St. Denis, France
Cravens	Cravens, Darnall, Sheffield, South Yorkshire.
DC	Drewry Car Company, London.
DK	Dick Kerr & Company, Preston, Lancashire.
Dodman	Alfred Dodman & Company, Highgate Works, Kings Lynn, Norfolk.
EE	English Electric Company, Bradford and Preston.
Electro	Electroputere, Craiova, Romania
EW	E.B. Wilson & Company, Railway Foundry, Leeds, West Yorkshire.
FB	Société Franco-Belge de Matériel de Chemins de Fer, Usine de Raismes, France
Florids	Wiener Lokomativfabrik A.G., Floridsdorf, Austria
Frichs	A/S Frichs Maskinfabrik & Kedelsmedie, Arhus, Denmark
FW	Fox, Walker & Company, Atlas Engine Works, Bristol.
GE	George England & Company, Hatcham Ironworks, London.
GRCW	Gloucester Railway Carriage & Wagon Company, Gloucester, Gloucestershire.
Hack	Timothy Hackworth, Soho Works, Shildon, Co. Durham.
Hartmann	Sachsische Maschinenfabrik, Hartmann AG, Chemnitz, Germany
HC	Hudswell-Clarke & Company, Hunslet, Leeds, West Yorkshire.
HE	Hunslet Engine Company,Hunslet, Leeds, West Yorkshire.
Hen	Henschel & Sohn GmbH, Kassel, Germany
HL	R & W Hawthorn, Leslie & Company, Forth Bank Works, Newcastle-Upon-Tyne.
HLT	Hughes Locomotive & Tramway Engine Works, Loughborough, Leicestershire.
JF	John Fowler & Company, (Leeds), Hunslet, Leeds, West Yorkshire.
Jung	Arn. Jung Lokomotivfabrik GmbH., Jungenthal, Germany
K	Kitson & Company, Airedale Foundry, Hunslet, Leeds, West Yorkshire.
Kitching	A. Kitching, Hope Town Foundry, Darlington, Co. Durham.
Krupp	Friedrich Krupp Maschinenfabriken, Essen, Germany
KS	Kerr Stuart & Company, California Works, Stoke-on-Trent, Staffordshire.
Leyland	Leyland Vehicles, Workington, Cumbria.
Lima	Lima Locomotive Works Inc., Lima, Ohio, USA.
LO	Lokomo Oy, Tampere, Finland
Loco. Ent.	Locomotion Enterprises (1975), Bowes Railway, Springwell, Gateshead, Tyne and Wear.
Manch	Greater Manchester Museum of Science & Industry, Manchester.
MC	Metropolitan–Cammel Carriage & Wagon Company, Birmingham (Metro-Cammel).
Matisa	Matisa Material Industriel S.A. Crissier, Lausanne, Switzerland
Mercury	The Mercury Truck & Tractor Company, Gloucester, Gloucestershire.

MF	Mercia Fabrication, Central Trading Estate, Shaw Road, Dudley, West Mids.
Minilok	Allrad-Rangiertechnik GmbH, Düsseldorf, Germany.
Motala	AB Motala Verkstad, Motala, Sweden
MR	Motor Rail & Tram Car Company, Simplex Works, Bedford, Bedfordshire.
MW	Manning, Wardle & Company, Boyne Engine Works, Hunslet, Leeds, West Yorks.
MV	Metropolitan-Vickers, Gorton, Manchester.
N	Neilson & Son, Springburn Locomotive Works, Glasgow, Scotland.
NBL	North British Locomotive Company, Glasgow, Scotland.
Niv	Les Ateliers Metallurgiques Nivelles, Tubize, Belgium
NNM	Noord Nederlandsche Maschienenfabriek BV, Winschoten, Netherlands.
NOHAB	Nydquist & Holm A.B., Trollhattan, Sweden
NR	Neilson Reid & Company, Springburn Works, Glasgow, Scotland.
P	Peckett & Sons, Atlas Locomotive Works, St George, Bristol.
Permaquip	The Permanent Way Equipment Company, Pweco Works, Bulwell, Nottingham.
PR	Park Royal Vehicles, Park Royal, London.
PS	Pressed Steel, Swindon, Wiltshire.
Resco	Resco (Railways), Erith, London.
Resita	Resita, Romania.
RH	Ruston & Hornsby Ltd., Lincoln, Lincolnshire.
RR	Rolls Royce, Sentinel Works, Shrewsbury, Shropshire.
RS	Robert Stephenson & Company, Newcastle, Tyne and Wear.
RSH	Robert Stephenson & Hawthorns, Darlington, County Durham.
RSHN	Robert Stephenson & Hawthorns, Newcastle-Upon-Tyne Works.
S	Sentinel (Shrewsbury), Battlefield, Shrewbury, Shropshire.
Sara	Sara & Company, Plymouth, Devon.
Schichau	F. Schichau, Maschinen-und Lokomotivfabrik, Elbing, Poland.
Science Museum	Science Museum, South Kensington, London
SM	Siemens, London.
SMH	Simplex Mechanical Handling, Elstow Road, Bedford, Bedfordshire.
SS	Sharp Stewart & Sons, Manchester, England and Glasgow, Scotland.
TH	Thomas Hill (Rotherham), Vanguard Works, Kilnhurst, South Yorkshire.
TK	OY Tampella AB, Tampere, Finland
TKL	Todd, Kitson and Laird, Leeds, West Yorkshire.
Unilok	Hugo Aeckerle & Company, Hamburg, Germany.
VF	Vulcan Foundry, Newton-le-Willows, Lancashire.
VIW	Vulcan Iron Works, Wilkes-Barre, Philadelphia, Pennsylvania, USA.
VL	Vickers, Barrow-in-Furness, Cumbria.
WB	W.G. Bagnall, Castle Engine Works, Stafford, Staffordshire.
Wkm	D. Wickham & Company, Ware, Hertfordshire.
WMD	Waggon und Maschienenbau G.m.b.H., Donauworth, Germany.
YE	Yorkshire Engine Company, Meadowhall, Sheffield, South Yorkshire.
YEC	Yorkshire Engine Company, Unit 7, Meadow Bank Industrial Estate, Hornson Street, Rotherham, South Yorkshire.

KEEP THIS BOOK UP TO DATE WITH...

entrain

Britain's premier railway magazine

entrain preservation stock changes

Movements

GWR 2800 CLASS 2861 (page 11)
GWR 4500 CLASS 5539 (page 12)
GWR 5101 CLASS 4115 (page 13)
GWR 5205 CLASS 5227 (page 13)
GWR 5600 CLASS 6686 (page 13)
GWR 6959 CLASS 7927 (page 16)
LMS 5MT 44901 (page 27)
LMS 8F 48518 (page 29)
BR 4MT 80150 (page 47)
BR 9F 92245 (page 47)

These ten locomotives have moved from storage at Atlantic Trading Estate, Sully, near Barry to the Vale of Glamorgan Railway, Barry. They are now located in the former EWS wagon works, close to Barry station, that is now being used by the Vale of Glamorgan Railway.

GWR 4500 CLASS 5553 (page 12)

Following the completion of the restoration of this locomotive at Tyseley Locomotive Works, Birmingham, it has moved to the West Somerset Railway.

GWR 5600 CLASS 6619 (page 13)

The restoration work being undertaken on this locomotive at the West Coast Railway Company, Carnforth has now been completed. The locomotive has now returned to the North Yorkshire Moors Railway.

LMS CLASS 5MT 45337 (page 28)

Following completion of mechanical attention at The Railway Age, Crewe, this locomotive has moved to the North Yorkshire Moors Railway.

BR 4MT 80098 (page 47)

This locomotive has been loaned to the Churnet Valley Railway from the Midland Railway Centre.

BR Class 50 D429-50029 (page 77)
BR Class 50 D430-50030 (page 77)

These two locomotives have moved from the Pontypool & Blaenavon Railway to Peak Railway, Darley Dale.

BR Class 06 D2420-06003-97804 (page 80)

This locomotive has moved from the Rutland Railway Museum to Barrow Hill Roundhouse.

BR Class 73/0 E6003-73003 (page 102)

This locomotive has moved from the Lavender Line to the Great Central Railway.

BR Class 73/1 E6048-73141

After a period of regular use at the Nottingham Heritage Centre this locomotive has moved to the Battlefield Steam Railway. It has already seen use at its new home.

BR Class 422 TSRB 69316 (page 145)

This vehicle has now moved to the newly established Waverley Route Heritage Association site at Whitrope near Hawick. It had

ALL THIS PLUS MUCH, MUCH MORE!

Published 2nd MONDAY of EVERY MONTH £3.10

entrain – THE WORD IS OUT!